LIVING *the* WORD

**Scripture Reflections and Commentaries
for Sundays and Holy Days**

**Laurie Brink, O.P. and
Paul A. Colloton, O.S.F.S.**

NOVEMBER 29, 2015 THROUGH NOVEMBER 20, 2016   YEAR C

LIVING the WORD

Scripture Reflections and Commentaries
for Sundays and Holy Days

Vol. 31   November 29, 2015–November 20, 2016

Published annually

Individual copy: $14.95
(2-9 copies: $10.95 per copy;
10-24 copies: $9.95 per copy;
25-99 copies: $8.95 per copy;
100 or more copies: $6.95 per copy)

Editor: Alan J. Hommerding
Copy and Production Editor: Marcia T. Lucey
Cover Design and Typesetting: Tejal Patel
Cover Image: Luke (Ox) by Nicholas T. Markell
        www.markellstudios.com/1.651.204.5113
Director of Publications: Mary Beth Kunde-Anderson

In accordance with c. 827, permission to publish is granted on May 7, 2015, by Most Reverend Francis J. Kane, Vicar General of the Archdiocese of Chicago. Permission to publish is an official declaration of ecclesiastical authority that the material is free from doctrinal and moral error. No legal responsibility is assumed by the grant of this permission.

World Library Publications,
the music and liturgy division of J. S. Paluch Company, Inc.
3708 River Road, Suite 400, Franklin Park, IL 60131-2158
800 566-6150 • fax 888 957-3291
wlpcs@jspaluch.com •wlpmusic.com

Printed in the United States of America
WLP 006774 • (ISSN) 1079-4670 • (ISBN) 978-1-58459-777-3

Our renewed liturgy has generated a great deal of interest in sacred scripture. In turn, a richer appreciation of the readings for Mass has done much for participation in our liturgical celebrations. *Living the Word* is designed to help facilitate this twofold deepening of the Christian life. It is our hope that individuals, homilists, catechumens, candidates, discussion groups, religious education classes, and similar gatherings will all benefit from the commentaries and reflections found on these pages.

The readings for each Sunday, holy day, and major celebration from November 2015 through November 2016, Year C of the Lectionary cycle, are presented here, along with a brief passage intended to suggest a focus or approach to consider while reading them. Following the readings is a commentary that provides a context for understanding them, incorporating both biblical scholarship and the Church's age-old wisdom. A reflection section develops the initial focus and ties it together with the commentary. The discussion questions that follow offer help in moving from reflection to action, inviting those who use this volume to go about truly "living the word."

Whether reflecting on the scriptures in a group setting or individually, it is best to do so in the context of prayer. Consider creating an atmosphere that will foster prayerful reflection when you are using this book. In a quiet space, perhaps with lit candles and simple seasonal decoration (incense or soft music may also be appropriate), begin with a prayer and read aloud the scriptures for that day, even if you are alone. Groups can encourage members to focus on one word or idea that speaks to them from each reading. Participants might want to share these ideas with one another before continuing.

After listening to the readings, ask yourself how they have changed you, enlightened you, moved you. Proceed to the commentary, reflection, and prayer. Use the discussion questions to shape your conversation or as a springboard for your own questions. How does the brief *Reflecting on the Word* section invite you to "live the word" in your relationship with God, with family and friends, at work, school, or church, or in the broader community?

Having started with prayer, perhaps once you have spent time in reflection or discussion it will be appropriate to lift up someone or something in a prayer that is related to the readings or your reflections. Pray spontaneously as you think about the texts' meaning for you, or invite people in the group to offer prayers informally.

Finally, what action will you take this week that grows out of your prayerful reflection on this week's scriptures? You may offer your own prayer for help to do something in response to the readings or simply stand and pray the Lord's Prayer. If you are in a group, offer one another a sign of peace before departing. If alone, extend yourself to another in a gesture of peace later in the day or week, in person, by phone, or by offering a simple prayer.

Repeating this pattern over time can help your prayerful reflection to deepen your appreciation for and commitment to God's word every day of your life.

Table of Contents

	Page
INTRODUCTION	**3**
PRAYERS BEFORE AND AFTER READING SCRIPTURE	**6**
INTRODUCTION TO ADVENT/CHRISTMAS	**7**
First Sunday of Advent (11/29/15)	8
Second Sunday of Advent (12/6/15)	11
The Immaculate Conception	
of the Blessed Virgin Mary (12/8/15)	15
Third Sunday of Advent (12/13/15)	19
Fourth Sunday of Advent (12/20/15)	22
The Nativity of the Lord (12/25/15)	25
The Holy Family of Jesus, Mary, and Joseph (12/27/15)	27
Mary, the Holy Mother of God (1/1/16)	32
The Epiphany of the Lord (1/3/16)	35
The Baptism of the Lord (1/10/16)	38
INTRODUCTION TO ORDINARY TIME I	**43**
Second Sunday in Ordinary Time (1/17/16)	44
Third Sunday in Ordinary Time (1/24/16)	49
Fourth Sunday in Ordinary Time (1/31/16)	51
Fifth Sunday in Ordinary Time (2/7/16)	55
INTRODUCTION TO LENT	**59**
First Sunday of Lent (2/14/16)	60
Second Sunday of Lent (2/21/16)	63
Third Sunday of Lent (2/28/16)	66/70
Fourth Sunday of Lent (3/6/16)	74/78
Fifth Sunday of Lent (3/13/16)	82/85
Palm Sunday of the Passion of the Lord (3/20/16)	89
INTRODUCTION TO EASTER	**97**
Easter Sunday of the Resurrection of the Lord (3/27/16)	99
Second Sunday of Easter (4/3/16)	101
Third Sunday of Easter (4/10/16)	105
Fourth Sunday of Easter (4/17/16)	109
Fifth Sunday of Easter (4/24/16)	112
Sixth Sunday of Easter (5/1/16)	115

The Ascension of the Lord (5/5/16 or 5/8/16)   118
Seventh Sunday of Easter (5/8/16)   122
Pentecost Sunday (5/15/16)   125

INTRODUCTION TO ORDINARY TIME II   129

The Most Holy Trinity (5/22/16)   130
The Most Holy Body and Blood of Christ (5/29/16)   133
Tenth Sunday in Ordinary Time (6/5/16)   136
Eleventh Sunday in Ordinary Time (6/12/16)   139
Twelfth Sunday in Ordinary Time (6/19/16)   143
Thirteenth Sunday in Ordinary Time (6/26/16)   146
Fourteenth Sunday in Ordinary Time (7/3/16)   149
Fifteenth Sunday in Ordinary Time (7/10/16)   152
Sixteenth Sunday in Ordinary Time (7/17/16)   155
Seventeenth Sunday in Ordinary Time (7/24/16)   158
Eighteenth Sunday in Ordinary Time (7/31/16)   162
Nineteenth Sunday in Ordinary Time (8/7/16)   165
Twentieth Sunday in Ordinary Time (8/14/16)   169
Twenty-first Sunday in Ordinary Time (8/21/16)   172
Twenty-second Sunday in Ordinary Time (8/28/16)   175
Twenty-third Sunday in Ordinary Time (9/4/16)   178
Twenty-fourth Sunday in Ordinary Time (9/11/16)   181
Twenty-fifth Sunday in Ordinary Time (9/18/16)   185
Twenty-sixth Sunday in Ordinary Time (9/25/16)   188
Twenty-seventh Sunday in Ordinary Time (10/2/16)   191
Twenty-eighth Sunday in Ordinary Time (10/9/16)   194
Twenty-ninth Sunday in Ordinary Time (10/16/16)   197
Thirtieth Sunday in Ordinary Time (10/23/16)   200
Thirty-first Sunday in Ordinary Time (10/30/16)   203
All Saints (11/1/16)   206
Thirty-second Sunday in Ordinary Time (11/6/16)   210
Thirty-third Sunday in Ordinary Time (11/13/16)   213
Our Lord Jesus Christ, King of the Universe (11/20/16)   216

Prayers Before Reading Scripture

Lord Jesus,
we give you praise.
Speak to us as we read your word,
and send your Spirit into our hearts.
Guide us today and each day in your service,
for you are our way, our truth, our life.

Lord Jesus, we love you:
keep us in your love for ever and ever. *Amen!*

or

Blessed are you, Lord God,
king of all creation:
you have taught us by your word.
Open our hearts to your Spirit,
and lead us on the paths of Christ your Son.

All praise and glory be yours for ever. *Amen!*

or

Lord, open our hearts:
let your Spirit speak to us
as we read your word. *Amen!*

or

Lord Jesus,
to whom shall we go?
You have the words of eternal life.

Speak, Lord,
your servants are listening:
here we are, Lord,
ready to do your will. *Amen!*

Prayers After Reading Scripture

Blessed are you, Lord God,
maker of heaven and earth,
ruler of the universe:
you have sent your Holy Spirit
to teach your truth to your holy people.
We praise you for letting us read your word today.

Grant that we may continue to think and pray
over the words we have read,
and to share your thoughts with others
throughout this day.

Loving God, we praise you
and thank you in Jesus' name. *Amen!*

or

God of all graciousness, we thank you
for speaking to us today
through your holy word. *Amen!*

Advent signals the beginning of the end. The promises foretold by the prophets are coming to realization with the birth of God incarnate. But as the readings in the beginning of Advent remind us, the gift of the promise unsettles the status quo and requires vigilance and the living of an upright life on the part of believers. As Advent progresses, the first readings reflect a steadfast hope in God, despite the experience of exile and persecutions. The first readings during the Christmas season celebrate God's redemption of Zion. The prophetic readings from Jeremiah, Second Isaiah, and Baruch emerge out of a specific moment in Israel's history: that of the destruction of Jerusalem beginning in 587 BC and the exile to Babylon of many of its inhabitants in 586 BC. It is these broken people whom Baruch envisions returning from the east. Their once-ruined city, Jerusalem, is enfolded in the splendor of the glory of God and wrapped in a cloak of justice.

Because the first reading is chosen to highlight or enhance the Gospel reading, we are not surprised to find similar themes echoed in the Gospel. The evangelist Luke, whose Gospel we read during this Year C, is also attentive to historical context, situating the life of John the Baptist and the life of Jesus clearly within Roman imperial temporal markers: the reign of Caesar Augustus (Luke 2:1) and Tiberius Caesar (Luke 3:1). Luke's attention to such details may be part of his overall plan to assure his patron, Theophilus, of the accuracy of his narrative (Luke 1:1–4).

Only Luke tells us about the nativity of John the Baptist (Luke 1:5–25, 57–80) and entwines it with the birth of Jesus (1:26–38; 2:1–20). The Fourth Sunday of Advent celebrates this connection by recalling the Visitation between Elizabeth, the soon-to-be mother of John, and Mary, the soon-to-be mother of Jesus (1:39–56). On Christmas Day, the Gospel is taken from John, where it is not Jesus' birth so much as his preexistence that is heralded. The Word takes on flesh in order to reveal God to us—the ultimate Christmas gift.

Most of the second readings for Advent come from the hand of the apostle Paul, whose concern is not historical but eschatological (looking forward to the end-times). Anticipating Jesus' imminent return, Paul urges that believers live a life worthy of their calling, partnering with Paul in the work of the gospel. Readings are taken from the Letter to the Ephesians for much of the Christmas season. The eschatological urgency has lessened but the author nonetheless exhorts his readers to be "copartners in the promise of Christ Jesus."

November 29, 2015

FIRST SUNDAY OF ADVENT

Today's Focus: Ready for the Return

As the season of Advent begins, we hear much about vigilance and preparedness. If today were your last day, would you be ready for the Lord's return?

FIRST READING
Jeremiah 33:14–16

The days are coming, says the LORD, when I will fulfill the promise I made to the house of Israel and Judah. In those days, in that time, I will raise up for David a just shoot; he shall do what is right and just in the land. In those days Judah shall be safe and Jerusalem shall dwell secure; this is what they shall call her: "The LORD our justice."

PSALM RESPONSE
Psalm 25:1b

To you, O Lord, I lift my soul.

SECOND READING
1 Thessalonians 3:12 — 4:2

Brothers and sisters: May the Lord make you increase and abound in love for one another and for all, just as we have for you, so as to strengthen your hearts, to be blameless in holiness before our God and Father at the coming of our Lord Jesus with all his holy ones. Amen.

Finally, brothers and sisters, we earnestly ask and exhort you in the Lord Jesus that, as you received from us how you should conduct yourselves to please God—and as you are conducting yourselves —you do so even more. For you know what instructions we gave you through the Lord Jesus.

GOSPEL
Luke 21:25–28, 34–36

Jesus said to his disciples: "There will be signs in the sun, the moon, and the stars, and on earth nations will be in dismay, per-plexed by the roaring of the sea and the waves. People will die of fright in anticipation of what is coming upon the world, for the pow-ers of the heavens will be shaken. And then they will see the Son of Man coming in a cloud with power and great glory. But when these signs begin to happen, stand erect and raise your heads because your redemption is at hand.

"Beware that your hearts do not become drowsy from carousing and drunkenness and the anxieties of daily life, and that day catch you by surprise like a trap. For that day will assault everyone who lives on the face of the earth. Be vigilant at all times and pray that you have the strength to escape the tribulations that are imminent and to stand before the Son of Man."

❖ Understanding the Word

The first reading from Jeremiah invokes a long-standing though seldom-met expectation of Israel's kings—that of justice (2 Samuel 7:10–11; Psalms 2, 21). The prophet Jeremiah lived and worked during four decades of political and personal turmoil (the rise of Babylonian hegemony to the destruction of Jerusalem, 626–585 BC). During much of this time, the kings of the southern kingdom of Judah failed to secure peace for the people. Jeremiah's lament (Jeremiah 20:7–9) poignantly depicts the sufferings that he endured as he attempted to turn the Jerusalem leadership back to right worship of God. Today's reading actually may have come from an anonymous post-exilic writer, applying Jeremiah's earlier prophecies to a new situation.

The second reading speaks of personal responsibility as well, but it is not the king but the people who are called "to be blameless in holiness before our God" (1 Thessalonians 3:13). Just as the reading from Jeremiah promised that "the days are coming" (Jeremiah 33:14), so too does the apostle Paul remind the Thessalonian believers that Christ will return soon. In readiness for Christ's return, Paul exhorts them to conduct themselves accordingly.

This end-of-time expectation is described more fully in the Gospel. In Mark 13, from which Luke takes this narrative, Jesus is sitting on the Mount of Olives looking across the Kidron Valley at the temple of Jerusalem (Mark 13:3). Luke places Jesus in the midst of the temple (Luke 21:1). This "resetting" by Luke serves to remind the reader of Jesus' first visit to the temple, where the righteous Simeon prophesied, "Behold, this child is destined for the fall and rise of many in Israel . . . so that the thoughts of many hearts may be revealed" (Luke 2:27). Now Jesus himself announces the coming wrath and warns his disciples, "Beware that your hearts do not become drowsy from carousing and drunkenness" (Luke 21:34).

❖ Reflecting on the Word

St. Francis de Sales advises us to live each day as if it were our last, to which I add, because it might be! Too many people focus their energy on when the end will come, whether of the world, the universe, life as we know it, or one's own life. However, Matthew 24:36 and Mark 13:32 make clear that no one knows the exact time or hour, not even the Son; only God knows. Following de Sales' advice to live each day as if were our last can make us ready and vigilant at all times (Luke 21:36).

During Advent we remember that God became one with us through Jesus in order that we might become one with God and give birth to the divine through our words, deeds, and attitudes. Following the instructions Jesus gave through words and the example of his life, death, and resurrection will help us grow in right relationship with God and one another. That is one definition of biblical justice. At the beginning of our liturgical new year, take time to reflect upon God's love for us. Name how you experience God's love and the light of Christ in concrete ways. Thank God by letting that light shine on others by the way we love one another and all creation (1 Thessalonians 3:12). Let it shine as brightly as the candle on the Advent wreath that we light today or the lights that decorate our homes. Reflect on any darkness in your life. Invite God's hope and peace to lessen that darkness. Pray with today's psalm, "To you, O Lord, I lift up my soul."

9

In this way we will be ready, for the Lord's return and ever-vigilant because we give flesh to "The LORD our justice" each and every day.

✦ Consider/Discuss

- Where do I see God's justice shatter the injustice that sometimes seems to overwhelm our world?
- How can I live each day in ways that reduce anxiety in my life and make me ready for the Lord's return?

✦ Living and Praying with the Word

Lord our justice, open our eyes to see the light of your Son, Jesus, each day during this Advent season. Help us diminish the darkness in the world by words, deeds, and attitudes that give flesh to the light of your love.

December 6, 2015

SECOND SUNDAY OF ADVENT

Today's Focus: Living the Consecutive Now

Even though we have no choice but to live here and now, we do have a choice as to how we will listen for and heed God's will for us—in the here and now, and in the hereafter.

FIRST
READING
Baruch 5:1–9

Jerusalem, take off your robe of mourning and misery;
    put on the splendor of glory from God forever:
wrapped in the cloak of justice from God,
    bear on your head the mitre
    that displays the glory of the eternal name.
For God will show all the earth your splendor:
    you will be named by God forever
    the peace of justice, the glory of God's worship.

Up, Jerusalem! stand upon the heights;
    look to the east and see your children
gathered from the east and the west
    at the word of the Holy One,
    rejoicing that they are remembered by God.
Led away on foot by their enemies they left you:
    but God will bring them back to you
    borne aloft in glory as on royal thrones.
For God has commanded
    that every lofty mountain be made low,
and that the age-old depths and gorges
    be filled to level ground,
    that Israel may advance secure in the glory of God.
The forests and every fragrant kind of tree
    have overshadowed Israel at God's command;
for God is leading Israel in joy
    by the light of his glory,
    with his mercy and justice for company.

PSALM
RESPONSE
Psalm 126:3

The Lord has done great things for us; we are filled with joy.

11

SECOND READING
Philippians 1:4–6, 8–11

Brothers and sisters: I pray always with joy in my every prayer for all of you, because of your partnership for the gospel from the first day until now. I am confident of this, that the one who began a good work in you will continue to complete it until the day of Christ Jesus. God is my witness, how I long for all of you with the affection of Christ Jesus. And this is my prayer: that your love may increase ever more and more in knowledge and every kind of perception, to discern what is of value, so that you may be pure and blameless for the day of Christ, filled with the fruit of righteousness that comes through Jesus Christ for the glory and praise of God.

GOSPEL
Luke 3:1-6

In the fifteenth year of the reign of Tiberius Caesar, when Pontius Pilate was governor of Judea, and Herod was tetrarch of Galilee, and his brother Philip tetrarch of the region of Ituraea and Trachonitis, and Lysanias was tetrarch of Abilene, during the high priesthood of Annas and Caiaphas, the word of God came to John the son of Zechariah in the desert. John went throughout the whole region of the Jordan, proclaiming a baptism of repentance for the forgiveness of sins, as it is written in the book of the words of the prophet Isaiah:

A voice of one crying out in the desert:
"Prepare the way of the Lord,
make straight his paths.
Every valley shall be filled
and every mountain and hill shall be made low.
The winding roads shall be made straight,
and the rough ways made smooth,
and all flesh shall see the salvation of God."

❖ Understanding the Word

The first reading is from the book of the prophet Baruch, who also may have served as Jeremiah's scribe or secretary (Jeremiah 32:12–16; 36:1–32). Along with Jeremiah, Baruch is taken to Egypt (Jeremiah 43:6). However, when the book of Baruch opens, the scribe turned prophet is now in Babylon (Baruch 1:1). The final form of the book may be dated as late as the second century BC and is composed of four sections: the letter to Jerusalem (Baruch 1 — 3:8), praise of Wisdom (Baruch 3:9 — 4:4), Baruch's poem of consolation (Baruch 4:5 — 5:9), and a letter of Jeremiah (Baruch 6:1–72). Today's first reading is part of Baruch's poem of consolation in which he encourages the mourning city of Jerusalem, echoing the language of Second Isaiah.

The overall tone of Paul's Letter to the Philippians is that of joy. In today's reading, Paul prays with joy because the Philippians have partnered with Paul in the gospel. This partnership, or *koinonia* in the Greek, is demonstrated by shared suffering with Paul (Philippians 1:29) and participation in the Spirit (Philippians 2:1). But *koinonia* can also mean "contribution," and it may be that Paul is particularly pleased by their generosity (Philippians 4:15–18).

The Gospel reading introduces John the Baptist by situating his ministry within political temporal markers. The fifteenth year of the reign of Tiberius can be reckoned between AD 27 and 29. Pontius Pilate was prefect of Judea from AD 26 to 36. Herod Antipas, the son of Herod the Great, was the tetrarch (leader of a quarter) of Galilee and Perea from 4 BC to 39 AD, and his brother Philip had the same title and ruled over regions north and east of the Sea of Galilee from 4 BC to 34 AD. Luke also references the temple priesthood (though Annas and his son-in-law Caiaphas were not both high priests at the same time). Unlike the other evangelists, Luke presents John has having been called by God ("the word of God came to John"), but similar to the other Gospel writers, John will remain only a prophetic messenger who proclaims a baptism of repentance and recognizes that "one mightier than I is coming" (Luke 3:16; Matthew 3:11; Mark 1:7; John 1:27).

❖ Reflecting on the Word

Do you notice how specific Luke is about when John the Baptist received the word of God? Luke's list of political and religious leaders makes clear that John ministered at a specific time and place, just as Jesus was born during a specific historical time. God seeks us out in various times and situations. Baruch offers consolation and hope to a people in exile. Paul writes to a generous Philippian community, which joins him in living the Good News of Jesus Christ. Our readings make clear that God constantly seeks to be with us and will come again to bring mercy and justice, knowledge and light, and offer saving love to all flesh. The timeless One becomes human in time, making us witnesses in every time, every now of our life.

Life could be described as a series of consecutive nows. Any now could be our last. I recently learned about a friend who had a massive heart attack while taking his nightly walk. He died a few days ago at age 55. So I ask myself, how can God's love increase more and more in me today? What do I really value? How can my faith in Jesus Christ make a concrete difference today to all those people who are in my life now? Do I prepare the way of the Lord by means of a willingness to face hurt in ways that offer mercy, injustice in ways that seek God's economy, and darkness and sin in ways that shine with the light of God's consolation, hope, and peace? Pick one of these questions. Allow the Holy Spirit to do great things for you so that we can be filled with joy today.

❖ Consider/Discuss

- Where do injustice, darkness, or evil seem stronger in the world than God's justice, light, and love?
- What is one thing that I can do today to offer hope and transformation like Baruch, Paul, and John?

God of all times and ages, you make mountains low, straighten crooked paths and smooth ways that are rough. Help me to receive your Word today and live in ways that prepare the way for your Son, Jesus Christ, today, this Advent, and every day of life that you give me.

December 8, 2015

IMMACULATE CONCEPTION OF THE BLESSED VIRGIN MARY

Today's Focus: Coming Full Circle

In Mary's open and honest obedience to God, the hiding, dishonesty, and disobedience of Eden were replaced—to prepare the way for the ultimate obedience of Christ on the cross.

FIRST READING
Genesis 3:9–15, 20

After the man, Adam, had eaten of the tree, the LORD God called to the man and asked him, "Where are you?" He answered, "I heard you in the garden; but I was afraid, because I was naked, so I hid myself." Then he asked, "Who told you that you were naked? You have eaten, then, from the tree of which I had forbidden you to eat!" The man replied, "The woman whom you put here with me—she gave me fruit from the tree, and so I ate it." The LORD God then asked the woman, "Why did you do such a thing?" The woman answered, "The serpent tricked me into it, so I ate it."

Then the LORD God said to the serpent:
"Because you have done this, you shall be banned
    from all the animals
    and from all the wild creatures;
on your belly shall you crawl,
    and dirt shall you eat
    all the days of your life.
I will put enmity between you and the woman,
    and between your offspring and hers;
he will strike at your head,
    while you strike at his heel."
The man called his wife Eve, because she became the mother of all the living.

PSALM RESPONSE
Psalm 98:1a

Sing to the Lord a new song, for he has done marvelous deeds.

SECOND READING — Brothers and sisters: Blessed be the God and Father of our Lord Jesus Christ, who has blessed us in Christ with every spiritual blessing in the heavens, as he chose us in him, before the foundation of the world, to be holy and without blemish before him. In love he destined us for adoption to himself through Jesus Christ, in accord with the favor of his will, for the praise of the glory of his grace that he granted us in the beloved.

In him we were also chosen, destined in accord with the purpose of the One who accomplishes all things according to the intention of his will, so that we might exist for the praise of his glory, we who first hoped in Christ.

GOSPEL
Luke 1:26–38

The angel Gabriel was sent from God to a town of Galilee called Nazareth, to a virgin betrothed to a man named Joseph, of the house of David, and the virgin's name was Mary. And coming to her, he said, "Hail, full of grace! The Lord is with you." But she was greatly troubled at what was said and pondered what sort of greeting this might be. Then the angel said to her, "Do not be afraid, Mary, for you have found favor with God. Behold, you will conceive in your womb and bear a son, and you shall name him Jesus. He will be great and will be called Son of the Most High, and the Lord God will give him the throne of David his father, and he will rule over the house of Jacob forever, and of his kingdom there will be no end." But Mary said to the angel, "How can this be, since I have no relations with a man?" And the angel said to her in reply, "The Holy Spirit will come upon you, and the power of the Most High will overshadow you. Therefore the child to be born will be called holy, the Son of God. And behold, Elizabeth, your relative, has also conceived a son in her old age, and this is the sixth month for her who was called barren; for nothing will be impossible for God." Mary said, "Behold, I am the handmaid of the Lord. May it be done to me according to your word." Then the angel departed from her.

❖ Understanding the Word

The first eleven chapters of the book of Genesis introduce the origins of creation and God's intent that all be seen as "good." Despite that hope, sin and disobedience enter into Creation. Genesis 3 describes God's discovery that the man and woman have disobeyed him and the subsequent results of their disobedience. Having eaten of the tree of the knowledge of good and bad, the first couple recognizes that they are naked and when they hear God's voice, they hide from God. The story becomes the foundation of the later understanding of original sin. But despite the disobedience and God's punishment, today's reading ends with a note of hope. The experience has earned the woman a new name: Eve. She is the mother of all the living (Genesis 3:20). This profound misstep has not ended human potential, and as today's feast of the Immaculate Conception celebrates, God can enter into human existence through divine grace and wipe the slate clean.

As the second reading confirms, despite our sin, God's grace is lavished upon humanity. Through Christ, we have been chosen "before the foundation of the world, to be holy and without blemish before God" (Ephesians 1:4). Christ redeems humanity from its transgressions, and the Holy Spirit stands as proof of our redemption.

But in order to achieve our salvation, Jesus needed to be free of the stain of original sin. The dogma of the Immaculate Conception holds that Mary, the mother of Jesus, was a human being conceived without sin, making her the fitting vessel for the sinless Son of God. The idea isn't found in in today's Gospel, which describes Mary's encounter with the angel Gabriel. What is reported is that a young woman is invited to become the bearer of a holy child, conceived in an extraordinary way by the Holy Spirit of the Most High. Our readings bring us full circle. The disobedience of the first human couple stands in stark contrast to the obedience of the young woman, whose Magnificat sets in motion the process of redemption. "For nothing is impossible for God" (Luke 1:37).

❖ Reflecting on the Word

Are you a pessimist or an optimist? Do you believe in the basic goodness of humanity or that we are basically evil? The *Eucharistic Prayers for Various Needs and Occasions* remind us that God loves the human race and walks with us on life's journey. God, who chose us in Christ before the foundation of the world (Ephesians 1:4), believes in us. Even the account of Adam and Eve's disobedience we've come to call original sin ends with words of hope: "The man called his wife Eve, because she became the mother of all the living" (Genesis 3:20).

The Immaculate Conception that we celebrate today is about Mary's conception without original sin in order to be a fitting vessel for giving birth to the Son of God. When Gabriel appears to her she is surprised and afraid. Gabriel offers comfort: You have found favor with God, the Holy Spirit will be with you, you are not alone. Adam and Eve hid when they heard God's voice. Mary hides nothing and enters into an honest dialogue that frees her to trust Gabriel's words and God's promise. She is freed to say "Yes!"

God chose us in Christ. Even when we are aware of our sinfulness, God comes to us and walks with us offering hope. Advent reminds us that we are not alone. Jesus, God-who-saves, is God's mercy made visible in time. God walks with us on life's journey. Take time to pray today. Listen for God's voice. Respond with honesty and hope. Invite God to give birth to Christ in you and me today, for nothing is impossible with God.

❖ Consider/Discuss

- How do you listen for God's voice in your life? What do you hear?
- What helps you believe that God forgives you and makes you an angel who announces God's merciful love to others?

God our mercy, we can find it difficult to believe that you constantly reach out to us with forgiveness and hope. Free us from fear and help us believe in your love so that our words, deeds, and attitudes announce your presence to those we meet.

December 13, 2015

THIRD SUNDAY OF ADVENT

Today's Focus: What Are We to Do?

John the Baptist instructs us today that we are called simply to live fairly, in God's justice. When we live that way, we know the Lord is near. A cause for rejoicing!

FIRST READING
Zephaniah 3: 14–18a

Shout for joy, O daughter Zion!
    Sing joyfully, O Israel!
Be glad and exult with all your heart,
    O daughter Jerusalem!
The LORD has removed the judgment against you,
    he has turned away your enemies;
the King of Israel, the LORD, is in your midst,
    you have no further misfortune to fear.
On that day, it shall be said to Jerusalem:
    Fear not, O Zion, be not discouraged!
The LORD, your God, is in your midst,
    a mighty savior;
he will rejoice over you with gladness,
    and renew you in his love,
he will sing joyfully because of you,
    as one sings at festivals.

PSALM RESPONSE
Isaiah 12:6

Cry out with joy and gladness: for among you is the great and Holy One of Israel.

SECOND READING
Philippians 4: 4–7

Brothers and sisters: Rejoice in the Lord always. I shall say it again: rejoice! Your kindness should be known to all. The Lord is near. Have no anxiety at all, but in everything, by prayer and petition, with thanksgiving, make your requests known to God. Then the peace of God that surpasses all understanding will guard your hearts and minds in Christ Jesus.

GOSPEL
Luke 3:10–18

The crowds asked John the Baptist, "What should we do?" He said to them in reply, "Whoever has two cloaks should share with the person who has none. And whoever has food should do likewise." Even tax collectors came to be baptized and they said to him, "Teacher, what should we do?" He answered them, "Stop collecting more than what is prescribed." Soldiers also asked him, "And what is it that we should do?" He told them, "Do not practice extortion, do not falsely accuse anyone, and be satisfied with your wages."

Now the people were filled with expectation, and all were asking in their hearts whether John might be the Christ. John answered them all, saying, "I am baptizing you with water, but one mightier than I is coming. I am not worthy to loosen the thongs of his sandals. He will baptize you with the Holy Spirit and fire. His winnowing fan is in his hand to clear his threshing floor and to gather the wheat into his barn, but the chaff he will burn with unquenchable fire." Exhorting them in many other ways, he preached good news to the people.

❖ Understanding the Word

The short prophetic book (53 verses) known as Zephaniah records the oracles of a prophet who lived at the same time as Jeremiah, about whom we have little historical information. In language and themes reminiscent of Amos (for example, Zephaniah 1:13 and Amos 5:11), the prophet announces a judgment on Judah, particularly its officials (see Ephesians 1:8) and the wealthy who have become complacent (Ephesians 1:12). Even Jerusalem will not escape the wrath of the coming Day of the Lord (Ephesians 3:1–7). But God's wrath is a purifying fire (Ephesians 3:8–9), and as today's reading describes, God will remove judgment against Jerusalem (Ephesians 3:15). The remnant of Israel, whom the prophet calls "the humble and lowly" (Ephesians 3:12), will be glad and rejoice, recognizing that God is in their midst!

The theme of rejoicing echoes through Paul's Letter to the Philippians. His joyous tone is remarkable when we consider the setting of the letter. Paul is writing from prison. He is an aging apostle writing back to a beloved community, thanking them for their financial and personal support and hoping to visit them soon. Today's second reading is part of Paul's *parenesis* (or exhortation). In the previous verses, Paul had urged Euodia and Syntyche, pleading that they come to terms, and calls on a member of the church to act as arbitrator (Philippians 4:2). In our reading, Paul invites the Philippians to rejoice because the Lord is near (Philippians 4:5); therefore, they should have no anxiety. This short letter was meant to reassure a beloved community that their aging and imprisoned founder "can do all things in him who strengthens me" (Philippians 4:13).

Today's Gospel both introduces a theme about appropriate use of possessions, and indicates the demands of discipleship. Those who have gathered to hear John the Baptist query, "What are we do to?" (Luke 3:10). The crowds, whom Luke generally depicts as favorable to Jesus, are told to share their wealth, here symbolized by having two cloaks (Luke 3:11). The tax collectors are to stop taking more than their due (Luke 3:12), and soldiers coming to John are told to stop abusing their power by extorting and falsely accusing the people (Luke 3:14). The preaching of John prepares the people for the ethical demands of the good news that Jesus brings.

Last week in Luke we saw that the ministry of John the Baptist took place at a specific time. This week Luke is also specific in the guidance John offers to each group who comes to him asking, "What are we to do?" The crowd is to share their resources. Tax collectors are to take nothing more than what is prescribed. Soldiers are not to abuse power. Each answer provides a hint about what people were doing that needed to change if they were going to repent and witness the Christ.

How would John the Baptist answer you if you asked the same question? I'd probably hear: Give from your resources, not just your abundance. Take more time to pray. Pay attention to the person who challenges or frightens you. Take time to ask God, "What do I need to do to live Jesus this Advent?" What might you hear? Asking someone you trust that question might point you in the needed direction.

When we were baptized with water and the Holy Spirit, we promised to live Jesus and to see and be his presence in concrete ways. Belonging to Christ is reason for great rejoicing. Hear Zephaniah's words addressed to you: God rejoices over us. The Lord has removed judgment against us. Then treat others as God has treated you so that others can rejoice. Believe these words. Live with rejoicing. Remove anxiety from your hearts. Let kindness abound in ways that help others see Jesus and experience God's love. Then dance with great rejoicing.

✤ Consider/Discuss

- Name the person(s) in your life who call(s) you to live more like Jesus or John the Baptizer did.
- What needs to change in your life for you to follow Christ more closely and be free from needless worry?

✤ Living and Praying with the Word

Open our hearts to hear your Word today, O God, so that we might rejoice in your loving care for us and live in ways that help others rejoice in you.

December 20, 2015

FOURTH SUNDAY OF ADVENT

Today's Focus: Promise in the Air

As the day of Christmas draws near, the tone of promise and hopefulness fills the readings, culminating in the joy of the Visitation of Elizabeth and Mary.

FIRST READING
Micah 5:1–4a

Thus says the LORD:
    You, Bethlehem-Ephrathah,
      too small to be among the clans of Judah,
  from you shall come forth for me
    one who is to be ruler in Israel;
  whose origin is from of old,
    from ancient times.
Therefore the Lord will give them up, until the time
    when she who is to give birth has borne,
  and the rest of his kindred shall return
    to the children of Israel.
He shall stand firm and shepherd his flock
    by the strength of the LORD,
    in the majestic name of the LORD, his God;
  and they shall remain, for now his greatness
    shall reach to the ends of the earth;
    he shall be peace.

PSALM RESPONSE
Psalm 80:4

Lord, make us turn to you; let us see your face and we shall be saved.

SECOND READING
Hebrews 10:5–10

Brothers and sisters: When Christ came into the world, he said:
  "Sacrifice and offering you did not desire,
    but a body you prepared for me;
  in holocausts and sin offerings you took no delight.
Then I said, 'As is written of me in the scroll,
behold, I come to do your will, O God.' "

First he says,
  "Sacrifices and offerings, holocausts and sin offerings,
    you neither desired nor delighted in."
These are offered according to the law. Then he says,
  "Behold, I come to do your will."
He takes away the first to establish the second.

By this "will," we have been consecrated through the offering of the body of Jesus Christ once for all.

Mary set out and traveled to the hill country in haste to a town of Judah, where she entered the house of Zechariah and greeted Elizabeth. When Elizabeth heard Mary's greeting, the infant leaped in her womb, and Elizabeth, filled with the Holy Spirit, cried out in a loud voice and said, "Blessed are you among women, and blessed is the fruit of your womb. And how does this happen to me, that the mother of my Lord should come to me? For at the moment the sound of your greeting reached my ears, the infant in my womb leaped for joy. Blessed are you who believed that what was spoken to you by the Lord would be fulfilled."

✤ Understanding the Word

The superscription (or heading) on the book of Micah identifies the author as Micah of Moreseth, a fortified town twenty-five miles southwest of Jerusalem. Micah prophesied during the reigns of Ahaz, the king of the northern kingdom of Israel, and Hezekiah, the king of Judah, the southern kingdom. Scholars surmise that Micah was an elder, one of the prominent men who sat in judgment over the people of a particular town. The prophecies of Micah appear to be situated during the time of Hezekiah when the Assyrians threatened the city of Jerusalem. While chapters 1–3 and 6–7 come from this historical period, chapters 4–5, from which today's reading is taken, come from a later hand, and are more positive in tone.

The second reading is taken from Hebrews, once attributed to the apostle Paul, but more likely an anonymous homily written in the late first century by a Hellenistic (Greek) Jewish Christian. The author's familiarity with both Old Testament imagery and ancient rhetoric is evident. The primary oppression facing the author's audience appears to have been apathy about the rigors of Christian life (Hebrews 2:1; 4:14; 10:23–32). In today's reading, the reason for Christ's coming into the world is made explicit: to be more pleasing to God than holocausts and sin offerings (Hebrews 10:8–9). Unlike the offerings of the priests at the altar, Christ's sacrifice was "once for all" (Hebrews 10:10).

Only the Gospel of Luke tells us about the nativity of John, and in today's Gospel, John's mother, Elizabeth, and Jesus' mother, Mary, are introduced as faithful women whose unusual pregnancies are a sign of God's favor. Scholars propose that the author of Luke recognized a periodization of salvation history: the period of the Law and the prophets, followed by the interim of John and Jesus' nativities; the period of the proclamation of Jesus Christ, followed by the time of Resurrection appearances and revelatory teaching to disciples by the risen Jesus; and, finally, the period of the proclamation of Kingdom of God by the church, from the descent of the Spirit to Jesus' return. Today's Gospel foreshadows the coming of the second period, for Elizabeth recognizes Mary as "the mother of my Lord."

Brother Mickey McGrath, OSFS, has created a wonderful painting of the Visitation, titled the "Windsock Visitation." The two dark-skinned women embrace. They are smiling. He includes words of St. Jane de Chantal, founder of the Visitation order, that describe their meeting as a place of delight and rest. I want to leap for joy whenever I see it.

John leaped in Elizabeth's womb. Elizabeth called Mary blessed because Mary believed that the words of God's promise would be fulfilled. She believed. We are five days from Christmas. The days can be hurried. The nights can be harried. Yet the promise of joy is in the air. We celebrate the time when God's promise of peace begins to be fulfilled. Do we believe that ours is the time of fulfillment? Do we believe that God's promised justice and peace, light and hope, mercy and visitation are meant for us? Do we believe that God's will for us is to know God-with-us, Emmanuel, every day? Do we believe that our believing this promise can lighten the darkness and lessen the evil that surround us and fill our world?

Believe it or try to live as if you believe today. Let God's love fill you, Christ's light shine through you, and the peace of the Spirit surround you so clearly that people say of you and me, "Blessed are you who believe that what was spoken to us by the Lord would be fulfilled." Visit someone who gives you hope. Leap for joy in honor of the Visitation of Elizabeth and Mary. Make clear that God is with us.

❖ Consider/Discuss

• Where do you see signs that God's promises continue to be fulfilled this Advent season?

• To whom might you turn for light, hope, or joy in any darkness or pain you carry this year?

❖ Living and Praying with the Word

God of promise and fulfillment, visit us with Christ in ways that bring us peace, light, and hope. Empower us to visit others with the fruit of Mary's womb, Jesus.

December 25, 2015

THE NATIVITY OF THE LORD

Today's Focus: Light on Your Feet

Christmas is a time to celebrate, proclaim, and share the joyful light of Christ. We do this by getting on our feet and spreading the light to all.

FIRST READING
Isaiah 52:7–10

How beautiful upon the mountains
    are the feet of him who brings glad tidings,
announcing peace, bearing good news,
    announcing salvation, and saying to Zion,
    "Your God is King!"

Hark! Your sentinels raise a cry,
    together they shout for joy,
for they see directly, before their eyes,
    the LORD restoring Zion.
Break out together in song,
    O ruins of Jerusalem!
For the LORD comforts his people,
    he redeems Jerusalem.
The LORD has bared his holy arm
    in the sight of all the nations;
all the ends of the earth will behold
    the salvation of our God.

PSALM RESPONSE
Psalm 98:3c

All the ends of the earth have seen the saving power of God.

SECOND READING
Hebrews 1:1–6

Brothers and sisters: In times past, God spoke in partial and various ways to our ancestors through the prophets; in these last days, he has spoken to us through the Son, whom he made heir of all things and through whom he created the universe, who is the refulgence of his glory, the very imprint of his being, and who sustains all things by his mighty word. When he had accomplished purification from sins, he took his seat at the right hand of the Majesty on high, as far superior to the angels as the name he has inherited is more excellent than theirs.

For to which of the angels did God ever say:
    You are my son; this day I have begotten you?
Or again:
    I will be a father to him, and he shall be a son to me?
And again, when he leads the firstborn into the world, he says:
    Let all the angels of God worship him.

GOSPEL
John 1:1–18
or 1:1–5, 9–14

In the beginning was the Word,
    and the Word was with God,
    and the Word was God.
He was in the beginning with God.
All things came to be through him,
    and without him nothing came to be.

What came to be through him was life,
    and this life was the light of the human race;
the light shines in the darkness,
    and the darkness has not overcome it.

[A man named John was sent from God. He came for testimony, to testify to the light, so that all might believe through him. He was not the light, but came to testify to the light.] The true light, which enlightens everyone, was coming into the world.

He was in the world,
    and the world came to be through him,
    but the world did not know him.
He came to what was his own,
    but his own people did not accept him.

But to those who did accept him he gave power to become children of God, to those who believe in his name, who were born not by natural generation nor by human choice nor by a man's decision but of God.

And the Word became flesh
    and made his dwelling among us,
    and we saw his glory,
    the glory as of the Father's only Son,
    full of grace and truth.

[John testified to him and cried out, saying, "This was he of whom I said, 'The one who is coming after me ranks ahead of me because he existed before me.' " From his fullness we have all received, grace in place of grace, because while the law was given through Moses, grace and truth came through Jesus Christ. No one has ever seen God. The only Son, God, who is at the Father's side, has revealed him.]

✦ Understanding the Word

The book of Isaiah is a compilation of oracles and poems composed over the span of one hundred years by at least three different writers. Chapters 1–39 are the work of Isaiah of Jerusalem, who lived in the eighth century, shortly after Assyria had destroyed the Northern Kingdom. Chapters 40–55 were composed by "Second Isaiah," an unnamed prophet writing in the late sixth century, on the cusp of the exiles' return to Jerusalem. The focus in Second Isaiah is on hope and restoration. Chapters 56–66 are from another anonymous prophet writing in the name of Isaiah. Today's first reading demonstrates the joy and expectancy characteristic of much of Second Isaiah. The good news is that God is king and comes to restore Zion.

The reading from Hebrews seems to pick up from Second Isaiah. This redeemer of whom Isaiah foretold is in reality God's Son. Originally part of a hymn, verses 3–4 describe this Son as pre-existent heir, in terms reminiscent of Wisdom in the Old Testament. Once he had accomplished the "purification of sin" he returned to the right hand of God. Since he is begotten of God, this Son ranks even higher than angels. The Letter to the Hebrews is actually a sermon in letter format, which at one time had been ascribed to Paul. It reflects on the death of Jesus as a saving act and finds support and direction from Old Testament texts.

Unlike Matthew and Luke, John's Gospel does not begin with the nativity of Jesus. Rather, it reaches further back to the moment before creation. In the beginning, God and the Word existed, and through the Word all things came to be. This Word stands as a beacon to human beings. John the Baptist testified to the coming of this light, and acknowledged that Jesus ranks ahead of him. This exalted, pre-existent Word became incarnate and lived among human beings. Like the reading from Hebrews, John describes Jesus through a particular philosophical lens. Luke and Matthew tell a story of the birth, but John the Evangelist interprets Jesus' birth as the profound act of humility: the Word taking on flesh in order to reveal God to us—the ultimate Christmas gift.

✥ Reflecting on the Word

Isaiah offers us one of my favorite lines in scripture: "How beautiful upon the mountains are the feet of him who brings glad tidings" (Isaiah 52:7). Feet carry the weight of our bodies. Feet help us move from place to place. Feet need washing, healing, and rest to do their job. Sometimes they need massaging, too. The feet of one who announces God's glad tidings of peace, saving love, and redeeming mercy are beautiful. How beautiful are your feet?

Today we celebrate that the Word—with God from the beginning, begotten not made, through whom all things come into being, Jesus Christ—took on our human flesh. Through him God shines a light on the world that no darkness can overcome, even when darkness seems stronger. God took on human limits to help us see, touch, and feel God's limitless mercy. God became one with us that we might become one with God and each another. This is a gift we won't find under the Christmas tree. However, if we give flesh to Jesus, others find that gift in us.

The light of Christ is given to us. Our feet carry that light by witnessing the power of Christ's light active in the world. Abuse, sickness, war, addiction and . . . try to diminish that light, but the light continues to shine. Offer hope to others by witnessing the Christ-light carried on your beautiful feet. If darkness is stronger in your life this year, look for that light in others who have experienced a similar hurt or weight. May all the ends of the earth behold the salvation of our God because our feet carry our faith and free us from fear.

- Name people and places where you see the light we celebrate at Christmas shining in our world.
- How can you give testimony to the presence of Christ today and throughout Christmastime?

✤ Living and Praying with the Word

God of our Lord Jesus Christ, you sent your Light into the world in human flesh and blood. Strengthen your presence within us. Help us radiate your hope, joy, and peace through bodies that are a light for all to see, carried on beautiful feet.

December 27, 2015

HOLY FAMILY OF JESUS, MARY, AND JOSEPH

Today's Focus: What Does a Family Look Like?

Like any family, Jesus, Mary, and Joseph had their own complications and fears to deal with, but they were always grounded in the loving faithfulness of their covenant with God and one another.

FIRST READING
1 Samuel 1: 20–22, 24–28

In those days Hannah conceived, and at the end of her term bore a son whom she called Samuel, since she had asked the LORD for him. The next time her husband Elkanah was going up with the rest of his household to offer the customary sacrifice to the LORD and to fulfill his vows, Hannah did not go, explaining to her husband, "Once the child is weaned, I will take him to appear before the LORD and to remain there forever; I will offer him as a perpetual nazirite."

Once Samuel was weaned, Hannah brought him up with her, along with a three-year-old bull, an ephah of flour, and a skin of wine, and presented him at the temple of the LORD in Shiloh. After the boy's father had sacrificed the young bull, Hannah, his mother, approached Eli and said: "Pardon, my lord! As you live, my lord, I am the woman who stood near you here, praying to the LORD. I prayed for this child, and the LORD granted my request. Now I, in turn, give him to the LORD; as long as he lives, he shall be dedicated to the LORD." Hannah left Samuel there.

PSALM RESPONSE
Psalm 84:5a

Blessed are they who dwell in your house, O Lord.

SECOND READING
1 John 3: 1–2,21–24

Beloved: See what love the Father has bestowed on us that we may be called the children of God. And so we are. The reason the world does not know us is that it did not know him. Beloved, we are God's children now; what we shall be has not yet been revealed. We do know that when it is revealed we shall be like him, for we shall see him as he is.

Beloved, if our hearts do not condemn us, we have confidence in God and receive from him whatever we ask, because we keep his commandments and do what pleases him. And his commandment is this: we should believe in the name of his Son, Jesus Christ, and love one another just as he commanded us. Those who keep his commandments remain in him, and he in them, and the way we know that he remains in us is from the Spirit he gave us.

29

GOSPEL
Luke 2:41–52

Each year Jesus' parents went to Jerusalem for the feast of Passover, and when he was twelve years old, they went up according to festival custom. After they had completed its days, as they were returning, the boy Jesus remained behind in Jerusalem, but his parents did not know it. Thinking that he was in the caravan, they journeyed for a day and looked for him among their relatives and acquaintances, but not finding him, they returned to Jerusalem to look for him. After three days they found him in the temple, sitting in the midst of the teachers, listening to them and asking them questions, and all who heard him were astounded at his understanding and his answers. When his parents saw him, they were astonished, and his mother said to him, "Son, why have you done this to us? Your father and I have been looking for you with great anxiety." And he said to them, "Why were you looking for me? Did you not know that I must be in my Father's house?" But they did not understand what he said to them. He went down with them and came to Nazareth, and was obedient to them; and his mother kept all these things in her heart. And Jesus advanced in wisdom and age and favor before God and man.

❖ Understanding the Word

Fittingly for the celebration of the feast of the Holy Family, the theme of children is found in all three of our readings. In her misery and sadness, Hannah had prayed ardently to God for a child (1 Samuel 1:9). She promised to dedicate a male child to the Lord (1 Samuel 1:10). In today's reading, the child is taken to Shiloh and presented to Eli, the priest, as a "perpetual nazirite" (1 Samuel 1:22). The term "nazirite" derives from the Hebrew *nazir*—to set apart as sacred. Nazirites were those men and women who vowed themselves to God, refraining from wine or cutting their hair (Numbers 6:4–5). The child Samuel will become a prophet and serve as the last judge of Israel (1 Samuel 7:6).

The reading from First John continues the theme of children but the focus is not on an individual. All are children of God if they keep the commandment to believe in the name of God's Son, Jesus Christ, and to love one another as Jesus commanded. In the ancient world, adoption was a common legal way to assure heirs. Here First John picks up the imagery from the Gospel of John. Belief in the name leads to adoption as children of God (John 1:12).

Little is known about the life of Jesus prior to his baptism in the Jordan River, the point at which the evangelist Mark begins his story. Both Matthew and Luke had access to different sources and describe scattered events in the childhood of Jesus. In today's reading, we hear of the twelve-year-old Jesus' encounter with the religious teachers in the temple. Luke describes every parent's nightmare—a lost child in a big city. Though Luke tends to present Mary as the first disciple—the obedient hearer of God's word—in today's Gospel she is a typical mother: "Son, why have you done this to us?" (Luke 2:48). The narrative serves to foreshadow the adult Jesus' own teaching in the temple (Luke 19:47).

✤ Reflecting on the Word

What does family look like? Single parents or a couple with one or more children, belonging by birth or adoption, an extended family or friends, all of the above? The Holy Family consisted of Jesus, his birth mother and his birth mother's husband. Our Gospel offers us one of the few glimpses we have into their life together. The teenage Jesus gives Mary and Joseph a scare. Their response is typical of many frightened parents: they retrace their steps and, filled with anxiety, scurry to find him. Mary's frustration is clear: "Why have you done this to us?" Jesus answers like many teens who wonder why their parents worry. Their family was complicated. Jesus' parents were not only human. He was the Son of God. Jesus is learning to respect his situation.

Hannah's prayers for a child were answered, unlike others who pray and do not conceive. Remember those families today. Such pain paralyzes some. Others find life through adoption, friendship, or outreach. Not all family relationships give life. Healing only comes through time.

Whatever our experience of human family, we are all children of God, called to love one another with a love that makes our belonging to the human family visible. Healing, life-giving, unconditional love takes a lifetime to learn. So we too need to advance in wisdom, age, and favor before God and others.

What does your family look like? Thank those who make your experience life-giving. Seek healing where your family has brought pain. Grow in love, however you can, so others can know the light of hope we celebrating at Christmas. Dedicated to the Lord by baptism, may we advance in wisdom, age, and love.

✤ Consider/Discuss

- Name the families to which you belong and describe the relationships that make you a family.
- How can you nurture love that is both affirming and challenging so people have the skills needed to advance in wisdom, age, and favor today?

✤ Living and Praying with the Word

Loving God, the Church gives us the life of Mary, Joseph, and Jesus as an example of holy living. Help us express the truth of Mary's anxiety, Jesus' confidence, and Joseph's faithfulness to you in ways that deepen our faith and free us to grow in your love.

31

January 1, 2016

MARY, THE HOLY MOTHER OF GOD

Today's Focus: A Year of Grace, Blessing, and Comfort

The readings today speak to us of God's rich and merciful love present in Mary, the Mother of God. It is also present to us throughout the days of our New Year.

FIRST READING
*Numbers 6:
22–27*

The LORD said to Moses: "Speak to Aaron and his sons and tell them: This is how you shall bless the Israelites. Say to them:

The LORD bless you and keep you!
The LORD let his face shine upon you, and be gracious to you!
The LORD look upon you kindly and give you peace!

So shall they invoke my name upon the Israelites, and I will bless them."

PSALM RESPONSE
Psalm 67:2a

May God bless us in his mercy.

SECOND READING
Galatians 4:4–7

Brothers and sisters: When the fullness of time had come, God sent his Son, born of a woman, born under the law, to ransom those under the law, so that we might receive adoption as sons. As proof that you are sons, God sent the Spirit of his Son into our hearts, crying out, "Abba, Father!" So you are no longer a slave but a son, and if a son then also an heir, through God.

GOSPEL
Luke 2:16–21

The shepherds went in haste to Bethlehem and found Mary and Joseph, and the infant lying in the manger. When they saw this, they made known the message that had been told them about this child. All who heard it were amazed by what had been told them by the shepherds. And Mary kept all these things, reflecting on them in her heart. Then the shepherds returned, glorifying and praising God for all they had heard and seen, just as it had been told to them.

When eight days were completed for his circumcision, he was named Jesus, the name given him by the angel before he was conceived in the womb.

The reading from Numbers is known as the "priestly blessing" and recounts the blessing the Aaronite priests were to say over the people of Israel. Written in poetic form, the blessing outlines God's actions toward the Chosen People (blessing, making the divine face shine upon them, lifting up God's countenance) and follows with the results of God's actions (keep you, be gracious, and give peace). In response to this blessing, the Israelites were to bear God's name, making them a sign of God's presence, grace, and peace (Numbers 6:27).

In Paul's Letter to the Galatians, the apostle reminds the believers that they are no longer bound by the law of Moses, despite what rival evangelists were claiming. Paul believed that the law of Moses had been given to the Jews to serve as a *paidagogos*, which means "one who leads children" (Galatians 3:24). We might say a tutor or disciplinarian. But with the coming of Christ the law was no longer necessary. God had sent the Son to be born of a woman, under the law, so as to release those under the law. As those baptized into Christ, the Galatians are now adopted children of God, who have received the Spirit of God enabling them to call God Abba.

The Gospel continues the story of the Nativity and focuses on the witness of the shepherds, ironically not the most well respected of possible witnesses. Yet they go to Bethlehem to find verification of the angel's announcement. When they find the Holy Family, they relate what had been told to them about the child, and then they return, glorifying and praising God. Sandwiched between this coming and going of the shepherds is Mary's response. She treasured these words and pondered them. When the baby is presented in the temple, Simeon will address Mary directly, "and you yourself a sword will pierce" (Luke 2:35). At the close of Luke's infancy narrative—the finding of Jesus in the temple—once again Mary is said to treasure all these things in her heart (Luke 2:51). Luke presents the role of Mary as both the mother of Jesus and the perfect disciple—one who treasures and ponders God's word.

✤ Reflecting on the Word

Our new calendar year begins with scriptural words of blessing, comfort, and empowerment. The priestly or Aaronic blessing in Numbers proclaims God's promise to be with us. God's face shines upon us with graciousness, kindness, and peace. A friend of mine prays for peace in hearts, homes, cities, church, and world. Peace is more than the absence of conflict. Peace means we will be all right no matter what because God is with us.

Paul comforts us with the reminder that we are adopted children of God. One with Christ, we are instruments of God's blessing, peace, and comfort for our world. Mary models the way. She held the message and visit of the shepherds close to her heart, treasuring their words and pondering what their visit meant.

We can find comfort by reflecting on God's visit and message offered through the birth of Jesus that we celebrate this season. Ponder this event. Reflect on today's readings. What do they invite us to treasure? What difference does being God's daughter or son make in how we live?

Baptism makes us disciples of Jesus and empowers us to witness who he is and the difference faith in Christ can make in our world. Do you feel unworthy? The shepherds offer hope. They were considered unclean, suspicious characters, treated like those we can tend to put down. If they could proclaim a message for Mary to ponder, so can we. On this eighth day of Christmas rest, read, and reflect on God's words of blessing and comfort, then rouse up your good self to witness Jesus Christ this day.

✤ Consider/Discuss

- Read the blessing in Numbers and ask, "Where do I find God's light, kindness, and peace in my life?"
- What would it take for you to seek the Lord, like the shepherds, and be God's messenger?

✤ Living and Praying with the Word

Son of Mary, open my eyes to your presence around and within me. Fill me with your Spirit so that I can be an instrument of your light and peace for those I meet today.

January 3, 2016

EPIPHANY OF THE LORD

Today's Focus: Heavenly Lights

The artificial light of the world around us can sometimes eclipse the natural light of heaven that still shines on us, shines in us, shines through us.

FIRST READING
Isaiah 60:1–6

Rise up in splendor, Jerusalem! Your light has come,
    the glory of the Lord shines upon you.
See, darkness covers the earth,
    and thick clouds cover the peoples;
but upon you the Lord shines,
    and over you appears his glory.
Nations shall walk by your light,
    and kings by your shining radiance.
Raise your eyes and look about;
    they all gather and come to you:
your sons come from afar,
    and your daughters in the arms of their nurses.

Then you shall be radiant at what you see,
    your heart shall throb and overflow,
for the riches of the sea shall be emptied out before you,
    the wealth of nations shall be brought to you.
Caravans of camels shall fill you,
    dromedaries from Midian and Ephah;
all from Sheba shall come
    bearing gold and frankincense,
    and proclaiming the praises of the Lord.

PSALM RESPONSE
Psalm 72:11

Lord, every nation on earth will adore you.

SECOND READING
Ephesians 3: 2–3a, 5–6

Brothers and sisters: You have heard of the stewardship of God's grace that was given to me for your benefit, namely, that the mystery was made known to me by revelation. It was not made known to people in other generations as it has now been revealed to his holy apostles and prophets by the Spirit: that the Gentiles are coheirs, members of the same body, and copartners in the promise in Christ Jesus through the gospel.

GOSPEL
Matthew 2:
1–12 When Jesus was born in Bethlehem of Judea, in the days of King Herod, behold, magi from the east arrived in Jerusalem, saying, "Where is the newborn king of the Jews? We saw his star at its rising and have come to do him homage." When King Herod heard this, he was greatly troubled, and all Jerusalem with him. Assembling all the chief priests and the scribes of the people, he inquired of them where the Christ was to be born. They said to him, "In Bethlehem of Judea, for thus it has been written through the prophet:

> And you, Bethlehem, land of Judah,
>> are by no means least among the rulers of Judah;
> since from you shall come a ruler,
>> who is to shepherd my people Israel."

Then Herod called the magi secretly and ascertained from them the time of the star's appearance. He sent them to Bethlehem and said, "Go and search diligently for the child. When you have found him, bring me word, that I too may go and do him homage." After their audience with the king they set out. And behold, the star that they had seen at its rising preceded them, until it came and stopped over the place where the child was. They were overjoyed at seeing the star, and on entering the house they saw the child with Mary his mother. They prostrated themselves and did him homage. Then they opened their treasures and offered him gifts of gold, frankincense, and myrrh. And having been warned in a dream not to return to Herod, they departed for their country by another way.

❖ Understanding the Word

Today's reading comes from what scholars call "Third Isaiah" and was written when the exiles had returned to Jerusalem. Whereas "First Isaiah" reflects the original prophet's oracles against the sins of Jerusalem, warning of punishment (chapters 1–39), the tone of Second Isaiah (chapters 40–55) and Third Isaiah (chapters 56–66) is that of hope. Deliverance has come. God has renewed the divine covenant with the people. God's light will again emanate from Zion and nations will be drawn by this light. A caravan from the East is envisioned, bringing gifts of gold and frankincense. The Gospel reading will describe just such a caravan.

The passage from Ephesians picks up this theme of recognition and inclusion described in Isaiah. The word, translated as "Gentiles" in Ephesians, is the Greek word *ethnoi*, which means both "nations" or non-Jews, hence Gentiles. From an ancient Jewish perspective, one was either a Jew or a member of the *ethnoi*. Through the preaching of the gospel, the Gentiles had become fellow heirs and members of the same body, sharing in the promises of the gospel.

The first Gentiles encountered in Matthew's Gospel are magi from the East who seek the new king of the Jews. The word *magos* originally referred to a member of the Persian priestly class, and later was used of those who engaged in Eastern philosophy and science—hence magicians and astrologers. The magi report seeing a star rising, which, in popular understanding, signaled the birth of a significant person. This star directs the magi to Bethlehem, where they found the "king" in very humble circumstances. The magi pay homage to baby Jesus, presenting him with gifts befitting a king: gold, frankincense, and myrrh. They are warned in a dream not to return to Herod, so they go home by a different route. It is likely that Matthew meant for these Gentiles from the East to foreshadow the inclusion of Gentiles in the later Christian mission.

❖ Reflecting on the Word

The magi must have paid close attention to see a new star. Nowadays, city lights blind us to the lights of heaven. When I was a young religious we sat on our roof deck and paid attention to the sky, pointing out shooting stars, falling stars, or lights that seemed brighter or new. We didn't leave that deck to follow new stars like the magi, but the experience taught me to pay attention to God's glory above, below, and around me, and then, like the magi, act upon what I discovered.

Their message troubled Herod. He did not want competition, so he sought to destroy, rather than honor, the child. The magi paid attention to God's message in a dream and did not return to Herod. They were changed by their encounter with Jesus and departed another way. When we pay attention to the Lord, we are often not the same. We are transformed and live another way. We use our gifts to pay God homage.

Epiphany celebrates God's utter inclusivity. God is Lord of the chosen people and all people, Jew and Gentile. All the people of God become a light for others to see, know, and adore. God's promise to rescue the poor, help the afflicted, govern with justice, and have compassion for everyone is made flesh in Jesus and in us. At baptism we promised to keep the light of Christ burning brightly. We promised to pay attention to Christ wherever his light shines. Live Jesus in your flesh, through your eyes, mouth, hands, feet, and the hair on your head, as St. Francis de Sales commands. Pay attention to everyone, even those you or I might think unworthy. Shine brightly with the light that has come. Be not afraid. Be affirmed.

❖ Consider/Discuss

- Who has surprised you by living the way of Jesus clearly? How?
- Name ways that you can relieve poverty, help those afflicted in any way, and shine with the light of God's justice.

❖ Living and Praying with the Word

Christ our Light, help me to be the star of wonder that shines with your compassionate love so that all people know your presence, justice, peace, and love.

January 10, 2016

BAPTISM OF THE LORD

Today's Focus: Joy to the World!

We both conclude and continue the season of Christmas today. Perhaps its continuation is more important, through our witness as God's beloved daughters and sons.

FIRST READING
Isaiah 40:1–5, 9–11

Comfort, give comfort to my people,
   says your God.
Speak tenderly to Jerusalem, and proclaim to her
   that her service is at an end,
   her guilt is expiated;
indeed, she has received from the hand of the LORD
   double for all her sins.

     A voice cries out:
In the desert prepare the way of the LORD!
   Make straight in the wasteland a highway for our God!
Every valley shall be filled in,
   every mountain and hill shall be made low;
the rugged land shall be made a plain,
   the rough country, a broad valley.
Then the glory of the LORD shall be revealed,
   and all people shall see it together;
   for the mouth of the LORD has spoken.

Go up onto a high mountain,
   Zion, herald of glad tidings;
cry out at the top of your voice,
   Jerusalem, herald of good news!
Fear not to cry out
   and say to the cities of Judah:
   Here is your God!
Here comes with power
   the Lord GOD,
   who rules by a strong arm;
here is his reward with him,
   his recompense before him.
Like a shepherd he feeds his flock;
   in his arms he gathers the lambs,
carrying them in his bosom,
   and leading the ewes with care.

PSALM RESPONSE
Psalm 104:1

O bless the Lord, my soul.

SECOND READING
Titus 2:11–14; 3:4–7

Beloved: The grace of God has appeared, saving all and training us to reject godless ways and worldly desires and to live temperately, justly, and devoutly in this age, as we await the blessed hope, the appearance of the glory of our great God and savior Jesus Christ, who gave himself for us to deliver us from all lawlessness and to cleanse for himself a people as his own, eager to do what is good.

When the kindness and generous love
    of God our savior appeared,
not because of any righteous deeds we had done
    but because of his mercy,
he saved us through the bath of rebirth
    and renewal by the Holy Spirit,
whom he richly poured out on us
    through Jesus Christ our savior,
so that we might be justified by his grace
    and become heirs in hope of eternal life.

GOSPEL
Luke 3:15–16, 21–22

The people were filled with expectation, and all were asking in their hearts whether John might be the Christ. John answered them all, saying, "I am baptizing you with water, but one mightier than I is coming. I am not worthy to loosen the thongs of his sandals. He will baptize you with the Holy Spirit and fire."

After all the people had been baptized and Jesus also had been baptized and was praying, heaven was opened and the Holy Spirit descended upon him in bodily form like a dove. And a voice came from heaven, "You are my beloved Son; with you I am well pleased."

✤ Understanding the Word

In today's first reading, God instructs the anonymous prophet known as Second Isaiah to offer comfort to the exiles in Babylon. This "proclamation of salvation" begins with God's instruction. Preparation is to be made for this glorious event. The reading concludes with further instructions for the prophet who is to "cry out . . . Here is your God!" Since the vision presented was not historically realized by the returning exiles, they came to understand that the glorious restoration was yet to be fulfilled in some distant future. In the Gospels, John the Baptist echoes Isaiah, "In the desert prepare the way of the Lord!" (Isaiah 40:3, see Matthew 3:3; Mark 1:3; Luke 3:4; John 1:23). The long-awaited promise is fulfilled in Jesus.

The author of the second reading also awaits the promise, but for the Letter to Titus that promise is the return of Christ. During the in-between time of Jesus' ascension and his second coming or *parousia*, the faithful in Christ were to behave in a strict ethical manner, living "temperately, justly, and devoutly in this age" (Titus 2:12). Titus describes the rite of initiation as "the bath of rebirth and renewal by the Holy Spirit" (Titus 3:5). The baptism of repentance for the forgiveness of sins (Luke 3:3) is now a gateway into new life in Christ.

Testimony about John exists outside the New Testament accounts. The first-century Jewish historian Josephus reports that John the Baptist urged others to live a life of justice toward one another and reverence toward God. Herod feared John's popularity and had him imprisoned and eventually killed. Today's Gospel reflects some of John's popularity. Those gathered wondered if John was the long-awaited Messiah. The test of multiple attestations suggests that when a passage is found in multiple sources it may be authentic to the time of Jesus. Mark 1:7 (the source for Matthew and Luke) and John 1:26 record John's acknowledgment that "one mightier than I is coming." Like the voice of the prophet in the first reading, John points toward another who "will baptize you with the Holy Spirit and fire" (Luke 3:16). The actual baptism of Jesus by John is not narrated in Luke, but we are told that afterward, while he was praying, Jesus sees the heavens open and the Holy Spirit descend. Though in Matthew's version the heavenly voice is directed to all (Matthew 3:17), in Luke's account only Jesus is told, "You are my beloved Son; with you I am well pleased" (Luke 3:22).

✤ Reflecting on the Word

Today ends the Christmas season. We put away the singing of Christmas carols, like "Joy to the World," but not living their words. The Lord has "saved us through the bath of rebirth and renewal by the Holy Spirit, whom he richly poured out on us through Jesus Christ our savior" (Titus 2:5b–6)—through Jesus Christ, to whom the heavenly voice in Luke's Gospel is addressed, "You are my beloved Son, with you I am well pleased." Because we put on Christ in baptism, we too are beloved daughters and sons of God. The Holy Spirit has been poured out on us. We do more than point the way to Christ like John the Baptizer; we are called to live Jesus.

Baptism makes us heralds of glad tidings who announce that God is with us, offering comfort and speaking tenderly. Our lives proclaim "here is your God" in small ways that speak loudly, for nothing is small in God's service, St. Francis de Sales says. Paying attention to every person we meet, sharing our resources like offering a smile, a call, an e-mail, a text, or a wave that acknowledges the other—all proclaim, "God is here." They can lift the valley of depression, topple the mountain of arrogance, smooth the rough ways of hurt or fear, and make the desert of loneliness bloom. By living our baptism we reveal the glory of the Lord for all to see and enjoy. And if you are stuck in a valley or struggling with some ruggedness in your life, listen for the voice of God that spoke at our baptism: "You are my beloved. With you I am well pleased." Be a living carol that sings joy to the world, the Lord is come for all.

- Do you believe that you are God's beloved daughter or son? How do you show it? If not, what gets in the way?
- Name five concrete ways you can be a herald of the message that God is in our midst, that the Lord is come.

✥ *Living and Praying with the Word*

O God, you have made us your adopted daughters and sons. Deepen your Spirit within us to live Jesus so clearly that people meet him when they meet us, hear his voice when they hear our voices, and know your comfort and love in our midst.

The liturgical year is punctuated with celebrations of significant moments in the life of Jesus: the annunciation and anticipation of his birth (Advent); his birth, epiphany, and baptism (Christmas); his journey to the cross (Lent); his passion and death (Triduum); and his resurrection (Easter). The thirty-three or thirty-four weeks of Ordinary Time are interrupted by Lent and then continue after Pentecost Sunday. The Baptism of the Lord closes the Christmas season, and the following Sunday is numbered as the Second Sunday of Ordinary Time. Special feasts or solemnities that occur during Ordinary Time are known by the feast title and are not numbered (Trinity Sunday, Body and Blood of Christ).

The first readings for Ordinary Time describe the calls of the prophets. For the sake of Zion (Second Sunday), the prophet must not remain silent until Jerusalem is vindicated by God, and no longer desolate or forsaken. The reading from the book of Nehemiah (Third Sunday) is a narrative example of Isaiah's poetic description. The people gather to hear the words of Torah and renew their commitment, for "Today is holy to the LORD your God!" The call of Jeremiah (Fourth Sunday) and the call of Isaiah (Fifth Sunday) remind us of the costs of hearing and responding to God's invitation.

During the first five weeks of Ordinary Time, the last few chapters of Paul's First Letter to the Corinthians are read almost continuously. Paul attempts to dissuade the Corinthians from their factious behavior. They are fighting over whose spiritual gift is greater (Second Sunday), and failing to recognize that they are all part of the same body (Third Sunday). As an antidote to the schisms dividing the community, Paul proposes that they strive for the great gift—love. The self-sacrificing love that Paul advocates puts the good of the community ahead of the ego and needs of the individual. The gospel that Paul preaches (Fifth Sunday) has been handed down to him and so he passes it on to the Corinthians. Here we find the earliest articulation of faith: "Christ died for our sins in accordance with the Scriptures; that he was buried; that he was raised on the third day in accordance with the Scriptures; that he appeared to Cephas, then to the Twelve" (1 Corinthians 15:3–5).

The Gospel readings for Year C are mostly taken from Luke, and introduce us to Jesus' first days: his inaugural in Nazareth (Third Sunday), his rejection there (Fourth Sunday), and the call of the first disciples (Fifth Sunday). Though he follows much of framework of the Gospel of Mark, the evangelist Luke introduces narratives and parables from his own sources, or from another source that Matthew also uses.

January 17, 2016

SECOND SUNDAY IN ORDINARY TIME

Today's Focus: Extraordinary Wines in Ordinary Time

By making an extraordinary wine for a wedding, Jesus demonstrates how we, as baptized members of his Body—the church—are made extraordinary by his grace for the heavenly feast.

FIRST READING
Isaiah 62:1–5

For Zion's sake I will not be silent,
   for Jerusalem's sake I will not be quiet,
until her vindication shines forth like the dawn
   and her victory like a burning torch.

Nations shall behold your vindication,
   and all the kings your glory;
you shall be called by a new name
   pronounced by the mouth of the LORD.
You shall be a glorious crown in the hand of the LORD,
   a royal diadem held by your God.
No more shall people call you "Forsaken,"
   or your land "Desolate,"
but you shall be called "My Delight,"
   and your land "Espoused."
For the LORD delights in you
   and makes your land his spouse.
As a young man marries a virgin,
   your Builder shall marry you;
and as a bridegroom rejoices in his bride
   so shall your God rejoice in you.

PSALM RESPONSE
Psalm 96:3

Proclaim his marvelous deeds to all the nations.

SECOND READING
1 Corinthians 12: 4–11

Brothers and sisters: There are different kinds of spiritual gifts but the same Spirit; there are different forms of service but the same Lord; there are different workings but the same God who produces all of them in everyone. To each individual the manifestation of the Spirit is given for some benefit. To one is given through the Spirit the expression of wisdom; to another, the expression of knowledge according to the same Spirit; to another, faith by the same Spirit; to another, gifts of healing by the one Spirit; to another, mighty deeds; to another, prophecy; to another, discernment of spirits; to another, varieties of tongues; to another, interpretation of tongues. But one and the same Spirit produces all of these, distributing them individually to each person as he wishes.

GOSPEL
John 2:1–11
There was a wedding at Cana in Galilee, and the mother of Jesus was there. Jesus and his disciples were also invited to the wedding. When the wine ran short, the mother of Jesus said to him, "They have no wine." And Jesus said to her, "Woman, how does your concern affect me? My hour has not yet come." His mother said to the servers, "Do whatever he tells you." Now there were six stone water jars there for Jewish ceremonial washings, each holding twenty to thirty gallons. Jesus told them, "Fill the jars with water." So they filled them to the brim. Then he told them, "Draw some out now and take it to the headwaiter." So they took it. And when the headwaiter tasted the water that had become wine, without knowing where it came from—although the servers who had drawn the water knew—, the headwaiter called the bridegroom and said to him, "Everyone serves good wine first, and then when people have drunk freely, an inferior one; but you have kept the good wine until now." Jesus did this as the beginning of his signs at Cana in Galilee and so revealed his glory, and his disciples began to believe in him.

❖ *Understanding the Word:*

On first reading, the passage from Isaiah appears redundant. "For Zion's sake, I will not be silent, for Jerusalem's sake I will not be quiet" (Isaiah 62:1). This method, common to Hebrew poetry, is known as synonymous parallelism, in which the second line essentially repeats the meaning of the first. Antithetic parallelism occurs when the second line is the opposite of the first. In synthetic parallelism, one line might be a comparison to the other and help advance the thought. "As a young man marries a virgin, your Builder shall marry you" (Isaiah 62:5). Parallelism can strengthen a particular point (synonymous), contrast ideas (antithetic), or advance understanding (synthetic).

In his Letter to the Corinthians, Paul uses a slightly different type of parallelism to underscore the gifts of the Spirit. The Corinthians appear to have been arguing over who possessed the "best" spiritual gift. Paul answers that though different in manifestation, all gifts are granted by the same Spirit for the good of the community (1 Corinthians 14:12). Though Paul uses the metaphor of the parts of the body to indicate the value of each individual (1 Corinthians 12:12–26), he nevertheless highlights prophecy as a chief spiritual gift (1 Corinthians 14:1).

The Gospel reading from John presents a hesitant Jesus, who though urged by his mother (John never uses her name) is reluctant to perform a sign. Jesus doesn't perform miracles in the Gospel of John; rather, he demonstrates "signs." The turning of water into wine becomes the first of seven signs in the Gospel that point to Jesus' true identity. Jesus informs his mother that his hour has not yet come (John 2:4), a circumlocution for the moment that Jesus begins his glorification. Scholars propose that the largest section of the Gospel of John can be divided into the Book of Signs (Chapters 1:19 — 12:50) and the Book of Glory (Chapters 13:1 — 20:29).

One time, while shopping for wine, I was struck by the sheer numbers and varieties: red, white, Californian, Argentinian, merlot, chardonnay, and even alcohol free. Not all are of the same quality, but all are wine. The first sign Jesus performs in John's Gospel is changing water into wine. Hesitant at first, he not only performs the sign, he also creates the best wine of the wedding feast. Thus Jesus begins to fulfill the promises we hear from the prophet Isaiah.

Have you thought of yourself as a fine wine? By water and the Holy Spirit we are members of the Church. We have different gifts but the same Spirit. We are one in Christ but have diverse gifts. Blessed Louis Brisson, osfs, founder of the Oblates of St. Francis de Sales, calls this unidiversity. All gifts, great or small, are needed in the Church. They complement one another, like the parts of a body. They are signs that God cares for each of us and for our world. Having drunk of the same Spirit, we become good wine for a thirsty world. It seems the Corinthians thought some were better than others. Not so, says St. Paul. Whether we are a vintage sparkling wine or a newly-pressed varietal, God rejoices in each of us when we live the life of the Spirit given to us. Take time. Drink in the wine of God's Spirit given to you. Let Christ continue to ferment you so your unidiverse gift becomes a fine wine that benefits any and all. Offer yourself during Ordinary Time as an extraordinarily fine wine that gives glory to God.

✤ Consider/Discuss

- What are the gifts that God has given you to build up the Church and transform our world?
- How do your gifts complement those of your family, friends, co-workers, classmates or neighbors?

✤ Living and Praying with the Word

Good and gracious God, you delight in us. Help us use the gifts you have given us to help our sisters and brothers drink in your love and offer you glory and praise.

THIRD SUNDAY IN ORDINARY TIME

Today's Focus: Fulfilled in Our Living

Jesus didn't merely proclaim that Isaiah's words were fulfilled in him, he went out and lived that fulfillment every day. As his disciples, we are called to do the same.

FIRST READING
Nehemiah 8: 2–4a, 5–6, 8–10

Ezra the priest brought the law before the assembly, which consisted of men, women, and those children old enough to understand. Standing at one end of the open place that was before the Water Gate, he read out of the book from daybreak till midday, in the presence of the men, the women, and those children old enough to understand; and all the people listened attentively to the book of the law. Ezra the scribe stood on a wooden platform that had been made for the occasion. He opened the scroll so that all the people might see it—for he was standing higher up than any of the people—; and, as he opened it, all the people rose. Ezra blessed the LORD, the great God, and all the people, their hands raised high, answered, "Amen, amen!" Then they bowed down and prostrated themselves before the LORD, their faces to the ground. Ezra read plainly from the book of the law of God, interpreting it so that all could understand what was read. Then Nehemiah, that is, His Excellency, and Ezra the priest-scribe and the Levites who were instructing the people said to all the people: "Today is holy to the LORD your God. Do not be sad, and do not weep"—for all the people were weeping as they heard the words of the law. He said further: "Go, eat rich foods and drink sweet drinks, and allot portions to those who had nothing prepared; for today is holy to our LORD. Do not be saddened this day, for rejoicing in the LORD must be your strength!"

PSALM RESPONSE
John 6:63c

Your words, Lord, are Spirit and life.

In the shorter form of the reading, the passages in brackets are omitted.

SECOND READING
1 Corinthians 12:12–30 or 12:12–14, 27

Brothers and sisters: As a body is one though it has many parts, and all the parts of the body, though many, are one body, so also Christ. For in one Spirit we were all baptized into one body, whether Jews or Greeks, slaves or free persons, and we were all given to drink of one Spirit.

Now the body is not a single part, but many. [If a foot should say, "Because I am not a hand I do not belong to the body," it does not for this reason belong any less to the body. Or if an ear should say, "Because I am not an eye I do not belong to the body," it does not for this reason belong any less to the body. If the whole body were an eye, where would the hearing be? If the whole body were hearing, where would the sense of smell be? But as it is, God placed the parts, each one of them, in the body as he intended. If they were all one part, where would the body be? But as it is, there are many parts, yet one body. The eye cannot say to the hand, "I do not need you," nor again the head to the feet, "I do not need you." Indeed, the parts of the body that seem to be weaker are all the more necessary, and those parts of the body that we consider less honorable we surround with greater honor, and our less presentable parts are treated with greater propriety, whereas our more presentable parts do not need this. But God has so constructed the body as to give greater honor to a part that is without it, so that there may be no division in the body, but that the parts may have the same concern for one another. If one part suffers, all the parts suffer with it; if one part is honored, all the parts share its joy.]

Now you are Christ's body, and individually parts of it. [Some people God has designated in the church to be, first, apostles; second, prophets; third, teachers; then, mighty deeds; then gifts of healing, assistance, administration, and varieties of tongues. Are all apostles? Are all prophets? Are all teachers? Do all work mighty deeds? Do all have gifts of healing? Do all speak in tongues? Do all interpret?]

GOSPEL
Luke 1:1–4; 4:14–21

Since many have undertaken to compile a narrative of the events that have been fulfilled among us, just as those who were eyewitnesses from the beginning and ministers of the word have handed them down to us, I too have decided, after investigating everything accurately anew, to write it down in an orderly sequence for you, most excellent Theophilus, so that you may realize the certainty of the teachings you have received.

Jesus returned to Galilee in the power of the Spirit, and news of him spread throughout the whole region. He taught in their synagogues and was praised by all.

He came to Nazareth, where he had grown up, and went according to his custom into the synagogue on the sabbath day. He stood up to read and was handed a scroll of the prophet Isaiah. He unrolled the scroll and found the passage where it was written:

The Spirit of the Lord is upon me,
because he has anointed me
to bring glad tidings to the poor.
He has sent me to proclaim liberty to captives
and recovery of sight to the blind,
to let the oppressed go free,
and to proclaim a year acceptable to the Lord.

Rolling up the scroll, he handed it back to the attendant and sat down, and the eyes of all in the synagogue looked intently at him. He said to them, "Today this Scripture passage is fulfilled in your hearing."

❖ Understanding the Word

The book of Nehemiah contains the stories of the returned exiles' attempts to rebuild the city of Jerusalem and the temple of God. Written during the Persian period, both Nehemiah and Ezra are the last books to be included in the Hebrew canon. The concerns of Nehemiah reflect those of a community attempting to redefine itself in the wake of near religious annihilation. In today's reading, Ezra the priest-scribe instructs the people in the correct way to read the Torah so that God's Law can guide the community.

The First Letter to the Corinthians is Paul's reply to the litany of questions the community sent to him. Paul admonishes them in the beginning of the letter because the community has broken into factions (1 Corinthians 1:11). To these crises and conflicts, Paul offers his advice, addressing each one separately. A man of his times, Paul uses rhetoric in order to persuade his community toward good. He uses images of the body and its various parts in order to strengthen the Corinthians' sense of common purpose (1 Corinthians 12:12). The imagery of the body used as a political metaphor to combat factionalism is found in various ancient writers. Paul's ultimate answer to the schisms in his community is rooted not in the parts, but in the whole: "now you are Christ's body, and individually parts of it" (1 Corinthians 12:27).

The reading from Nehemiah depicts the returned exiles gathered around the Torah as their central law and religious guide. Paul advocates that the Corinthians be unified in the body of Christ. The Gospel reading combines both those images. Luke depicts Jesus' inaugural proclamation in the synagogue in Nazareth. Jesus reads from the prophet Isaiah and then returns the scroll to the attendant. "Today this Scripture passage is fulfilled in your hearing" (Luke 4:21). The very actions described by Isaiah (bringing glad tidings to the poor, proclaiming liberation and recovery of sight) will be manifested in the words and deeds of Jesus.

❖ Reflecting on the Word

An ancient maxim—*Lex orandi, lex credendi*—states that we pray what we believe. Our prayer and belief affect how we live. Celebrating liturgy forms us as Catholic Christians. Its ritual actions, songs, scriptures, and prayers, along with how we use our bodies, all make a difference and prepare us to announce the gospel with our lives.

The first reading today describes a liturgy. The Israelites, returned from exile, relearn how to honor, hear, reverence, and live God's law. They weep, overcome with emotion at being able to gather again and celebrate this ritual. They eat and drink to celebrate their return to temple, land, and religious practice. Maybe you have had a similar experience after being away from celebrating the Eucharist for a while.

Liturgy is also the setting for today's Gospel. Jesus reads from Isaiah and invites us to identify his life and ministry as the time when God's promised favor, freedom, justice, and mercy are fulfilled. Because the people thought they knew Jesus well they find his identifying himself with these words difficult. Adding "Today this Scripture passage is fulfilled in your hearing" adds fuel to the fire.

We gather as the Body of Christ to celebrate the liturgy. We have a personal relationship with God's saving love because we belong to Christ's Body. Our unique gifts help the entire Body live what we celebrate. We can live or ignore what we pray. When we live it, do people meet us and say, "Today the scriptures are fulfilled by your living"? We pray what we believe to know how to live. Being filled with the Spirit can free captives, announce good news, open eyes, and anoint the world with the presence of Christ.

❖ Consider/Discuss

- What parts of the liturgy bring you to tears or invite overwhelming rejoicing? Why?
- Does celebrating Mass make a difference in how you live? How?

❖ Living and Praying with the Word

Your words are Spirit and life, O Lord. Give us humble courage to announce your word through attitudes and actions that respect all the members of your Body and God's creation, from least to greatest.

January 31, 2016

FOURTH SUNDAY IN ORDINARY TIME

Today's Focus: Held Captive

Sometimes our thoughts, or the stereotypes we operate from, or preconceptions or misconceptions, can imprison us or those around us. We must be freed to speak the Good News!

FIRST READING
Jeremiah 1:4–5, 17–19

The word of the LORD came to me, saying:
Before I formed you in the womb I knew you,
 before you were born I dedicated you,
 a prophet to the nations I appointed you.

But do you gird your loins;
 stand up and tell them
 all that I command you.
Be not crushed on their account,
 as though I would leave you crushed before them;
for it is I this day
 who have made you a fortified city,
a pillar of iron, a wall of brass,
 against the whole land:
against Judah's kings and princes,
 against its priests and people.
They will fight against you but not prevail over you,
 for I am with you to deliver you, says the LORD.

PSALM RESPONSE
Psalm 71:15ab

I will sing of your salvation.

SECOND READING
1 Corinthians 12:31 — 13:13 or 13:4–13

In the shorter form of the reading, the passages in brackets are omitted.
Brothers and sisters: [Strive eagerly for the greatest spiritual gifts. But I shall show you a still more excellent way.

If I speak in human and angelic tongues, but do not have love, I am a resounding gong or a clashing cymbal. And if I have the gift of prophecy, and comprehend all mysteries and all knowledge; if I have all faith so as to move mountains, but do not have love, I am nothing. If I give away everything I own, and if I hand my body over so that I may boast, but do not have love, I gain nothing.]

Love is patient, love is kind. It is not jealous, it is not pompous, it is not inflated, it is not rude, it does not seek its own interests, it is not quick-tempered, it does not brood over injury, it does not rejoice over wrongdoing but rejoices with the truth. It bears all things, believes all things, hopes all things, endures all things.

Love never fails. If there are prophecies, they will be brought to nothing; if tongues, they will cease; if knowledge, it will be brought to nothing. For we know partially and we prophesy partially, but when the perfect comes, the partial will pass away. When I was a child, I used to talk as a child, think as a child, reason as a child; when I became a man, I put aside childish things. At present we see indistinctly, as in a mirror, but then face to face. At present I know partially; then I shall know fully, as I am fully known. So faith, hope, love remain, these three; but the greatest of these is love.

GOSPEL
Luke 4:21–30

Jesus began speaking in the synagogue, saying: "Today this Scripture passage is fulfilled in your hearing." And all spoke highly of him and were amazed at the gracious words that came from his mouth. They also asked, "Isn't this the son of Joseph?" He said to them, "Surely you will quote me this proverb, 'Physician, cure yourself,' and say, 'Do here in your native place the things that we heard were done in Capernaum.' " And he said, "Amen, I say to you, no prophet is accepted in his own native place. Indeed, I tell you, there were many widows in Israel in the days of Elijah when the sky was closed for three and a half years and a severe famine spread over the entire land. It was to none of these that Elijah was sent, but only to a widow in Zarephath in the land of Sidon. Again, there were many lepers in Israel during the time of Elisha the prophet; yet not one of them was cleansed, but only Naaman the Syrian."

When the people in the synagogue heard this, they were all filled with fury. They rose up, drove him out of the town, and led him to the brow of the hill on which their town had been built, to hurl him down headlong. But Jesus passed through the midst of them and went away.

✤ Understanding the Word

The lot of the prophet is a dismal one. Jeremiah often laments his call, wishing he hadn't been born. He is derided by the people and cursed (Jeremiah 15:10). He's commanded not to marry or have a family (Jeremiah 16:2). He is thrown into a cistern and left to die (Jeremiah 38). And eventually, he will be dragged to Egypt (Jeremiah 43:6). Today's reading recounts the origin of Jeremiah's call. Even before his birth, God had dedicated Jeremiah as a prophet to the nations (Jeremiah 1:5). Jeremiah's youth does not disqualify him (Jeremiah 1:6). God will place the word in his mouth (Jeremiah 1:10) and make of the prophet a pillar of iron, a wall of brass against the land (Jeremiah 1:18).

The entirety of the First Letter to the Corinthians is a sustained argument for unity. Paul's thesis, "Be united in the same mind and in the same purpose" (1 Corinthians 1:10), is exemplified in the metaphor of the body. The Corinthians are all part of the body of Christ (1 Corinthians 12:27). And as members of that body, they are to strive for the spiritual gifts. But even if they possess gifts of tongues (1 Corinthians 13:1) or prophecy (1 Corinthians 13:2) or faith (1 Corinthians 13:3)

and fail to possess love, they are empty. The love of which Paul writes is *agape*
the kind of love that sacrifices for the good of the whole. The *agape* that Paul
advocates is the antidote to schism and leads to *homonoia*, one-mindedness. Jesus
doesn't evidence any of the hesitancy of the reluctant Jeremiah, though he meets
with the same disbelief among his own. In today's Gospel, Jesus stands before
his own townspeople, who marvel at his "gracious words" but are quick to add,
"Isn't this the son of Joseph?" How could a local boy possess such authority? The
people ask him to "perform" as he had in Capernaum, in order to demonstrate
his abilities (Luke 4:23). Jesus invokes the story of Elijah and Elisha, who worked
miracles among foreigners. In Luke 2:32, Simeon had prophesied that Jesus would
be a light to the nations. In Luke 7:1–10, it will be the Gentile centurion who demonstrates great faith in Jesus. Here Luke is laying the foundation for the future
mission to the Gentiles, because Jesus' own had rejected him.

✤ Reflecting on the Word

How often have you said "I know him" or "I can tell you stories about her." How
often has fear of what people might think or say about you kept you from speaking out in faith or on behalf of something or someone in whom you believe? We
can be prisoners to how we think people will respond. We can imprison others by
thinking we really know them.

Jesus' hearers think they know him and they think they know what fidelity to
the Covenant means. So when he speaks boldly, using examples that stretch their
preconceived understanding about God, it is too much for them. Rather than
listen, they drive him out, hoping to kill him. He does not give them power by
keeping silent or lashing out. He simply "passed through the midst of them and
went away," living the love described in Paul's Letter to the Corinthians.

Jeremiah spoke in the face of great odds, too. He was too young. His message,
God's message, challenged the preconceptions of his day. He was tempted to
throw in the towel. But God's promise to strengthen and be with him freed him to
speak out, no matter the cost.

We only know partially. None of us has the big, much less the complete, picture. God's love described in today's second reading can free us from partial
understandings and the prisons of fear that keep us from living our beliefs. It can
free us from misconceptions about what we think we know. Step out in faith like
Jeremiah. Speak with confidence like Jesus. Turn to God's love today and be free.

✤ Consider/Discuss

- Describe times when you have had the courage of Jesus and Jeremiah
  to speak out in faith.
- How has God surprised you when you thought you knew someone or
  learned how the love of God transformed them?

Loving God, you promise to be with us and deliver us. Give me trust in your promise to live my faith clearly today and speak the truth of your ways in love. Surprise me.

February 7, 2016

FIFTH SUNDAY IN ORDINARY TIME

Today's Focus: Admit One

It's not easy to admit our sinfulness and shortcomings; but with Isaiah, Paul, and Peter, when we do so we also open our lives to the saving, merciful grace of God.

FIRST READING
Isaiah 6:1–2a, 3–8

In the year King Uzziah died, I saw the Lord seated on a high and lofty throne, with the train of his garment filling the temple. Seraphim were stationed above.

They cried one to the other, "Holy, holy, holy is the LORD of hosts! All the earth is filled with his glory!" At the sound of that cry, the frame of the door shook and the house was filled with smoke.

Then I said, "Woe is me, I am doomed! For I am a man of unclean lips, living among a people of unclean lips; yet my eyes have seen the King, the LORD of hosts!" Then one of the seraphim flew to me, holding an ember that he had taken with tongs from the altar.

He touched my mouth with it, and said, "See, now that this has touched your lips, your wickedness is removed, your sin purged."

Then I heard the voice of the Lord saying, "Whom shall I send? Who will go for us?" "Here I am," I said; "send me!"

PSALM RESPONSE
Psalm 138:1c

In the sight of the angels I will sing your praises, Lord.

SECOND READING
1 Corinthians 15:1–11 or 15:3–8, 11

In the shorter form of the reading, the passages in brackets are omitted.

[I am reminding you,] brothers and sisters,[of the gospel I preached to you, which you indeed received and in which you also stand. Through it you are also being saved, if you hold fast to the word I preached to you, unless you believed in vain. For] I handed on to you as of first importance what I also received: that Christ died for our sins in accordance with the Scriptures; that he was buried; that he was raised on the third day in accordance with the Scriptures; that he appeared to Cephas, then to the Twelve. After that, he appeared to more than five hundred brothers at once, most of whom are still living, though some have fallen asleep. After that he appeared to James, then to all the apostles. Last of all, as to one born abnormally, he appeared to me. [For I am the least of the apostles, not fit to be called an apostle, because I persecuted the church of God. But by the grace of God I am what I am, and his grace to me has not been ineffective. Indeed, I have toiled harder than all of them; not I, however, but the grace of God that is with me.] Therefore, whether it be I or they, so we preach and so you believed.

While the crowd was pressing in on Jesus and listening to the word of God, he was standing by the Lake of Gennesaret. He saw two boats there alongside the lake; the fishermen had disembarked and were washing their nets. Getting into one of the boats, the one belonging to Simon, he asked him to put out a short distance from the shore. Then he sat down and taught the crowds from the boat. After he had finished speaking, he said to Simon, "Put out into deep water and lower your nets for a catch." Simon said in reply, "Master, we have worked hard all night and have caught nothing, but at your command I will lower the nets." When they had done this, they caught a great number of fish and their nets were tearing. They signaled to their partners in the other boat to come to help them. They came and filled both boats so that the boats were in danger of sinking. When Simon Peter saw this, he fell at the knees of Jesus and said, "Depart from me, Lord, for I am a sinful man." For astonishment at the catch of fish they had made seized him and all those with him, and likewise James and John, the sons of Zebedee, who were partners of Simon. Jesus said to Simon, "Do not be afraid; from now on you will be catching men." When they brought their boats to the shore, they left everything and followed him.

❖ Understanding the Word

Isaiah of Jerusalem narrates his prophetic call in today's first reading. The fantastic description of the high and lofty throne and seraphim stationed above may reflect the actual interior of the holy of holies in the temple, where God was thought to dwell. Smoke in the sanctuary signals the presence of the divine (Exodus 40:34–38; 1 Kings 8:10–11). To this terrifying vision, Isaiah is right to proclaim his unworthiness: "Woe is me, I am doomed! For I am a man of unclean lips, living among a people with unclean lips" (Isaiah 6:5). The belief that beholding the glory of God would lead to one's death (Exodus 33:20) may be why Isaiah considered himself "doomed." He is purified by an ember from the altar and made clean. Now purified, Isaiah is privileged to hear the voice of God asking, "Whom shall I send?" Isaiah responds without hesitation, "Here I am . . . send me" (Isaiah 6:8).

Paul of Tarsus shares in common with Isaiah of Jerusalem recognition of his unworthiness. In today's second reading, Paul reminds the Corinthians of the gospel that he has been given and that he faithfully passes on to them: Christ died for our sins, was buried, was raised on the third day, and appeared to witnesses. "Last of all, as to one born abnormally, he appeared to me. For I am the least of the apostles, not fit to be called an apostle, because I persecuted the church of God" (1 Corinthians 15:8). Isaiah is cleansed by a burning ember and Paul by the grace of God.

The reading from today's Gospel is also a call story similar to that of Isaiah and of Paul. Ordinarily a call story possesses the following elements: invitation, expression of unworthiness on the part of the invitee, reassurance, and commission. Jesus chooses Simon's boat to serve as a platform for his preaching. After teaching the crowds on the shore, Jesus invites Simon to "put out into deep water and lower the nets" (Luke 5:4). With some hesitation, Simon lowers his nets and is astounded by the catch. Simon recognizes that he is in the presence of a holy man: "Depart from me, Lord, for I am a sinful man" (Luke 5:8). Jesus reassures him, "Do not be afraid," and commissions him (Luke 5:10). The experience has an effect not only on Simon, but also on James and John, the sons of Zebedee. They all leave their boats on the shore and follow Jesus.

✤ Reflecting on the Word

Common to today's readings is an admission that we are sinful, unworthy, unclean people. Isaiah calls himself "a man of unclean lips." Peter says, "Depart from me, Lord, for I am a sinful man." Paul identifies himself as "the least of the apostles, not fit to be called an apostle." Also common to our readings is the power of God's mercy. Touching Isaiah's mouth the angel says, "Your wickedness is removed, your sin is purged." Isaiah is freed to proclaim God's presence, responding to God's call. Jesus tells Simon, "Do not be afraid; from now you will be catching" people. Paul proclaims, "By the grace of God I am what I am, and his grace to me has not been ineffective."

We respond to the invitation to Communion, "Lord, I am not worthy that you should enter under my roof." We proclaim our sinfulness. "Only say the word and my soul shall be healed." We proclaim our trust in God's mercy. This coming Wednesday we begin Lent, a springtime retreat to renew the life of Christ we promised to live at Baptism. We name our sinfulness. We invite God's healing touch. We walk with sisters and brothers preparing for Baptism, Confirmation, and Eucharist at the Easter Vigil. We witness that God can take away whatever is sinful and defective in our lives in order to bring out what is upright, strong, and good.

These last days of Ordinary Time, name your sinfulness like Isaiah, Peter, and Paul. Thank God for marvelous, merciful love as they did, too. Hear God's invitation: "Whom shall I send?" Respond like Isaiah, "Here I am, send me." Fish for people, casting wide your net as Christ casts wide the net of God's mercy.

✤ Consider/Discuss

- Name the ways in which you have felt unworthy, unfit to be called a faithful follower of Jesus Christ.
- How has God brought out what is upright, strong, and good in you?

✤ Living and Praying with the Word

Merciful God, thank you for your generous mercy. Help me proclaim your merciful love to those I meet.

Notes

Breaking the flow of Ordinary Time, Lent offers us an opportunity to remember and renew our faith. The readings for this season have a mixture of themes—both celebrating God's fidelity and pointing toward the Cross. The readings from the Old Testament reflect on God's promises and the fulfillment of those promises. In Deuteronomy, the first fruits of the harvest are to be offered to God in gratitude for God's gift of land (First Sunday of Lent). Genesis relates that Abram is given both a sign and an oath to testify to God's fidelity. God will provide Abram with an heir and give his people a land of their own (Second Sunday of Lent). Moses is called forth out of his personal exile to guide the Hebrews out of slavery (Third Sunday of Lent). And in the reading from the book of Joshua, once the Israelites are gathered in the land of Canaan, the manna ceases and they are fed on the bounty of the land (Fourth Sunday of Lent). But God's saving action in the Exodus is nothing compared to what God has in store for the exiles in Babylon. For God is doing something new (Fifth Sunday of Lent). On Palm Sunday, we learn that the Servant of the Lord in Isaiah has been given a mission to proclaim a word to the weary that will rouse them, only to suffer abuse and personal attacks for his fidelity to God.

The second readings are taken from Paul's letters, in which Paul, the apostle to the Gentiles, affirms that both Jew and Gentile are heirs to God's promises (First Sunday of Lent), and believers need only look to Paul as an example (Second Sunday of Lent). The Corinthians are not to follow the example of the Israelites, who grumbled despite God's presence in the wilderness (Third Sunday of Lent), for they are a new creation (Fourth Sunday of Lent). Rather, like an athlete straining for the prize, they are to continue in the race (Fifth Sunday of Lent), taking the example of Christ (Palm Sunday).

In our Gospel readings for Lent we are shown various aspects of Jesus' character. When he is tempted (First Sunday of Lent), Jesus masters the devil, using the word of God as his defense. At the Transfiguration, we learn that Jesus experienced a moment of glory and recognized that his "exodus" would be accomplished in Jerusalem (Second Sunday of Lent). For the next three Sundays, we learn from Jesus that God gives second chances. The barren fig tree is given a reprieve (Third Sunday of Lent), the wayward son is welcomed home extravagantly (Fourth Sunday of Lent), and the woman caught in adultery is forgiven (Fifth Sunday of Lent). Finally, the character of Jesus is poignantly and painfully revealed in the depiction of his passion on Palm Sunday.

FIRST SUNDAY OF LENT

Today's Focus: Crying Out to God

As we enter our Lenten time of renewal and rebirth, we cry out to God for mercy and forgiveness, but must also remember to cry out in gratitude when they are granted.

FIRST READING
Deuteronomy 26: 4–10

Moses spoke to the people, saying: "The priest shall receive the basket from you and shall set it in front of the altar of the Lord, your God. Then you shall declare before the Lord, your God, 'My father was a wandering Aramean who went down to Egypt with a small household and lived there as an alien. But there he became a nation great, strong, and numerous. When the Egyptians maltreated and oppressed us, imposing hard labor upon us, we cried to the Lord, the God of our fathers, and he heard our cry and saw our affliction, our toil, and our oppression. He brought us out of Egypt with his strong hand and outstretched arm, with terrifying power, with signs and wonders; and bringing us into this country, he gave us this land flowing with milk and honey. Therefore, I have now brought you the firstfruits of the products of the soil which you, O Lord, have given me.' And having set them before the Lord, your God, you shall bow down in his presence."

PSALM RESPONSE
Psalm 91:15b

Be with me, Lord, when I am in trouble.

SECOND READING
Romans 10: 8–13

Brothers and sisters: What does Scripture say?
The word is near you,
in your mouth and in your heart
—that is, the word of faith that we preach—, for, if you confess with your mouth that Jesus is Lord and believe in your heart that God raised him from the dead, you will be saved. For one believes with the heart and so is justified, and one confesses with the mouth and so is saved. For the Scripture says,
No one who believes in him will be put to shame.
For there is no distinction between Jew and Greek; the same Lord is Lord of all, enriching all who call upon him. For "everyone who calls on the name of the Lord will be saved."

GOSPEL
Luke 4:1–13

Filled with the Holy Spirit, Jesus returned from the Jordan and was led by the Spirit into the desert for forty days, to be tempted by the devil. He ate nothing during those days, and when they were over he was hungry. The devil said to him, "If you are the Son of God, command this stone to become bread." Jesus answered him, "It is written, *One does not live on bread alone.*"

Then he took him up and showed him all the kingdoms of the world in a single instant. The devil said to him, "I shall give to you all this power and glory; for it has been handed over to me, and I may give it to whomever I wish. All this will be yours, if you worship me." Jesus said to him in reply, "It is written:

You shall worship the Lord, your God,
and him alone shall you serve."

Then he led him to Jerusalem, made him stand on the parapet of the temple, and said to him, "If you are the Son of God, throw yourself down from here, for it is written:

He will command his angels concerning you, to guard you,
and:
With their hands they will support you,
lest you dash your foot against a stone."

Jesus said to him in reply, "It also says,
You shall not put the Lord, your God, to the test."

When the devil had finished every temptation, he departed from him for a time.

❖ Understanding the Word

The first reading is taken from the book of Deuteronomy, which means literally the "second law," since many of its laws are found in other books of the Pentateuch. The section read today concludes the declaration of the laws, which Moses gave to the people after his divine revelation on Mount Horeb (the book of Exodus refers to it as Mount Sinai). The recitation of God's actions from the promises to Abraham through the Exodus and then settlement in the land serve to remind the people of the debt they owe to God, which is paid through proper sacrifice and obedience.

In the second reading from the Letter to the Romans, Paul cites passages of the Hebrew scriptures in order to explain how confession and belief lead to justification or righteousness and salvation. But the scripture, which had formerly been the source of direction only for the Jews, is now also a guide for Gentile believers. Paul cites the prophet Joel: "For everyone who calls on the name of the Lord will be saved" (Joel 3:5). In Romans, the apostle to the Gentiles explains that salvation was offered first to the Jews, and to them belong the sonship, glory, covenants, giving of the Law, and the promises (Romans 9:4). But the Gentiles are now co-heirs to the promise of salvation, grafted onto the branch of faith (Romans 11:17).

The Gospel reading also uses citations from the Hebrew scriptures, but to different effect. Where Paul demonstrated that scripture supported the inclusion of the Gentiles in God's plan of salvation, Jesus shows that God's word provides direction for life. When he is provoked by the devil in the desert, Jesus counters each temptation with scripture. "It is written" introduces the biblical warrants with which Jesus defends himself. In the third temptation, the devil anticipates Jesus' response and attempts to use Jesus' defense against him. This time it is the devil who quotes scripture, "for it is written," citing Psalm 91:11. Jesus replies, "It also says, 'You shall not put the Lord, your God, to the test.'" Even when the devil uses the same techniques, he is no match for Jesus.

❖ Reflecting on the Word

In our responsorial psalm we sing: "Be with me, Lord, when I am in trouble" (Psalm 91:15b). We cry out to God in our need. Moses reminds the people that when their ancestors cried out to the Lord, God heard their cry and freed them. Be grateful, Moses tells them. Paul proclaims how near the word is to the Romans, inviting them to cry out in their need to experience God's freeing, saving presence. The Spirit leads Jesus into the desert for forty days, like the forty years recalled in the first reading, to be tempted by the devil. Jesus cries out in his need, quoting God's word to guide him and counter the devil's temptations.

Lent is our forty-day experience to recall the story of God's saving love affair with us and to grow in gratitude for mercy so near. God's Word is near to us. We name the sin and darkness that tempt us to trust what is not God when what we really need to do is to invite God to be with us in our trouble and heal us. Feeding on the word of God and the liturgy can guide us to live the death and resurrection of Jesus more clearly this year.

Name the ways that you have known God's love throughout your life. Face whatever gets in the way of believing that God's Spirit dwells within you. Cry out to the Lord our God in honesty, faith, gratitude, and need. The Word is near you. May it help you grow more grateful for God's unconditional and merciful love and experience God's nearness this Lent.

❖ Consider/Discuss

- How can you express your gratitude for God's mercy and love in your life this Lent?
- Name the ways that you know that the Word is as near as your mouth and your heart.

❖ Living and Praying with the Word

God, our mercy, feed me with your word and sacrament this Lent. Help my worship of you deepen my trust that you are with me, so that I see you in all creation and make your nearness known to all.

February 21, 2016

SECOND SUNDAY OF LENT

Today's Focus: Emmanuel, God-with-Us

Too often we forget, once Advent and Christmas are over, that God is with us in Jesus. That presence shines forth in glory once again in today's scriptures.

FIRST READING
Genesis 15: 5–12, 17–18

The Lord God took Abram outside and said, "Look up at the sky and count the stars, if you can. Just so," he added, "shall your descendants be." Abram put his faith in the LORD, who credited it to him as an act of righteousness.

He then said to him, "I am the LORD who brought you from Ur of the Chaldeans to give you this land as a possession." "O Lord GOD," he asked, "how am I to know that I shall possess it?" He answered him, "Bring me a three-year-old heifer, a three-year-old she-goat, a three-year-old ram, a turtledove, and a young pigeon." Abram brought him all these, split them in two, and placed each half opposite the other; but the birds he did not cut up. Birds of prey swooped down on the carcasses, but Abram stayed with them. As the sun was about to set, a trance fell upon Abram, and a deep, terrifying darkness enveloped him.

When the sun had set and it was dark, there appeared a smoking fire pot and a flaming torch, which passed between those pieces. It was on that occasion that the LORD made a covenant with Abram, saying: "To your descendants I give this land, from the Wadi of Egypt to the Great River, the Euphrates."

PSALM RESPONSE
Psalm 27:1a

The Lord is my light and my salvation.

In the shorter form of the reading, the passages in brackets are omitted.

SECOND READING
Philippians 3:17 — 4:1 or 3:20 — 4:1

[Join with others in being imitators of me, brothers and sisters, and observe those who thus conduct themselves according to the model you have in us. For many, as I have often told you and now tell you even in tears, conduct themselves as enemies of the cross of Christ. Their end is destruction. Their God is their stomach; their glory is in their "shame." Their minds are occupied with earthly things. But] our citizenship is in heaven, and from it we also await a savior, the Lord Jesus Christ. He will change our lowly body to conform with his glorified body by the power that enables him also to bring all things into subjection to himself.

Therefore, my brothers and sisters, whom I love and long for, my joy and crown, in this way stand firm in the Lord.

GOSPEL
Luke 9:28b–36

Jesus took Peter, John, and James and went up the mountain to pray. While he was praying his face changed in appearance and his clothing became dazzling white. And behold, two men were conversing with him, Moses and Elijah, who appeared in glory and spoke of his exodus that he was going to accomplish in Jerusalem. Peter and his companions had been overcome by sleep, but becoming fully awake, they saw his glory and the two men standing with him. As they were about to part from him, Peter said to Jesus, "Master, it is good that we are here; let us make three tents, one for you, one for Moses, and one for Elijah." But he did not know what he was saying. While he was still speaking, a cloud came and cast a shadow over them, and they became frightened when they entered the cloud. Then from the cloud came a voice that said, "This is my chosen Son; listen to him." After the voice had spoken, Jesus was found alone. They fell silent and did not at that time tell anyone what they had seen.

❖ Understanding the Word

In Genesis 12, Abram had been called by God to leave his family and his homeland and to travel to a land that God would reveal to him, there to become both a great nation and a blessing (Genesis 12:1–3). And Abram went. In today's reading, God again speaks to Abram. This time God makes two promises: Abram's descendants will be as numerous the stars (Genesis 15:1–6), and Abram will possess a land of his own (Genesis 15:7–21). In response to the first promise, Abram "put his faith in the LORD, who credited it to him as an act of righteousness" (Genesis 15:6). But to the second, Abram asks for a sign (Genesis 15:8). To attest to God's trustworthiness and to seal the covenant, God takes an oath (Genesis 15:9–21).

Paul's Letter to the Philippians demonstrates the affection the apostle felt toward this community of Gentile believers in the Roman colony of Philippi. More than a half a dozen times, he refers to his joy over their commitment and faith. He holds them in great affection (Philippians 1:8). And though the impetus for the letter seems to be to iron out some difficulty between the church's leaders (Philippians 4:2–3), Paul takes the occasion to remind his beloved community that they are to look to him as a model who "forgetting what lies behind, but straining forward to what lies ahead, I continue my pursuit toward the goal, the prize of God's upward calling, in Christ Jesus" (Philippians 3:13).

Today's Gospel reading is found toward the end of Jesus' ministry in Galilee. Shortly after the Transfiguration, Jesus will turn his face resolutely toward Jerusalem and begin his journey to the city that kills the prophets (Luke 13:34). After Peter's confession that Jesus is the Messiah of God (Luke 9:20), Jesus utters his first prediction of his passion, death, and resurrection (Luke 9:22), followed by his description of the difficult conditions of discipleship (Luke 9:23–27). The Transfiguration, with its heavenly appearances of Elijah and Moses and divine approbation ("This is my chosen Son") serves as confirmation that Jesus' suffering will end in glory.

How often have we heard the promise that God is with us and transforms us? I relate to Abram's response: "How am I to know?" In other words, I want to believe you, Lord, but . . . I feel so unworthy, I am a sinner, I can't get it together . . . I bet that you could add to this list. Every Lent I seem to face the same sins, character defects or failings. Awareness is a good beginning. St. Francis de Sales notes that there is no better way of growing toward perfection in the spiritual life than to always be starting over again.

Today's Gospel gives us a glimpse of the Resurrection we celebrate at the end of Lent. Jesus is transformed while at prayer. God visits him through Moses and Elijah, in a cloud, and with a voice, "This is my chosen Son; listen to him." He leaves the mountain transfigured and journeys to Jerusalem, to his passion and death. Our journey, like his, is not easy, but we are not alone. Follow Jesus' example. Turn to God in prayer; voice your needs, frustrations, fears, dreams, and desires. Listen for God's voice: "You are my daughter, my son. I am with you." Follow Paul's advice to the Philippians to imitate Jesus.

I need today's reminder that God is with me. I need to remember the promise of resurrection. I need Lenten prayer to turn to Jesus and start over again. The Lord is here to light our way. Pray. Listen. Trust and imitate Jesus. It is good that we are here to stand firm in the Lord.

✤ Consider/Discuss

- When have I known without a doubt that I am God's beloved son or daughter?
- What and who help me trust that God's promises will be fulfilled?

✤ Living and Praying with the Word

Dear Jesus, it is good that we are here and that you are here, too. Make me dazzling with the light of your love so that others can come to see you in my words, deeds, and attitudes this Lent, and find hope.

February 28, 2016

THIRD SUNDAY OF LENT/YEAR C

Today's Focus: Both/And

It would be enough if God were kind toward us, or merciful; but God is both, and we need to respond by living in God's image as kind and merciful disciples.

FIRST READING
Exodus 3:1–8a, 13–15

Moses was tending the flock of his father-in-law Jethro, the priest of Midian. Leading the flock across the desert, he came to Horeb, the mountain of God. There an angel of the LORD appeared to Moses in fire flaming out of a bush. As he looked on, he was surprised to see that the bush, though on fire, was not consumed. So Moses decided, "I must go over to look at this remarkable sight, and see why the bush is not burned."

When the LORD saw him coming over to look at it more closely, God called out to him from the bush, "Moses! Moses!" He answered, "Here I am." God said, "Come no nearer! Remove the sandals from your feet, for the place where you stand is holy ground. I am the God of your fathers," he continued, "the God of Abraham, the God of Isaac, the God of Jacob." Moses hid his face, for he was afraid to look at God. But the LORD said, "I have witnessed the affliction of my people in Egypt and have heard their cry of complaint against their slave drivers, so I know well what they are suffering. Therefore I have come down to rescue them from the hands of the Egyptians and lead them out of that land into a good and spacious land, a land flowing with milk and honey."

Moses said to God, "But when I go to the Israelites and say to them, 'The God of your fathers has sent me to you,' if they ask me, 'What is his name?' what am I to tell them?" God replied, "I am who am." Then he added, "This is what you shall tell the Israelites: I AM sent me to you."

God spoke further to Moses, "Thus shall you say to the Israelites: The LORD, the God of your fathers, the God of Abraham, the God of Isaac, the God of Jacob, has sent me to you.

"This is my name forever; thus am I to be remembered through all generations."

PSALM RESPONSE
Psalm 103:8a

The Lord is kind and merciful.

SECOND READING
1 Corinthians 10: 1–6, 10–12 I do not want you to be unaware, brothers and sisters, that our ancestors were all under the cloud and all passed through the sea, and all of them were baptized into Moses in the cloud and in the sea. All ate the same spiritual food, and all drank the same spiritual drink, for they drank from a spiritual rock that followed them, and the rock was the Christ. Yet God was not pleased with most of them, for they were struck down in the desert.

These things happened as examples for us, so that we might not desire evil things, as they did. Do not grumble as some of them did, and suffered death by the destroyer. These things happened to them as an example, and they have been written down as a warning to us, upon whom the end of the ages has come. Therefore, whoever thinks he is standing secure should take care not to fall.

GOSPEL
Luke 13:1–9 Some people told Jesus about the Galileans whose blood Pilate had mingled with the blood of their sacrifices. Jesus said to them in reply, "Do you think that because these Galileans suffered in this way they were greater sinners than all other Galileans? By no means! But I tell you, if you do not repent, you will all perish as they did! Or those eighteen people who were killed when the tower at Siloam fell on them—do you think they were more guilty than everyone else who lived in Jerusalem? By no means! But I tell you, if you do not repent, you will all perish as they did!"

And he told them this parable: "There once was a person who had a fig tree planted in his orchard, and when he came in search of fruit on it but found none, he said to the gardener, 'For three years now I have come in search of fruit on this fig tree but have found none. So cut it down. Why should it exhaust the soil?' He said to him in reply, 'Sir, leave it for this year also, and I shall cultivate the ground around it and fertilize it; it may bear fruit in the future. If not you can cut it down.' "

❖ Understanding the Word

The first reading introduces Moses, who, having fled from Egypt after committing murder, is now a wandering shepherd working for his father-in-law. A murderous outlaw hardly seems like one whom God would call into divine service. Nonetheless, today's reading narrates the remarkable encounter on Mount Horeb. It appears that God must be introduced to Moses: "I am the God of your fathers . . . the God of Abraham, the God of Isaac, the God of Jacob" (Exodus 3:6). The suffering witnessed by Moses that led to his striking the Egyptians (Exodus 2:11) is the same affliction and cry of complaint to which God is now responding. Thus begins the prophetic ministry of Moses, who, armed with God's promises will lead the people from slavery into "a land flowing with milk and honey" (Exodus 3:8).

Paul refers to the Exodus that followed Moses' encounter with God in his Letter to the Corinthians: "our ancestors were all under the cloud and all passed through the sea" (1 Corinthians 10:1). But Paul interprets the event through the lens of a believer in Christ. "They drank from a spiritual rock that followed them, and the rock was the Christ" (1 Corinthians 10:4). Despite the guidance of Moses and the presence of God, therefore, not all the Hebrews survived the desert. The privilege of presence does not guarantee that one pleases God, thus Paul charges the Corinthians not to grumble—another reference to the wandering Hebrews (Exodus 16:7).

The Gospel reading also serves as a reminder to repent or risk perishing. Jesus responds to the story of Pilate's killing of a group of Galileans (an event unknown outside of the New Testament, though consistent with other heinous actions of Pilate). Those killed were not more guilty than any others; nonetheless, the capricious event should serve as a reminder to repent. But the sharpness of Jesus' warning is softened a bit by the parable of the unproductive fig tree. Finding no fruit, the owner intended to cut the tree down. Only at the insistence (and compassion) of the gardener did the owner relent. "I shall cultivate the ground around it and fertilize it; it may bear fruit in the future" (Luke 13:8–9).

❖ Reflecting on the Word

A cantor friend was practicing today's psalm response with her daughter: "The Lord is kind and merciful." She heard her daughter sing: "The Lord is kind of merciful." There is a big difference between being kind *and* merciful and kind *of* merciful. Which wording reflects your experience of God?

Moses was in exile because he murdered an Egyptian who abused a Hebrew slave. When he meets God in a burning bush, God asks this murderer to lead the people. Talk about mercy and a mercy that is constant, for God is "I am who am," that is, constant being.

The ever-living God took flesh in Jesus. The parable about the fig tree is a statement about God's desire to save us. Through Jesus the ever-living God cultivates us and fertilizes us with mercy. When we repent, we reorient our lives to live Jesus' values and teaching. The same God who asked a murderer to lead the Israelites forgives and empowers us to bear fruit. Talk about mercy!

The Corinthians thought they were better than anyone else. But they were sinners like everyone else. Paul advises them to learn from their ancestors who complained in the desert; many of them were saved, though not all. Some chose not to repent. Paul is the gardener who offers the Corinthians another chance to know God as kind *and* merciful.

None of us is perfect. All of us need the gift of God's unconditional love and mercy. Turn to the Lord. Learn from our ancestors. Repent. God is kind *and* merciful. Believe and live the kindness and mercy of God.

✤ Consider/Discuss

- When have you experienced God's kindness and mercy in your life?
- How can you share that love and mercy in ways that help others know God's forgiveness?

✤ Living and Praying with the Word

God of our Lord Jesus Christ, open my eyes to see you in my life today, and open my heart to repent so that all may know your love and mercy this Lent.

February 28, 2016

THIRD SUNDAY OF LENT/YEAR A

Today's Focus: I'm Thirsty. I'm Thirsty? I'm Thirsty!

As Lent re-focuses us on our own baptismal calling, we need to reflect more deeply on the ways that the waters of Baptism continue to instill a thirst for God in us.

FIRST READING
Exodus 17: 3–7

In those days, in their thirst for water, the people grumbled against Moses, saying, "Why did you ever make us leave Egypt? Was it just to have us die here of thirst with our children and our livestock?" So Moses cried out to the LORD, "What shall I do with this people? A little more and they will stone me!" The LORD answered Moses, "Go over there in front of the people, along with some of the elders of Israel, holding in your hand, as you go, the staff with which you struck the river. I will be standing there in front of you on the rock in Horeb. Strike the rock, and the water will flow from it for the people to drink." This Moses did, in the presence of the elders of Israel. The place was called Massah and Meribah, because the Israelites quarreled there and tested the LORD, saying, "Is the LORD in our midst or not?"

PSALM RESPONSE
Psalm 95:8

If today you hear his voice, harden not your hearts.

SECOND READING
Romans 5: 1–2, 5–8

Brothers and sisters: Since we have been justified by faith, we have peace with God through our Lord Jesus Christ, through whom we have gained access by faith to this grace in which we stand, and we boast in hope of the glory of God.

And hope does not disappoint, because the love of God has been poured out into our hearts through the Holy Spirit who has been given to us. For Christ, while we were still helpless, died at the appointed time for the ungodly. Indeed, only with difficulty does one die for a just person, though perhaps for a good person one might even find courage to die. But God proves his love for us in that while we were still sinners Christ died for us.

In the shorter form of the reading, the passages in brackets are omitted.

GOSPEL
John 4:5–42 or 4:5–15, 19b–26, 39a, 40–42

Jesus came to a town of Samaria called Sychar, near the plot of land that Jacob had given to his son Joseph. Jacob's well was there. Jesus, tired from his journey, sat down there at the well. It was about noon.

A woman of Samaria came to draw water. Jesus said to her, "Give me a drink." His disciples had gone into the town to buy food. The Samaritan woman said to him, "How can you, a Jew, ask me, a Samaritan woman, for a drink?"—For Jews use nothing in common with Samaritans.—Jesus answered and said to her, "If you knew the gift of God and who is saying to you, 'Give me a drink,' you would have asked him and he would have given you living water." The woman said to him, "Sir, you do not even have a bucket and the cistern is deep; where then can you get this living water? Are you greater than our father Jacob, who gave us this cistern and drank from it himself with his children and his flocks?" Jesus answered and said to her, "Everyone who drinks this water will be thirsty again; but whoever drinks the water I shall give will never thirst; the water I shall give will become in him a spring of water welling up to eternal life." The woman said to him, "Sir, give me this water, so that I may not be thirsty or have to keep coming here to draw water."

[Jesus said to her, "Go call your husband and come back." The woman answered and said to him, "I do not have a husband." Jesus answered her, "You are right in saying, 'I do not have a husband.' For you have had five husbands, and the one you have now is not your husband. What you have said is true." The woman said to him, "Sir,] I can see that you are a prophet. Our ancestors worshiped on this mountain; but you people say that the place to worship is in Jerusalem." Jesus said to her, "Believe me, woman, the hour is coming when you will worship the Father neither on this mountain nor in Jerusalem. You people worship what you do not understand; we worship what we understand, because salvation is from the Jews. But the hour is coming, and is now here, when true worshipers will worship the Father in Spirit and truth; and indeed the Father seeks such people to worship him. God is Spirit, and those who worship him must worship in Spirit and truth."

The woman said to him, "I know that the Messiah is coming, the one called the Christ; when he comes, he will tell us everything." Jesus said to her, "I am he, the one speaking with you."

[At that moment his disciples returned, and were amazed that he was talking with a woman, but still no one said, "What are you looking for?" or "Why are you talking with her?" The woman left her water jar and went into the town and said to the people, "Come see a man who told me everything I have done. Could he possibly be the Christ?" They went out of the town and came to him. Meanwhile, the disciples urged him, "Rabbi, eat." But he said to them, "I have food to eat of which you do not know." So the disciples said to one another, "Could someone have brought him something to eat?" Jesus said to them, "My food is to do the will of the one who sent me and to finish his work. Do you not say, 'In four months the harvest will be here'? I tell you, look up and see the fields ripe for the harvest. The reaper is already receiving payment and gathering crops for eternal life, so that the sower and reaper can rejoice together. For here the saying is verified that 'One sows and another reaps.' I sent you to reap what you have not worked for; others have done the work, and you are sharing the fruits of their work."]

Many of the Samaritans of that town began to believe in him
[because of the word of the woman who testified, "He told me
everything I have done."] When the Samaritans came to him, they
invited him to stay with them; and he stayed there two days. Many
more began to believe in him because of his word, and they said
to the woman, "We no longer believe because of your word; for we
have heard for ourselves, and we know that this is truly the savior
of the world."

❖ Understanding the Word

The narrative of the Exodus of the Hebrews from Egypt is the foundation story
of Israel, but not long after their harrowing escape, the people turn on Moses,
their leader. First, they grumble that they have no food (Exodus 16:3), and God
provides manna in the morning and quail in the evening. In today's reading, their
complaint is thirst. Moses is justified in asking God, "What shall I do with this
people?" And as God had provided food, now through the actions of Moses, God
provides drink. The place was called Massah (the place of the test) and Meribah
(the place of quarreling), and served as a reminder to future Israelites of God's
provident care despite the people's grumbling.

The second reading from Paul's Letter to the Romans is another example of
God's care, despite humanity's sinful state. Christ's willingness to die for "godless
people" is beyond imagining. Perhaps a good person may sacrifice his or her life
for someone who is just. But for a sinner? Christ's death evidences God's love for
us. And through his death, believers are justified and are at peace with God. As
Paul explains, God has poured out the Holy Spirit into the hearts of believers.
The presence of the Holy Spirit gives reason to hope that all believers will stand
in the glory of God.

The topic of thirst appears again in the Gospel reading. The woman of Samaria
meets the man of Galilee at the well of Jacob. The evangelist John may be playing
off the motif of meeting one's future spouse at the well. A wife for Isaac is found
at the well (Genesis 23:11–14). Jacob met Rachel at a well (Genesis 29:9–12).
Moses met Zipporah, the daughter of Jethro, at a well (Exodus 2:16–22). Indeed,
Jesus asks the woman about her husbands (she's had five). The evangelist seems
to be explaining to his own community how the Samaritans "married" into the
Johannine community. But the encounter also serves a larger purpose. The
Samaritan woman is contrasted with Nicodemus in John 3:1–14. Like the Pharisee,
she appears at an unusual time. At first she misunderstands Jesus' offer of living
water. However, where Nicodemus was stumped by Jesus' teaching, the woman
of Samaria engages in a theological conversation with Jesus. Jesus even reveals
to her that he is the Messiah. She leaves her water jar behind (perhaps a symbol
of having received the "living water"), returns to the town, and invites others to
come to Jesus.

✤ Reflecting on the Word

For what do you thirst? Some thirsts are physical: a cup of water or a favorite beverage. Some thirsts run deeper: freedom, security, forgiveness, acceptance, respect. In Egypt they had food and water, but in the desert they thirst, so they grumble to Moses. He grumbles to God. God provides water and restores their trust in Moses. Complaint, when made to someone who cares, can help us change or accept our situation, quench thirst and restore trust.

The Samaritan woman longs to be freed from her peers' judgmentalism when she comes to fill her bucket. She goes out at high noon, when no one went outside because of the heat. She meets a Jewish man. Women and men and Samaritans and Jews did not speak in public. But Jesus' caring engagement quells her fear, quenches her thirst, and offers such acceptance that she freely names the truth that others ridicule. Not only is her thirst for acceptance and respect quenched, she offers the living water of Jesus to those she had tried to avoid. They listen and follow. Acceptance, respect, and forgiveness turned the desert of her life into a life-giving stream.

Paul talks about the hope we have through Jesus Christ. Hope does not mean that everything will be all right. Hope means that however things turn out, we will be all right and find life in the deserts of our lives, forgiveness for sin, and respect from the God who cared enough to die even when we were sinners. Voice your needs to God like Moses and the Israelites. Engage in conversation with Jesus like the Samaritan woman. Invite the life-giving stream of God's loving mercy to quench your thirst. Then share it with our sisters and brothers.

✤ Consider/Discuss

- What are your deepest longings and thirsts?
- How has God quenched them and invited you to be life-giving water for others?

✤ Living and Praying with the Word

Give me living water, O God, and the courage to enter into the kind of exchange with you that will free me to be the vessel you use to quench the thirsts of others.

March 6, 2016

FOURTH SUNDAY OF LENT/YEAR C

Today's Focus: Upset by God's Mercy

Too often we are like the older son in today's Gospel passage: we criticize God's merciful nature rather than trying to reflect it.

FIRST READING
Joshua 5:9a, 10–12

The Lord said to Joshua, "Today I have removed the reproach of Egypt from you."

While the Israelites were encamped at Gilgal on the plains of Jericho, they celebrated the Passover on the evening of the fourteenth of the month. On the day after the Passover, they ate of the produce of the land in the form of unleavened cakes and parched grain. On that same day after the Passover, on which they ate of the produce of the land, the manna ceased. No longer was there manna for the Israelites, who that year ate of the yield of the land of Canaan.

PSALM RESPONSE
Psalm 34:9a

Taste and see the goodness of the Lord.

SECOND READING
2 Corinthians 5: 17–21

Brothers and sisters: Whoever is in Christ is a new creation: the old things have passed away; behold, new things have come. And all this is from God, who has reconciled us to himself through Christ and given us the ministry of reconciliation, namely, God was reconciling the world to himself in Christ, not counting their trespasses against them and entrusting to us the message of reconciliation. So we are ambassadors for Christ, as if God were appealing through us. We implore you on behalf of Christ, be reconciled to God. For our sake he made him to be sin who did not know sin, so that we might become the righteousness of God in him.

GOSPEL

Luke 15:1–3, 11–32

Tax collectors and sinners were all drawing near to listen to Jesus, but the Pharisees and scribes began to complain, saying, "This man welcomes sinners and eats with them." So to them Jesus addressed this parable: "A man had two sons, and the younger son said to his father, 'Father give me the share of your estate that should come to me.' So the father divided the property between them. After a few days, the younger son collected all his belongings and set off to a distant country where he squandered his inheritance on a life of dissipation. When he had freely spent everything, a severe famine struck that country, and he found himself in dire need. So he hired himself out to one of the local citizens who sent him to his farm to tend the swine. And he longed to eat his fill of the pods on which the swine fed, but nobody gave him any. Coming to his senses he thought, 'How many of my father's hired workers have more than enough food to eat, but here am I, dying from hunger. I shall get up and go to my father and I shall say to him, "Father, I have sinned against heaven and against you. I no longer deserve to be called your son; treat me as you would treat one of your hired workers." ' So he got up and went back to his father. While he was still a long way off, his father caught sight of him, and was filled with compassion. He ran to his son, embraced him and kissed him. His son said to him, 'Father, I have sinned against heaven and against you; I no longer deserve to be called your son.' But his father ordered his servants, 'Quickly bring the finest robe and put it on him; put a ring on his finger and sandals on his feet. Take the fattened calf and slaughter it. Then let us celebrate with a feast, because this son of mine was dead, and has come to life again; he was lost, and has been found.' Then the celebration began. Now the older son had been out in the field and, on his way back, as he neared the house, he heard the sound of music and dancing. He called one of the servants and asked what this might mean. The servant said to him, 'Your brother has returned and your father has slaughtered the fattened calf because he has him back safe and sound.' He became angry, and when he refused to enter the house, his father came out and pleaded with him. He said to his father in reply, 'Look, all these years I served you and not once did I disobey your orders; yet you never gave me even a young goat to feast on with my friends. But when your son returns who swallowed up your property with prostitutes, for him you slaughter the fattened calf.' He said to him, 'My son, you are here with me always; everything I have is yours. But now we must celebrate and rejoice, because your brother was dead and has come to life again; he was lost and has been found.' "

The reading from the book of Joshua recounts the last appearance of manna, the miraculous food by which God fed the wandering Israelites, and the celebration of the first Passover in the land. Prior to the celebration, the LORD instructs Joshua to circumcise the sons of the Israelites born during the forty-year sojourn, explaining, "Today I have removed the reproach of Egypt from you," and thus marking a new moment in Israel's history. On the day after Passover, the Israelites eat of the produce of the land of Canaan, symbolizing the fulfillment of the promise (Deuteronomy 32:13).

The second reading is taken from Paul's Second Letter to the Corinthians, which scholars propose is as many as five different letter fragments edited into a whole. Most of Second Corinthians 2:14 — 7:4 (from which this reading is taken) is believed to have been a separate letter, written shortly after First Corinthians. In today's reading, Paul exhorts the Corinthians that "whoever is in Christ is a new creation" (2 Corinthians 5:17). This new creation is the result of baptism into Christ, who "died for all, so that those who live might no longer live for themselves but for him who for their sake died and was raised" (2 Corinthians 5:15). Paul explains his ministry as that of an ambassador, who in the ancient context stood as the representative of the one who sent him. Standing between people and God, Paul urges that as the Father reconciled the world to himself in Christ, the Corinthians are to be reconciled to God; thus, they too participate in the ministry of reconciliation (2 Corinthians 5:19).

Often referred to as "the parable of the prodigal son," today's Gospel might more appropriately be called "the parable of the prodigal father," for it is the father who extravagantly showers riches upon his returned son. While it may appear that the point of the story is the younger son's coming to his senses, it is not his return that irks his brother. Rather, it is the father's compassion, generosity, and celebration that anger the older son. Jesus recounts the parable in response to the complaint of the Pharisees and scribes that he welcomed tax collectors and sinners. Like the reading from Second Corinthians, the parable witnesses to the hope of reconciliation—the lost are found, and the dead brought back to life.

✤ Reflecting on the Word

I saw the familiar God through fresh eyes. I noticed for the first time that Jesus addressed this parable to the Pharisees and scribes who complained that he welcomed sinners and ate with them. Now the older jealous son became the prodigal one, who was angry with his father for lavishing forgiveness on the younger prodigal. He stayed home. He didn't waste his inheritance on prostitutes. He was obedient and faithful but did not receive so much as a young goat, much less the fattened calf. Their father pleads with him to see through the father's eyes, grateful that the prodigal has returned and is alive. Could the father have shown the older son gratitude for fidelity earlier? Maybe. Could the older son have expressed gratitude for what his father always shared? Maybe. That's not our story.

The Pharisees and scribes are upset that the God Jesus shows is generous in mercy. Jesus welcomes those they judge and exclude. They missed the point. Obedience is simply doing our duty. We are asked to do more, welcome the lost, forgive the sinner—treat them as God treats us. After all, we all need to "be reconciled to God" (2 Corinthians 5:20c). We all sin. We are "ambassadors for Christ," (2 Corinthians 5:20a) by sharing the forgiveness we are freely given.

God feeds us with the manna of forgiveness to help us pass over from the land of sin to feast on God's promised merciful love. Having tasted and seen the goodness of the Lord we can feed others with God's unconditional love known in Jesus Christ. Can we see others and ourselves with God's eyes? Welcome others as God welcomes the least, the last, and the lost among and within us.

Celebrate! What was lost is found, what was dead is alive.

✤ Consider/Discuss

- When have you been jealous of someone you deemed unworthy to experience God's forgiveness and mercy? Why?
- How can you be an ambassador of reconciliation for Christ?

✤ Living and Praying with the Word

Generous God, you are rich in mercy even when we turn away from you. Open our eyes this day to see as you see, and help me choose to celebrate the mercy you offer all.

77

March 6, 2016

FOURTH SUNDAY OF LENT/YEAR A

Today's Focus: Blinded by Bias

Many things keep us from seeing, understanding, and reacting to the world around us as God wills. Today is the time to ask God to remove whatever impairs our vision.

FIRST READING
1 Samuel 16: 1b, 6–7, 10–13a

The LORD said to Samuel: "Fill your horn with oil, and be on your way. I am sending you to Jesse of Bethlehem, for I have chosen my king from among his sons."

As Jesse and his sons came to the sacrifice, Samuel looked at Eliab and thought, "Surely the Lord's anointed is here before him." But the LORD said to Samuel: "Do not judge from his appearance or from his lofty stature, because I have rejected him. Not as man sees does God see, because man sees the appearance but the LORD looks into the heart." In the same way Jesse presented seven sons before Samuel, but Samuel said to Jesse, "The LORD has not chosen any one of these." Then Samuel asked Jesse, "Are these all the sons you have?" Jesse replied, "There is still the youngest, who is tending the sheep." Samuel said to Jesse, "Send for him; we will not begin the sacrificial banquet until he arrives here." Jesse sent and had the young man brought to them. He was ruddy, a youth handsome to behold and making a splendid appearance. The LORD said, "There—anoint him, for this is the one!" Then Samuel, with the horn of oil in hand, anointed David in the presence of his brothers; and from that day on, the spirit of the LORD rushed upon David.

PSALM RESPONSE
Psalm 23:1

The Lord is my shepherd; there is nothing I shall want.

SECOND READING
Ephesians 5: 8–14

Brothers and sisters: You were once darkness, but now you are light in the Lord. Live as children of light, for light produces every kind of goodness and righteousness and truth. Try to learn what is pleasing to the Lord. Take no part in the fruitless works of darkness; rather expose them, for it is shameful even to mention the things done by them in secret; but everything exposed by the light becomes visible, for everything that becomes visible is light. Therefore, it says:

"Awake, O sleeper,
and arise from the dead,
and Christ will give you light."

GOSPEL
John 9:1–41 or
9:1, 6–9, 13–17,
34–38

As Jesus passed by he saw a man blind from birth. [His disciples asked him, "Rabbi, who sinned, this man or his parents, that he was born blind?" Jesus answered, "Neither he nor his parents sinned; it is so that the works of God might be made visible through him. We have to do the works of the one who sent me while it is day. Night is coming when no one can work. While I am in the world, I am the light of the world." When he had said this,] he spat on the ground and made clay with the saliva, and smeared the clay on his eyes, and said to him, "Go wash in the Pool of Siloam"—which means Sent—. So he went and washed, and came back able to see.

His neighbors and those who had seen him earlier as a beggar said, "Isn't this the one who used to sit and beg?" Some said, "It is," but others said, "No, he just looks like him." He said, "I am." [So they said to him, "How were your eyes opened?" He replied, "The man called Jesus made clay and anointed my eyes and told me, 'Go to Siloam and wash.' So I went there and washed and was able to see." And they said to him, "Where is he?" He said, "I don't know."]

They brought the one who was once blind to the Pharisees. Now Jesus had made clay and opened his eyes on a sabbath. So then the Pharisees also asked him how he was able to see. He said to them, "He put clay on my eyes, and I washed, and now I can see." So some of the Pharisees said, "This man is not from God, because he does not keep the sabbath." But others said, "How can a sinful man do such signs?" And there was a division among them. So they said to the blind man again, "What do you have to say about him, since he opened your eyes?" He said, "He is a prophet."

[Now the Jews did not believe that he had been blind and gained his sight until they summoned the parents of the one who had gained his sight. They asked them, "Is this your son, who you say was born blind? How does he now see?" His parents answered and said, "We know that this is our son and that he was born blind. We do not know how he sees now, nor do we know who opened his eyes. Ask him, he is of age; he can speak for himself." His parents said this because they were afraid of the Jews, for the Jews had already agreed that if anyone acknowledged him as the Christ, he would be expelled from the synagogue. For this reason his parents said, "He is of age; question him."

So a second time they called the man who had been blind and said to him, "Give God the praise! We know that this man is a sinner." He replied, "If he is a sinner, I do not know. One thing I do know is that I was blind and now I see." So they said to him, "What did he do to you? How did he open your eyes?" He answered them, "I told you already and you did not listen. Why do you want to hear it again? Do you want to become his disciples, too?" They ridiculed him and said, "You are that man's disciple; we are disciples of Moses! We know that God spoke to Moses, but we do not know where this one is from." The man answered and said to them, "This is what is so amazing, that you do not know where he is from, yet he

79

opened my eyes. We know that God does not listen to sinners, but if one is devout and does his will, he listens to him. It is unheard of that anyone ever opened the eyes of a person born blind. If this man were not from God, he would not be able to do anything." | They answered and said to him, "You were born totally in sin, and are you trying to teach us?" Then they threw him out.

When Jesus heard that they had thrown him out, he found him and said, "Do you believe in the Son of Man?" He answered and said, "Who is he, sir, that I may believe in him?" Jesus said to him, "You have seen him, the one speaking with you is he." He said, "I do believe, Lord," and he worshiped him. [Then Jesus said, "I came into this world for judgment, so that those who do not see might see, and those who do see might become blind."

Some of the Pharisees who were with him heard this and said to him, "Surely we are not also blind, are we?" Jesus said to them, "If you were blind, you would have no sin; but now you are saying, 'We see,' so your sin remains."]

❖❖❖ *Understanding the Word*

The reading from the first book of Samuel introduces David, the youngest son of Jesse of Bethlehem. At the request of the people, God had allowed the prophet Samuel to anoint Saul as ruler over the people (1 Samuel 10:1), but Saul proved unworthy. Samuel is sent to Bethlehem to anoint a new king from among the sons of Jesse. Judging by appearance, Samuel mistakes the oldest as the Lord's chosen. But God corrects him, "Not as human beings see does God see." It is the youngest son, David, whom God has chosen. As Samuel anoints him, the Spirit of the Lord rushes upon him. David will prove a worthy ruler, but he must first deal with Saul's jealousy, for as the Spirit descended upon David, so it withdrew from Saul. After Saul's death, David will be made king of Judah (2 Samuel 2:4).

The Letter to the Ephesians purported to be have been written by Paul actually comes from the second generation of Pauline Christians. Writing in the voice of the Apostle, the author reminds the community to live according to the light, which produces goodness, justice, and truth—virtues that even pagans admire.

The Gospel reading from John introduces the narrative of the man born blind. This is the sixth sign or miracle that Jesus has performed (water into wine in Cana, 2:1–11; royal official's son restored to life, 4:46–54; healing of the crippled man at Bethesda, 5:1–9; feeding the multitude, 6:1–15; walking on the water, 6:16–21). Each sign serves to reveal Jesus' identity, and confirms his disciples' belief in him. But with each sign, those who do not believe strengthen their animosity against him. After the seventh and final sign, the raising of Lazarus (11:1–14), the chief priests and Pharisees gather the Great Council and decide to have Jesus put to death (11:53). The man healed in today's Gospel is twice brought before the Pharisees to explain who restored his vision. With his new sight, he recognizes his healer as a prophet and a man from God. Now it is the Pharisees, unable to recognize Jesus as the Son of Man, who are truly blind.

I began ministry to and with people living with HIV/AIDS in 1985. Most of those infected then were gay men. Judgment and misconception abounded. Not until people saw their loved ones' faithful care for someone whose death was imminent or whose pain was great were hearts changed—unless one would not or could not let go of ingrained biases. Bias judges by appearance, hearsay, and falsehood.

The man born blind, his parents, and Jesus experienced similar reactions. Although Jesus broke the connection between sickness and punishment for personal sin, some still hold onto that belief. The Pharisees would not let truth correct their blindness. They believed that they saw correctly. The man's parents' fear of rejection would not let the light of truth lead them to stand up for their son. Only the man himself was open to physical and spiritual healing. Jesus was not only a physical healer, he was the Son of Man whose touch transformed the man born blind as surely as the witness of our sisters and brothers living with HIV/AIDS transformed many over these past thirty years.

God does not see as we do. God looks beyond appearance into the heart. The youngest is the leader. Darkness gives way to light. Sickness and hardship are doorways that invite an unconditionally loving God to touch even the hardest of hearts. We'd often prefer another way, but it seems we only appreciate light after we have been blinded by darkness.

All of us are blind in some way. Bias and prejudice are part of each of us. Naming our darkness can invite God's touch to wash us clean and open our eyes, like the man born blind.

✥ Consider/Discuss

- What blindness would you rather deny than admit to as a part of your life?
- Where has God touched you and opened your eyes to look into another's heart?

✥ Living and Praying with the Word

Give me your eyes, healing God, to see beyond appearance into the hearts of those whom I resist seeing, accepting, or loving as you do.

FIFTH SUNDAY OF LENT/YEAR C

Today's Focus: Caught in the Act

We much prefer to catch others in sinful acts than to be caught ourselves. Yet we all have sinned, and should show others the same mercy we would like to receive.

FIRST READING
Isaiah 43:16–21

Thus says the LORD,
  who opens a way in the sea
    and a path in the mighty waters,
who leads out chariots and horsemen,
  a powerful army,
till they lie prostrate together, never to rise,
  snuffed out and quenched like a wick.
Remember not the events of the past,
  the things of long ago consider not;
see, I am doing something new!
  Now it springs forth, do you not perceive it?
In the desert I make a way,
  in the wasteland, rivers.
Wild beasts honor me,
  jackals and ostriches,
for I put water in the desert
  and rivers in the wasteland
    for my chosen people to drink,
the people whom I formed for myself,
  that they might announce my praise.

PSALM RESPONSE
Psalm 126:3

The Lord has done great things for us; we are filled with joy.

SECOND READING
Philippians 3: 8–14

Brothers and sisters: I consider everything as a loss because of the supreme good of knowing Christ Jesus my Lord. For his sake I have accepted the loss of all things and I consider them so much rubbish, that I may gain Christ and be found in him, not having any righteousness of my own based on the law but that which comes through faith in Christ, the righteousness from God, depending on faith to know him and the power of his resurrection and the sharing of his sufferings by being conformed to his death, if somehow I may attain the resurrection from the dead.

It is not that I have already taken hold of it or have already attained perfect maturity, but I continue my pursuit in hope that I may possess it, since I have indeed been taken possession of by Christ Jesus. Brothers and sisters, I for my part do not consider myself to have taken possession. Just one thing: forgetting what lies behind but straining forward to what lies ahead, I continue my pursuit toward the goal, the prize of God's upward calling, in Christ Jesus.

GOSPEL
John 8:1–11

Jesus went to the Mount of Olives. But early in the morning he arrived again in the temple area, and all the people started coming to him, and he sat down and taught them. Then the scribes and the Pharisees brought a woman who had been caught in adultery and made her stand in the middle. They said to him, "Teacher, this woman was caught in the very act of committing adultery. Now in the law, Moses commanded us to stone such women. So what do you say?" They said this to test him, so that they could have some charge to bring against him. Jesus bent down and began to write on the ground with his finger. But when they continued asking him, he straightened up and said to them, "Let the one among you who is without sin be the first to throw a stone at her." Again he bent down and wrote on the ground. And in response, they went away one by one, beginning with the elders. So he was left alone with the woman before him. Then Jesus straightened up and said to her, "Woman, where are they? Has no one condemned you?" She replied, "No one, sir." Then Jesus said, "Neither do I condemn you. Go, and from now on do not sin any more."

❖ Understanding the Word

In the reading from Isaiah, the LORD is described as the one "who leads out chariots and horsemen . . . till they lie prostrate together, never to rise" (Isaiah 43:17), referring to the crossing of the Red Sea. But despite this introduction, God commands, "Remember not the events of the past" (Isaiah 43:18). Instead God is doing something new. Addressed to the exiles in Babylon, this new act of God will overshadow their memory of the Exodus. Already springs gush forth in the desert and rivers flow in the wasteland. Though the wild beasts honor God for watering the desert, these miraculous gifts are "for my chosen people" (Isaiah 43:20).

In his letters, Paul often uses the rhetorical technique of "boasting" (Philippians 2:16; 3:3) as a means of defending his apostolic authority. In today's second reading, however, he demonstrates true humility. Though he begins by summarizing his religious pedigree (Philippians 3:4–6), he quickly sets it aside: "I consider everything as a loss because of the supreme good of knowing Christ Jesus my Lord" (Philippians 3:8). That "knowing" manifests in "sharing his sufferings," which lead to "resurrection from the dead" (Philippians 3:10–11). Paul admits that he hasn't obtained maturity. He uses the metaphor of an athlete striving for the finish line, "straining forward to what lies ahead" (Philippians 3:13) toward the goal of union with Christ Jesus.

Many scholars question the authenticity of today's Gospel reading. Like John 21, this story may have been added after the Gospel of John had been completed, since it is missing from all the early Greek manuscripts. In its current placement, the story of the woman caught in adultery is part of a section (John 5 — 10) in which Jesus participates in a series of Jewish festivals. Having just celebrated the festival of Tabernacles, which included a ritual of lights, Jesus announces after his encounter with the woman that he is the light of the world (John 8:12). The ancient editor may have recognized that Jesus' actions and speech toward the woman shed light on how the Law should be authentically interpreted and compassionate justice meted out.

Have you ever been "caught in the act"? There is no way to get out of it, though we often try. The woman was caught in the act. So was the man. Where was he? He deserved the same punishment. But I digress. Jesus catches the leaders in the act of misunderstanding the Law in a way that imprisons them.

Jesus offers a new way. Taking his time he writes on the ground. We don't know what he wrote. Whatever it was, they are moved to change their intentions after Jesus invites anyone *without* sin to cast the first stone. They walk away and no longer condemn her. Neither does Jesus. He forgives her and tells her to sin no more. Note: nothing indicates that her forgiveness depends on her obeying that command.

Jesus did something new. He put her situation in a context we all share: we all sin and need God's freely offered mercy. If we turn to Jesus, admit our need for forgiveness, and take on the suffering that changing our hearts and our ways can entail, we can experience the promised resurrection that Paul proclaims in today's second reading.

We have a choice. We can be honest when caught in the act and suffer the consequences of sin or judgment, thus opening the way to forgiveness and acceptance; or we can try to wiggle our way out and miss God's freely offered mercy. Admitting our sin and need for God turns weeping into rejoicing at the great things God does for us. Drink of God's mercy and turn to the One who helps us run the race and reach the prize of God's merciful love.

✤ Consider/Discuss

- What is your natural response to being "caught in the act"?
- Who has helped you change your heart, return to God, and live God's merciful love?

✤ *Living and Praying with the* Word

Our God, our mercy, all of us are sinners and need your merciful love. Make us turn to you today to hear you say to us, "Neither do I condemn you." Let us not cast stones.

March 13, 2016

FIFTH SUNDAY OF LENT/YEAR A

Today's Focus: Death Becomes New Life

It is easy enough to see death transformed into new life in the world of nature during spring-time: How much more carefully must we look to see it happen every day, all around us!

FIRST READING
Ezekiel 37: 12–14

Thus says the LORD GOD: O my people, I will open your graves and have you rise from them, and bring you back to the land of Israel. Then you shall know that I am the LORD, when I open your graves and have you rise from them, O my people! I will put my spirit in you that you may live, and I will settle you upon your land; thus you shall know that I am the LORD. I have promised, and I will do it, says the LORD.

PSALM RESPONSE
Psalm 130:7

With the Lord there is mercy and fullness of redemption.

SECOND READING
Romans 8:8–11

Brothers and sisters: Those who are in the flesh cannot please God. But you are not in the flesh; on the contrary, you are in the spirit, if only the Spirit of God dwells in you. Whoever does not have the Spirit of Christ does not belong to him. But if Christ is in you, although the body is dead because of sin, the spirit is alive because of righteousness. If the Spirit of the one who raised Jesus from the dead dwells in you, the one who raised Christ from the dead will give life to your mortal bodies also, through his Spirit dwelling in you.

GOSPEL
John 11:1–45 or 11:3–7, 17, 20–27, 33b–45

In the shorter version of the reading, the five passages in brackets are omitted.

[Now a man was ill, Lazarus from Bethany, the village of Mary and her sister Martha. Mary was the one who had anointed the Lord with perfumed oil and dried his feet with her hair; it was her brother Lazarus who was ill. So] the sisters sent word to him saying, "Master, the one you love is ill." When Jesus heard this he said, "This illness is not to end in death, but is for the glory of God, that the Son of God may be glorified through it." Now Jesus loved Martha and her sister and Lazarus. So when he heard that he was ill, he remained for two days in the place where he was. Then after this he said to his disciples, "Let us go back to Judea." [The disciples said to him, "Rabbi, the Jews were just trying to stone you, and you want to go back there?" Jesus answered, "Are there not twelve hours in a day? If one walks during the day, he does not stumble, because he sees the light of this world. But if one walks at night, he stumbles, because the light is not in him." He said this, and then told them, "Our friend Lazarus is asleep, but I am going to awaken him." So the disciples said to him, "Master, if he is asleep, he will be saved." But Jesus was talking about his death, while they thought that he meant ordinary

85

sleep. So then Jesus said to them clearly, "Lazarus has died. And I am glad for you that I was not there, that you may believe. Let us go to him." So Thomas, called Didymus, said to his fellow disciples, "Let us also go to die with him."]

When Jesus arrived, he found that Lazarus had already been in the tomb for four days. [Now Bethany was near Jerusalem, only about two miles away. And many of the Jews had come to Martha and Mary to comfort them about their brother.] When Martha heard that Jesus was coming, she went to meet him; but Mary sat at home. Martha said to Jesus, "Lord, if you had been here, my brother would not have died. But even now I know that whatever you ask of God, God will give you." Jesus said to her, "Your brother will rise." Martha said to him, "I know he will rise, in the resurrection on the last day." Jesus told her, "I am the resurrection and the life; whoever believes in me, even if he dies, will live, and everyone who lives and believes in me will never die. Do you believe this?" She said to him, "Yes, Lord. I have come to believe that you are the Christ, the Son of God, the one who is coming into the world."

[When she had said this, she went and called her sister Mary secretly, saying, "The teacher is here and is asking for you." As soon as she heard this, she rose quickly and went to him. For Jesus had not yet come into the village, but was still where Martha had met him. So when the Jews who were with her in the house comforting her saw Mary get up quickly and go out, they followed her, presuming that she was going to the tomb to weep there. When Mary came to where Jesus was and saw him, she fell at his feet and said to him, "Lord, if you had been here, my brother would not have died." When] Jesus [saw her weeping and the Jews who had come with her weeping, he] became perturbed and deeply troubled, and said, "Where have you laid him?" They said to him, "Sir, come and see." And Jesus wept. So the Jews said, "See how he loved him." But some of them said, "Could not the one who opened the eyes of the blind man have done something so that this man would not have died?"

So Jesus, perturbed again, came to the tomb. It was a cave, and a stone lay across it. Jesus said, "Take away the stone." Martha, the dead man's sister, said to him, "Lord, by now there will be a stench; he has been dead for four days." Jesus said to her, "Did I not tell you that if you believe you will see the glory of God?" So they took away the stone. And Jesus raised his eyes and said, "Father, I thank you for hearing me. I know that you always hear me; but because of the crowd here I have said this, that they may believe that you sent me."

And when he had said this, he cried out in a loud voice, "Lazarus, come out!" The dead man came out, tied hand and foot with burial bands, and his face was wrapped in a cloth. So Jesus said to them, "Untie him and let him go."

Now many of the Jews who had come to Mary and seen what he had done began to believe in him.

❖ Understanding the Word

Shortest sentence – "Jesus wept."

The prophet Ezekiel proclaims a vision of hope to the exiles in Babylon. Dry bones wholly without life are knit together again. Graves are opened and the dead not only are raised, they are brought back to the land of Israel. God will place God's spirit in this new people and they will come to life. This figurative description of the exiles' return to the land is viewed by some as the foundation of Jewish and Christian understanding of resurrection from the dead.

Paul's Letter to the Romans continues the theme of a new creation, not as new sinews on dry bones or dead bodies emerging from graves. Rather, Paul understands that baptism into Christ makes the believer one with Christ. Earlier in the letter, he had written, "We were indeed buried with him through baptism into death, so that, just as Christ was raised from the dead by the glory of the Father, we too might live in newness of life" (Romans 6:4). The Spirit of God dwells within the believer, so that the "fleshly" things of the world are no longer of import. If God's spirit could raise Jesus from the dead, that same spirit will raise the bodies of believers. Though Paul's writing sounds dualistic, he means to distinguish between the things of God (the spiritual) and the things of this world (the fleshly).

The Gospel presents a poignant picture of Jesus, who, despite his love for Lazarus, delays his return until Lazarus has died, in order that his disciples might come to greater belief. Sandwiched between Lazarus' death and Jesus' raising him from the dead is Jesus' encounter with Martha, Lazarus' sister. In conversation between Jesus and the Samaritan woman, Jesus had identified himself as the Messiah. Here in another theological discussion with Martha he declares: "I am the resurrection and the life." Martha responds affirmatively, "I have come to believe that you are the Messiah, the Son of God." And yet this Messiah is not beyond human emotion. Jesus begins to weep at the tomb of Lazarus, causing the onlookers to remark, "See how he loved him." The final sign in John's Gospel reveals Jesus as a human Messiah, and points to his own death and resurrection.

❖ Reflecting on the Word

How human these readings are. We want the dead to rise and to know that God's Spirit is with us. We delay gratification when it promises greater good. We weep when someone we love dies. We experience affirmation and ridicule for our emotions. Freedom from a death-dealing reality often requires the help of those who put us there in the first place.

Jesus delays going to Lazarus, some scholars say, because raising Lazarus from the dead could be the greater sign that would free them to believe in Jesus as the Messiah. Why? To make clear that God was with him. We hear Martha and Mary's frustration, "Lord, if you had been here." Voicing it frees them to express faith: "Yes, Lord, I have come to believe." When Jesus weeps at his friend's death some affirm him—"See how he loved him"—while others ridicule him: "If he could open the eyes of the blind man." Lazarus chose to come out and needed people to remove the stone, his bandages, and his burial cloth. The townsfolk needed to let him be anew.

I can't imagine how that experience changed him. But maybe I can. When God's forgiveness healed something I thought unforgiveable, it took time to believe it and more time to live out of that belief. When God's love changes people I resist; I have to let them be in new ways. When the Spirit brings new life, try as I might, I can't go back to the way things were.

God offers us new life. Let us invite Jesus to heal us and bring us to life by leaving our tombs, becoming unbound, and letting each other go free.

✤ Consider/Discuss

- How has God touched your humanity in ways that gave you surprising life?
- Where do you resist helping another person become unbound and live in new ways?

✤ Living and Praying with the Word

Jesus, our resurrection and our life, help us listen for your voice inviting us out of the graves we dig for ourselves or others, so that we can choose to come out and be free.

March 20, 2016

PALM SUNDAY OF THE PASSION OF THE LORD

Today's Focus: Are You Being Served? Are You Serving?

In the life of the disciple, there are opportunities to serve others, and there are times to allow others to serve us. The one thing discipleship doesn't call for is being self-serving.

FIRST READING
Isaiah 50:4–7

The Lord God has given me
   a well-trained tongue,
that I might know how to speak to the weary
   a word that will rouse them.
Morning after morning
   he opens my ear that I may hear;
and I have not rebelled,
   have not turned back.
I gave my back to those who beat me,
   my cheeks to those who plucked my beard;
my face I did not shield
   from buffets and spitting.

The Lord God is my help,
   therefore I am not disgraced;
I have set my face like flint,
   knowing that I shall not be put to shame.

PSALM RESPONSE
Psalm 22:2a

My God, my God, why have you abandoned me?

SECOND READING
Philippians 2: 6–11

Christ Jesus, though he was in the form of God,
   did not regard equality with God
   something to be grasped.
Rather, he emptied himself,
   taking the form of a slave,
   coming in human likeness;
   and found human in appearance,
   he humbled himself,
   becoming obedient to the point of death,
   even death on a cross.

Because of this, God greatly exalted him
   and bestowed on him the name
   which is above every name,
   that at the name of Jesus
   every knee should bend,
   of those in heaven and on earth and under the earth,
   and every tongue confess that
   Jesus Christ is Lord,
   to the glory of God the Father.

In the shorter form of the Passion, the passages in brackets are omitted.

GOSPEL

Luke 22:
14 — 23:56 or
23:1–49

[When the hour came, Jesus took his place at table with the apostles. He said to them, "I have eagerly desired to eat this Passover with you before I suffer, for, I tell you, I shall not eat it again until there is fulfillment in the kingdom of God." Then he took a cup, gave thanks, and said, "Take this and share it among yourselves; for I tell you that from this time on I shall not drink of the fruit of the vine until the kingdom of God comes." Then he took the bread, said the blessing, broke it, and gave it to them, saying, "This is my body, which will be given for you; do this in memory of me." And likewise the cup after they had eaten, saying, "This cup is the new covenant in my blood, which will be shed for you.

"And yet behold, the hand of the one who is to betray me is with me on the table; for the Son of Man indeed goes as it has been determined; but woe to that man by whom he is betrayed." And they began to debate among themselves who among them would do such a deed.

Then an argument broke out among them about which of them should be regarded as the greatest. He said to them, "The kings of the Gentiles lord it over them and those in authority over them are addressed as 'Benefactors'; but among you it shall not be so. Rather, let the greatest among you be as the youngest, and the leader as the servant. For who is greater: the one seated at table or the one who serves? Is it not the one seated at table? I am among you as the one who serves. It is you who have stood by me in my trials; and I confer a kingdom on you, just as my Father has conferred one on me, that you may eat and drink at my table in my kingdom; and you will sit on thrones judging the twelve tribes of Israel.

"Simon, Simon, behold Satan has demanded to sift all of you like wheat, but I have prayed that your own faith may not fail; and once you have turned back, you must strengthen your brothers." He said to him, "Lord, I am prepared to go to prison and to die with you." But he replied, "I tell you, Peter, before the cock crows this day, you will deny three times that you know me."

He said to them, "When I sent you forth without a money bag or a sack or sandals, were you in need of anything?" "No, nothing," they replied. He said to them, "But now one who has a money bag should take it, and likewise a sack, and one who does not have a sword should sell his cloak and buy one. For I tell you that this Scripture must be fulfilled in me, namely,

He was counted among the wicked;

and indeed what is written about me is coming to fulfillment." Then they said, "Lord, look, there are two swords here." But he replied, "It is enough!"

Then going out, he went, as was his custom, to the Mount of Olives, and the disciples followed him. When he arrived at the place he said to them, "Pray that you may not undergo the test." After withdrawing about a stone's throw from them and kneeling, he prayed, saying, "Father, if you are willing, take this cup away from me; still, not my will but yours be done." And to strengthen him an angel from heaven appeared to him. He was in such agony and he prayed so fervently that his sweat became like drops of blood falling on the ground. When he rose from prayer and returned to his disciples, he found them sleeping from grief. He said to them, "Why are you sleeping? Get up and pray that you may not undergo the test."

While he was still speaking, a crowd approached and in front was one of the Twelve, a man named Judas. He went up to Jesus to kiss him. Jesus said to him, "Judas, are you betraying the Son of Man with a kiss?" His disciples realized what was about to happen, and they asked, "Lord, shall we strike with a sword?" And one of them struck the high priest's servant and cut off his right ear. But Jesus said in reply, "Stop, no more of this!" Then he touched the servant's ear and healed him. And Jesus said to the chief priests and temple guards and elders who had come for him, "Have you come out as against a robber, with swords and clubs? Day after day I was with you in the temple area, and you did not seize me; but this is your hour, the time for the power of darkness."

After arresting him they led him away and took him into the house of the high priest; Peter was following at a distance. They lit a fire in the middle of the courtyard and sat around it, and Peter sat down with them. When a maid saw him seated in the light, she looked intently at him and said, "This man too was with him." But he denied it saying, "Woman, I do not know him." A short while later someone else saw him and said, "You too are one of them"; but Peter answered, "My friend, I am not." About an hour later, still another insisted, "Assuredly, this man too was with him, for he also is a Galilean." But Peter said, "My friend, I do not know what you are talking about." Just as he was saying this, the cock crowed, and the Lord turned and looked at Peter; and Peter remembered the word of the Lord, how he had said to him, "Before the cock crows today, you will deny me three times." He went out and began to weep bitterly. The men who held Jesus in custody were ridiculing and beating him. They blindfolded him and questioned him, saying, "Prophesy! Who is it that struck you?" And they reviled him in saying many other things against him.

When day came the council of elders of the people met, both chief priests and scribes, and they brought him before their Sanhedrin. They said, "If you are the Christ, tell us," but he replied to them, "If I tell you, you will not believe, and if I question, you will not respond. But from this time on the Son of Man will be seated at the right hand of the power of God." They all asked, "Are you then the Son of God?" He replied to them, "You say that I am." Then they said, "What further need have we for testimony? We have heard it from his own mouth."]

Then the whole assembly of them arose and brought him before Pilate. They brought charges against him, saying, "We found this man misleading our people; he opposes the payment of taxes to Caesar and maintains that he is the Christ, a king." Pilate asked him, "Are you the king of the Jews?" He said to him in reply, "You say so." Pilate then addressed the chief priests and the crowds, "I find this man not guilty." But they were adamant and said, "He is inciting the people with his teaching throughout all Judea, from Galilee where he began even to here."

On hearing this Pilate asked if the man was a Galilean; and upon learning that he was under Herod's jurisdiction, he sent him to Herod who was in Jerusalem at that time. Herod was very glad to see Jesus; he had been wanting to see him for a long time, for he had heard about him and had been hoping to see him perform some sign. He questioned him at length, but he gave him no answer. The chief priests and scribes, meanwhile, stood by accusing him harshly. Herod and his soldiers treated him contemptuously and mocked him, and after clothing him in resplendent garb, he sent him back to Pilate. Herod and Pilate became friends that very day, even though they had been enemies formerly. Pilate then summoned the chief priests, the rulers, and the people and said to them, "You brought this man to me and accused him of inciting the people to revolt. I have conducted my investigation in your presence and have not found this man guilty of the charges you have brought against him, nor did Herod, for he sent him back to us. So no capital crime has been committed by him. Therefore I shall have him flogged and then release him."

But all together they shouted out, "Away with this man! Release Barabbas to us."—Now Barabbas had been imprisoned for a rebellion that had taken place in the city and for murder.—Again Pilate addressed them, still wishing to release Jesus, but they continued their shouting, "Crucify him! Crucify him!" Pilate addressed them a third time, "What evil has this man done? I found him guilty of no capital crime. Therefore I shall have him flogged and then release him." With loud shouts, however, they persisted in calling for his crucifixion, and their voices prevailed. The verdict of Pilate was that their demand should be granted. So he released the man who had been imprisoned for rebellion and murder, for whom they asked, and he handed Jesus over to them to deal with as they wished.

As they led him away they took hold of a certain Simon, a Cyrenian, who was coming in from the country; and after laying the cross on him, they made him carry it behind Jesus. A large crowd of people followed Jesus, including many women who mourned and lamented him. Jesus turned to them and said, "Daughters of Jerusalem, do not weep for me; weep instead for yourselves and for your children, for indeed, the days are coming when people will say, 'Blessed are the barren, the wombs that never bore and the breasts that never nursed.' At that time people will say to the mountains, 'Fall upon us!' and to the hills, 'Cover us!' for if these things are done when the wood is green what will happen when it is dry?" Now two others, both criminals, were led away with him to be executed.

When they came to the place called the Skull, they crucified him and the criminals there, one on his right, the other on his left. Then Jesus said, "Father, forgive them, they know not what they do." They divided his garments by casting lots. The people stood by and watched; the rulers, meanwhile, sneered at him and said, "He saved others, let him save himself if he is the chosen one, the Christ of God." Even the soldiers jeered at him. As they approached to offer him wine they called out, "If you are King of the Jews, save yourself." Above him there was an inscription that read, "This is the King of the Jews."

Now one of the criminals hanging there reviled Jesus, saying, "Are you not the Christ? Save yourself and us." The other, however, rebuking him, said in reply, "Have you no fear of God, for you are subject to the same condemnation? And indeed, we have been condemned justly, for the sentence we received corresponds to our crimes, but this man has done nothing criminal." Then he said, "Jesus, remember me when you come into your kingdom." He replied to him, "Amen, I say to you, today you will be with me in Paradise."

It was now about noon and darkness came over the whole land until three in the afternoon because of an eclipse of the sun. Then the veil of the temple was torn down the middle. Jesus cried out in a loud voice, "Father, into your hands I commend my spirit"; and when he had said this he breathed his last.

The centurion who witnessed what had happened glorified God and said, "This man was innocent beyond doubt." When all the people who had gathered for this spectacle saw what had happened, they returned home beating their breasts; but all his acquaintances stood at a distance, including the women who had followed him from Galilee and saw these events.

[Now there was a virtuous and righteous man named Joseph who, though he was a member of the council, had not consented to their plan of action. He came from the Jewish town of Arimathea and was awaiting the kingdom of God. He went to Pilate and asked for the body of Jesus. After he had taken the body down, he wrapped it in a linen cloth and laid him in a rock-hewn tomb in which no one had yet been buried. It was the day of preparation, and the sabbath was about to begin. The women who had come from Galilee with him followed behind, and when they had seen the tomb and the way in which his body was laid in it, they returned and prepared spices and perfumed oils. Then they rested on the sabbath according to the commandment.]

In today's first reading, we hear the voice of the prophet explaining his mission. He is to speak to the weary for which he is beaten and abused. Isaiah 50 is one of four songs that describe the Suffering Servant of the Lord (42:1–9; 49:1–7; 50:4–11; 52:13 — 53:12), and is attributed to Second Isaiah, an anonymous prophet preaching in the spirit of Isaiah of Jerusalem but two centuries later. Christians see the Suffering Servant as foreshadowing the passion of Christ.

Last week, Paul was an athlete striving for the goal of union with Christ. Today's second reading comes from the previous chapter. Incorporating an older hymn, Paul reminds the Philippian faithful that they are to have the same attitude as Christ, whose obedience to God led to his exaltation. Paul's correspondence with the Philippians evidences a fondness for the community, his first converts on European soil. As such, this reading is meant to encourage them to continue their "partnership in the Gospel" (Philippians 1:5).

Each Gospel presents Jesus' passion as the culmination of its narrative. The conflict initiated in Galilee is brought to a head in Jerusalem. But each evangelist also tells that narrative through a particular lens. Luke presents the Passion as a supreme assault by Satan (22:3, 31, 53). Though both are antagonists, Roman authorities are presented more positively than the Sanhedrin. Three times Pilate announces that Jesus is innocent of the charge (Luke 23:4, 14, 22). But the Sanhedrin, composed of the elders, chief priests, and scribes, is accusatory (Luke 22:67–71), asking religious questions but charging Jesus with political crimes (Luke 23:2). Luke edits his source, Mark's Passion, and places the beating and shaming of Jesus at the hands of Herod and not Pilate (Luke 23:11). Luke also minimizes the failure of the Eleven. Mark states expressly that those with Jesus in the garden left him and fled (Mark 14:50), while Luke portrays the disciples as ready to defend Jesus with the sword (Luke 22:49). Luke's editorial changes reflect his audience's continuing discomfort with the Passion. Though understanding the death of Jesus as necessary for his glorification (Luke 9:31), early Christians saw crucifixion as the ultimate Roman humiliation and the most painful and agonizing method of execution. The horror of the event remained fresh in the early Christian memory.

✤ Reflecting on the Word

Are you someone who serves or seeks to be served? Are you more attentive to others, yourself, or both? In Luke's Passion narrative, Jesus says: "Let the greatest among you be as the youngest, and the leader as the servant." Jesus lives as one who serves. He feeds the disciples with his body and blood. He heals those who arrest him. He prays that God's will be done. He continues to teach while in agony in the garden. He prepares Peter before his betrayal of Jesus. He is neither defensive nor combative before Herod and Pilate. He attends to the women of Jerusalem and welcomes the so-called good thief. Finally he commends his spirit into God's hands. Throughout his passion Jesus serves others and God. Like the servant of God in Isaiah who did not turn back but set his face like flint to speak God's word, Jesus empties himself, like God's self-emptying in becoming human.

Unlike Jesus, the disciples serve themselves out of fear that they might suffer the same fate as Jesus, and out of fear of the crowd's reaction. They keep their distance. Herod and Pilate do not want to lose power. Simon must be forced into service, and even Joseph of Arimathea comes to Jesus' aid only after the crucifixion. It is the centurion who announces Jesus' innocence.

I want to have Jesus' other-centeredness in the face of rejection and ridicule. But when I'm honest I know that I keep quiet too often in order to avoid both. I am more concerned about defending myself than humbly submitting to the example Jesus offered. During this week we call holy, watch Jesus. Listen to his words. Note his example and let the Lord God be our help so that we might commend our spirits to God and learn to serve in all circumstances.

✤ Consider/Discuss

- Name times when you have followed Jesus' example of service in the face of opposition.
- What freed you to do so, or what kept you from doing so when that was your choice?

✤ Living and Praying with the Word

Almighty God, you took on every human limitation with the exception of sin. Give us courage to follow Jesus even when it is not easy, so that our lives might reveal the power that comes from committing ourselves totally to your Son, Jesus Christ.

It's Time to Order
Living the Word 2017: Year A

By now you have discovered what a prayerful and valuable scriptural resource *Living the Word* provides for you each Sunday of the year.

Don't miss a single week! Subscribe to *Living the Word 2017* today for yourself, your staff, parishioners, family, and friends, and share the gift of God's Word.

Order now to receive the same low price as 2016:

100 or more copies	$6.95 each
25–99 copies	$8.95 each
10–24 copies	$9.95 each
2–9 copies	$10.95 each
Single copies..	$14.95

MAKE A COPY OF THIS ORDER FORM AND FAX IT TODAY TO 888-957-3291 OR SCAN AND SEND TO WLPCS@JSPALUCH.COM.
(This will keep your current book intact!)

OR, CALL WLP CUSTOMER CARE AT
800-566-6160 TO PLACE YOUR ORDER.

[ ] Yes, I'd like to order *Living the Word 2017: Year A*. Please send me _____ copies at _____ each, plus shipping, handling and any applicable sales tax.

NAME _____ POSITION _____

PARISH/INSTITUTION_____

ADDRESS _____

CITY _____ STATE _____ ZIP _____

PHONE _____ FAX_____ E-MAIL_____

Please keep a copy of your order for reference.

Living the Word 2017 will be shipped and billed after October 1, 2016.

Add $7.95 for orders up to $20.00. Add 16% of total for orders over $20.00. Payment in U.S. currency only. No cash or stamps, please. Make checks payable to World Library Publications. Prices subject to change without notice.
Applicable sales tax will be added to orders based on individual state tax requirements.

WLP World Library Publications
the music and liturgy division of J.S.Paluch Company, Inc.
3708 River Road, Suite 400 • Franklin Park, IL 60131-2158
800-566-6150 • wlpcs@jspaluch.com • wlpmusic.com

LTWC17

The Easter season opens with the grand liturgical celebration of the Resurrection of the Lord, symbolized by the lighting of the Easter candle at the Vigil. The readings at the Vigil serve to remind us of the long history of God's actions of deliverance that are brought to profound completion with the resurrection of Jesus. As the Sundays of the Easter season unfold, our first readings are taken from Acts of the Apostles, the second volume by the evangelist tradition names as Luke. The twenty-eight chapters narrate the experiences of the early apostles after the resurrection of Jesus and his ascension, and the coming of the Holy Spirit (Pentecost). In the name of Jesus, the apostles, led by Peter, are able to heal and cast out demons (Second Sunday of Easter). The actions and preaching of the apostles angers the religious authorities (Third and Fourth Sunday of Easter), who stone Stephen (Seventh Sunday of Easter). Another theme seen in the first readings for Easter is the question of the Gentiles. Peter baptizes the Roman centurion Cornelius (Easter), and Paul preaches to the God-fearers on his first missionary journey (Fifth Sunday of Easter), which leads to the Jerusalem Council (Sixth Sunday of Easter) and its approbation of the Gentile mission.

With the exception of a couple of readings from Pauline letters, most of the texts for the second reading are taken from the book of Revelation. The apocalyptic work uses highly symbolic language and images to convey the hope of a persecuted people for the realization of God's reign. Jesus is envisioned as the victorious Lamb (Third Sunday of Easter), and faithful believers stand before the throne of God, having been washed in the blood of the Lamb (Fourth Sunday of Easter). The visions culminate with the images of a new heaven and a new earth (Fifth Sunday of Easter) and a new Jerusalem (Sixth Sunday of Easter). Revelation closes with the warning and the hope: Jesus is coming! (Seventh Sunday of Easter).

The Gospel readings during the Easter season are taken from the Gospel according to John. The fourth evangelist had access to different sources than the Synoptic writers, so his presentation of Jesus and his mission are slightly different. While he shares with the evangelists that Mary discovered the empty tomb (Easter Sunday), he includes a post-Resurrection encounter with Thomas (Second Sunday of Easter). The Synoptics do not record a reconciliation between Jesus and Peter after Peter's denial, but John 21 (Third Sunday of Easter) presents us with just such a scene. Peter is told to "feed my sheep." Jesus uses the imagery of sheep and shepherd to describe his own care of the disciples (Fourth Sunday of Easter). John's Gospel lacks a sermon on ethics or the Beatitudes. Instead, Jesus gives one commandment: love one another (Fifth Sunday of Easter). Those who heed this command will dwell in God and receive the Advocate, whom Jesus promised to send (Sixth Sunday of Easter). The final Sunday before Pentecost, we hear Jesus' prayer to his Father in which he prays for those who will come to belief through the preaching of his disciples. We are the ones for whom Jesus prayed.

March 27, 2016

EASTER SUNDAY OF THE RESURRECTION OF THE LORD

Today's Focus: Witnesses When We Testify

In discipleship, as in all of life, nobody knows what we've witnessed until we give our testimony to it.

FIRST READING
Acts 10:34a, 37–43

Peter proceeded to speak and said: "You know what has happened all over Judea, beginning in Galilee after the baptism that John preached, how God anointed Jesus of Nazareth with the Holy Spirit and power. He went about doing good and healing all those oppressed by the devil, for God was with him. We are witnesses of all that he did both in the country of the Jews and in Jerusalem. They put him to death by hanging him on a tree. This man God raised on the third day and granted that he be visible, not to all the people, but to us, the witnesses chosen by God in advance, who ate and drank with him after he rose from the dead. He commissioned us to preach to the people and testify that he is the one appointed by God as judge of the living and the dead. To him all the prophets bear witness, that everyone who believes in him will receive forgiveness of sins through his name.

PSALM RESPONSE
Psalm 118:24

This is the day the Lord has made; let us rejoice and be glad.

SECOND READING
Colossians 3: 1–4

Brothers and sisters: If then you were raised with Christ, seek what is above, where Christ is seated at the right hand of God. Think of what is above, not of what is on earth. For you have died, and your life is hidden with Christ in God. When Christ your life appears, then you too will appear with him in glory.

– or –

1 Corinthians 5: 6b–8

Brothers and sisters: Do you not know that a little yeast leavens all the dough? Clear out the old yeast, so that you may become a fresh batch of dough, inasmuch as you are unleavened. For our paschal lamb, Christ, has been sacrificed. Therefore, let us celebrate the feast, not with the old yeast, the yeast of malice and wickedness, but with the unleavened bread of sincerity and truth.

On the first day of the week, Mary of Magdala came to the tomb early in the morning, while it was still dark, and saw the stone removed from the tomb. So she ran and went to Simon Peter and to the other disciple whom Jesus loved, and told them, "They have taken the Lord from the tomb, and we don't know where they put him." So Peter and the other disciple went out and came to the tomb. They both ran, but the other disciple ran faster than Peter and arrived at the tomb first; he bent down and saw the burial cloths there, but did not go in. When Simon Peter arrived after him, he went into the tomb and saw the burial cloths there, and the cloth that had covered his head, not with the burial cloths but rolled up in a separate place. Then the other disciple also went in, the one who had arrived at the tomb first, and he saw and believed. For they did not yet understand the Scripture that he had to rise from the dead.

✥ Understanding the Word

In order to understand the significance of the first reading, we need to know what preceded Peter's encounter with the Gentile centurion Cornelius, whom we are told was a God-fearer, one who worshiped with the Jews but was not Jewish (Acts 10:1–2). Peter had been in Joppa where he saw a vision of a sheet floating down from heaven. On the sheet were all the animals, reptiles, and birds. Three times a heavenly voice had commanded Peter to slaughter and eat. Peter refused, since some of the animals were not kosher. Finally, the voice announces, "What God has made clean, you are not to call profane" (Acts 10:14). Peter comes to understand this vision as God's approbation that Gentiles can join the Way. In today's reading, Peter begins his speech by recounting the story of Jesus' public life and assures Cornelius' household that Peter and the apostles are witnesses of all that Jesus said and did, and that Peter has been commissioned by Jesus to preach to the people. The proclamation of the gospel to a Gentile and his family in this Greco-Roman city fulfills the prophecy of Simeon that Jesus would will be "a light for revelation to the Gentiles" (Luke 2:32), and opens the way of the gospel for all Gentiles.

Though there are two choices for second readings, both Colossians 3:1–4 and 1 Corinthians 5:6–8 speak of the same theme: the newness that comes with being part of the body of Christ. In Colossians, we are reminded that our focus should be on the things of heaven, since our life is now in Christ and Christ is seated at God's right hand. In First Corinthians, we are to be fresh dough without old yeast. Christ is the Passover who was sacrificed and we are to respond with the bread of sincerity and truth.

The Gospel of John recounts the discovery of the empty tomb by Mary Magdalene. All four of our Gospels attributed this discovery to Mary, but Paul will announce that Cephas or Peter was the first one to whom Jesus appeared (1 Corinthians 15:5). Today's Gospel highlights the important roles of both parties. Mary visits the tomb of Jesus, but we are not told why, since Jesus was anointed before his burial (John 19:40). When she discovers the empty tomb, she runs to Simon Peter and the beloved disciple. The men hasten to the tomb and verify what Mary has told them. In the Greco-Roman context, the testimony of a woman did not hold up in court. Rather, two male witnesses were needed to corroborate a fact.

Did you notice how often witnessing or testifying appear in today's readings? Peter calls the disciples witnesses, commissioned to testify that Jesus is the one appointed by God. The prophets are said to witness God's forgiving love. Mary is the first to witness the empty tomb. After she goes to tell Peter, and the beloved disciple, they need to see with their own eyes. Seeing, they believe. Mary, Peter and the beloved are witnesses to the Resurrection. They did not see Jesus rise. They did see that the tomb was empty. All that remained were the burial cloths, and the cloth covering Jesus' head was separate, which implies an intentional act, not a body snatching. The first preacher of the Resurrection, Mary is named apostle to the apostles and patron of the Order of Preachers.

We are also to witness the Resurrection. We did not see Jesus walk the earth like Mary, Peter, or the beloved disciple. However, because we experience the effects of the Resurrection, we see hope where others see despair. The forgiveness in Jesus' dying and rising brings light where others see darkness. Death-dealing realities like disease, divorce, addiction, or loss give way to acceptance, healing, survival, and recovery. When we admit that we are powerless, and that our lives are hidden in Christ (Colossians 3:3b), living sincerity and truth lessen the power of malice and wickedness (1 Corinthians 5:8).

"This is the day the Lord has made; let us rejoice and be glad." Review your life since last Easter. Name where you found new life because of your faith in the resurrected Lord. Testify to that truth. Witness the Resurrection so that others may come to see and believe through you.

✤ Consider/Discuss

- How has your faith in the Resurrection made a concrete difference in your life?
- Who is a living witness to the power of faith in Jesus Christ for you? Give thanks for their testimony.

✤ Living and Praying with the Word

Thank you for raising your Son Jesus from the dead, dear God. Let our words and deeds sing "Alleluia" in gratitude for this gift of new life.

April 3, 2016

SECOND SUNDAY OF EASTER

Today's Focus: As Close as Breath

There are many ways to know if somebody's breathing: you presume it because they're conscious; you can see their bodies move; but only when you're very close can you feel another person's breath.

FIRST READING
Acts 5:12–16

Many signs and wonders were done among the people at the hands of the apostles. They were all together in Solomon's portico. None of the others dared to join them, but the people esteemed them. Yet more than ever, believers in the Lord, great numbers of men and women, were added to them. Thus they even carried the sick out into the streets and laid them on cots and mats so that when Peter came by, at least his shadow might fall on one or another of them. A large number of people from the towns in the vicinity of Jerusalem also gathered, bringing the sick and those disturbed by unclean spirits, and they were all cured.

PSALM RESPONSE
Psalm 118:1

Give thanks to the Lord for he is good, his love is everlasting.

SECOND READING
Revelation 1: 9–11a, 12–13, 17–19

I, John, your brother, who share with you the distress, the kingdom, and the endurance we have in Jesus, found myself on the island called Patmos because I proclaimed God's word and gave testimony to Jesus. I was caught up in spirit on the Lord's day and heard behind me a voice as loud as a trumpet, which said, "Write on a scroll what you see." Then I turned to see whose voice it was that spoke to me, and when I turned, I saw seven gold lampstands and in the midst of the lampstands one like a son of man, wearing an ankle-length robe, with a gold sash around his chest.

When I caught sight of him, I fell down at his feet as though dead. He touched me with his right hand and said, "Do not be afraid. I am the first and the last, the one who lives. Once I was dead, but now I am alive forever and ever. I hold the keys to death and the netherworld. Write down, therefore, what you have seen, and what is happening, and what will happen afterwards."

On the evening of that first day of the week, when the doors were locked, where the disciples were, for fear of the Jews, Jesus came and stood in their midst and said to them, "Peace be with you." When he had said this, he showed them his hands and his side. The disciples rejoiced when they saw the Lord. Jesus said to them again, "Peace be with you. As the Father has sent me, so I send you." And when he had said this, he breathed on them and said to them, "Receive the Holy Spirit. Whose sins you forgive are forgiven them, and whose sins you retain are retained."

Thomas, called Didymus, one of the Twelve, was not with them when Jesus came. So the other disciples said to him, "We have seen the Lord." But he said to them, "Unless I see the mark of the nails in his hands and put my finger into the nailmarks and put my hand into his side, I will not believe."

Now a week later his disciples were again inside and Thomas was with them. Jesus came, although the doors were locked, and stood in their midst and said, "Peace be with you." Then he said to Thomas, "Put your finger here and see my hands, and bring your hand and put it into my side, and do not be unbelieving, but believe." Thomas answered and said to him, "My Lord and my God!" Jesus said to him, "Have you come to believe because you have seen me? Blessed are those who have not seen and have believed."

Now Jesus did many other signs in the presence of his disciples that are not written in this book. But these are written that you may come to believe that Jesus is the Christ, the Son of God, and that through this belief you may have life in his name.

❖ Understanding the Word

The first reading from Acts is a summary of the signs and wonders effected by the apostles after the coming of the Holy Spirit (Acts 2). Even Peter's shadow is thought to be efficacious (Acts 5:15). The author of Acts careful crafts the portrait of the apostles so that their actions and words are shown to be in continuity with those of Jesus. As we saw in the Gospel, so too here in Acts, those who are sick or possessed by unclean spirits are cured. But as Peter carefully noted earlier, it is in the name of Jesus Christ the Nazorean (Acts 3:6) that all signs and wonders are done.

The second reading introduces the visionary John, who is imprisoned on Patmos, an island in the Aegean Sea, which then served as a Roman penal colony. Though the author never states explicitly why he is imprisoned, most scholars presume John had refused to engage in emperor worship, which revered emperors as gods. Revelation is the only complete apocalyptic work in the New Testament. This genre uses highly symbolic language and images to portray the cataclysmic coming of the end-times. In today's reading, the seer is commanded to write down the various visions that will occur. Reminiscent of Daniel 7:13–14, John sees "one like the son of man" whom we recognize as the Risen Christ ("Once I was dead, but now I am alive forever" [Revelation 1:18]).

The Gospel reading presents the evangelist John's narration of the coming of the Spirit. The disciples are together behind locked doors when Jesus appears before them. He offers a typical Jewish greeting: *Shalom*—Peace be with you. After showing them his wounds, he repeats the greeting. Jesus then commissions the disciples. As the Father has sent him, so he now empowers and sends the disciples. The Resurrected Jesus breathes the Holy Spirit upon them, and with that they share in his power. The story doesn't then depict the great works enacted by this now inspired group of disciples, as will be narrated in Acts. Instead, we hear of one disciple, Thomas, who missed the encounter. His doubt is only erased when Jesus returns a week later. Instead of simply showing his wounds as Jesus did the first time, he now invites Thomas to touch them. Thomas responds with an exclamation of belief: "My Lord and My God." To this acknowledgment, Jesus utters a beatitude: "Blessed are those who have not seen and have believed," thereby blessing all who come to faith after the Resurrection.

❖ Reflecting on the Word

Jesus breathed on them and said, "Receive the Holy Spirit." Breathe gently through your mouth. Now raise a hand to your mouth until you feel that breath. This gives you an idea about how close Jesus had to be for the disciples to feel the breath of the Spirit. The Spirit empowers the Church to forgive and proclaim God's love. Do you believe that power is ours? It comes by facing the wounds of our sin, hurt, and doubt. Had Thomas not doubted, he might not have been invited to touch Jesus' wounds. Often woundedness invites healing, sin invites forgiveness, and doubt invites deeper faith. If you believe this, live in ways that help others see Jesus, hear his voice, and feel his breath so they can touch him and be healed.

The wounded disciples became powerful witnesses. The shadow of Peter the denier could heal others as Jesus did. The fearful disciples leave the safety of the upper room to walk among the people and proclaim the mighty deeds of the Christ. Jesus sent them into the world as the Father sent him. Hearing his tender words— "Peace be with you "—they were no longer afraid and went out to witness the power of Christ's life, death, and resurrection.

We received the Holy Spirit at baptism. We were sealed in the Spirit at confirmation. In the sacrament of reconciliation we are told that God sent the Holy Spirit among us for the forgiveness of sins. Feel Jesus breathe the Spirit anew in you. Name your own sin and hear his invitation to touch his healing wounds. Believe and live in ways that help others feel Christ's merciful, loving, life-giving breath written on the pages of your own lives.

❖ *Consider/Discuss*

- Name where have you felt the peace of Jesus in your life.
- What doubts, fears, sins, or wounds keep you from believing that Christ's loving forgiveness is meant for you?

❖ *Living and Praying with the Word*

Almighty God, your love is everlasting. It took flesh in the life, death, and resurrection of your Son Jesus to heal the wounds of our sin, doubt, and fear. Touch me in ways today so that like Thomas I can proclaim, "My Lord and my God," and help others feel your life-giving breath.

April 10, 2016

THIRD SUNDAY OF EASTER

Today's Focus: How Do You Love?

In the dialogue between Peter and Jesus today, Peter speaks of his love for Jesus, At the end of the passage, Jesus foretells how Peter would ultimately show his love: dying on a cross, as Jesus had.

FIRST READING
Acts 5:27–32, 40b–41

When the captain and the court officers had brought the apostles in and made them stand before the Sanhedrin, the high priest questioned them, "We gave you strict orders, did we not, to stop teaching in that name? Yet you have filled Jerusalem with your teaching and want to bring this man's blood upon us." But Peter and the apostles said in reply, "We must obey God rather than men. The God of our ancestors raised Jesus, though you had him killed by hanging him on a tree. God exalted him at his right hand as leader and savior to grant Israel repentance and forgiveness of sins. We are witnesses of these things, as is the Holy Spirit whom God has given to those who obey him."

The Sanhedrin ordered the apostles to stop speaking in the name of Jesus, and dismissed them. So they left the presence of the Sanhedrin, rejoicing that they had been found worthy to suffer dishonor for the sake of the name.

PSALM RESPONSE
Psalm 30:2a

I will praise you, Lord, for you have rescued me.

SECOND READING
Revelation 5: 11–14

I, John, looked and heard the voices of many angels who surrounded the throne and the living creatures and the elders. They were countless in number, and they cried out in a loud voice:

"Worthy is the Lamb that was slain
   to receive power and riches, wisdom and strength,
   honor and glory and blessing."

Then I heard every creature in heaven and on earth and under the earth and in the sea, everything in the universe, cry out:

"To the one who sits on the throne and to the Lamb
   be blessing and honor, glory and might,
   forever and ever."

The four living creatures answered, "Amen," and the elders fell down and worshiped.

In the shorter form of the reading, the passage in brackets is omitted.

GOSPEL
John 21:1–19 or 21:1–14

At that time, Jesus revealed himself again to his disciples at the Sea of Tiberias. He revealed himself in this way. Together were Simon Peter, Thomas called Didymus, Nathanael from Cana in Galilee, Zebedee's sons, and two others of his disciples. Simon Peter said to them, "I am going fishing." They said to him, "We also will come with you." So they went out and got into the boat, but that night they caught nothing. When it was already dawn, Jesus was standing on the shore; but the disciples did not realize that it was Jesus. Jesus said to them, "Children, have you caught anything to eat?" They answered him, "No." So he said to them, "Cast the net over the right side of the boat and you will find something." So they cast it, and were not able to pull it in because of the number of fish. So the disciple whom Jesus loved said to Peter, "It is the Lord." When Simon Peter heard that it was the Lord, he tucked in his garment, for he was lightly clad, and jumped into the sea. The other disciples came in the boat, for they were not far from shore, only about a hundred yards, dragging the net with the fish. When they climbed out on shore, they saw a charcoal fire with fish on it and bread. Jesus said to them, "Bring some of the fish you just caught." So Simon Peter went over and dragged the net ashore full of one hundred fifty-three large fish. Even though there were so many, the net was not torn. Jesus said to them, "Come, have breakfast." And none of the disciples dared to ask him, "Who are you?" because they realized it was the Lord. Jesus came over and took the bread and gave it to them, and in like manner the fish. This was now the third time Jesus was revealed to his disciples after being raised from the dead.

[When they had finished breakfast, Jesus said to Simon Peter, "Simon, son of John, do you love me more than these?" Simon Peter answered him, "Yes, Lord, you know that I love you." Jesus said to him, "Feed my lambs." He then said to Simon Peter a second time, "Simon, son of John, do you love me?" Simon Peter answered him, "Yes, Lord, you know that I love you." Jesus said to him, "Tend my sheep." Jesus said to him the third time, "Simon, son of John, do you love me?" Peter was distressed that Jesus had said to him a third time, "Do you love me?" and he said to him, "Lord, you know everything; you know that I love you." Jesus said to him, "Feed my sheep. Amen, amen, I say to you, when you were younger, you used to dress yourself and go where you wanted; but when you grow old, you will stretch out your hands, and someone else will dress you and lead you where you do not want to go." He said this signifying by what kind of death he would glorify God. And when he had said this, he said to him, "Follow me."]

✤ Understanding the Word

The author of Acts of the Apostles portrays the Sanhedrin as "filled with jealousy" (Acts 5:17), infuriated and desirous of the apostles' deaths (Acts 5:33) because of the success of the early preaching in Jerusalem. The Council has the apostles put in jail but an angel of the Lord releases them, so by morning they are again preaching in the temple (Acts 5:17–21). In today's first reading, the guards have rounded up the apostles once again and brought them before the Sanhedrin. Though commanded "to stop preaching in that name" (Acts 5:28), Peter, emboldened by the Spirit, announces, "We must obey God rather than men" (Acts 5:29).

In Chapter 5 of Revelation, Christ is depicted as both a lion and a lamb. One of the elders tells the seer in his heavenly vision that "the lion of the Tribe of Judah" is worthy to open the sealed scroll (Revelation 5:5). "Lion of Judah" was a messianic title applied to Christ that symbolized victory (Revelation 22:16). But in today's second reading, John sees not a lion but a lamb, the symbol of the Paschal Lamb that was sacrificed (Exodus 12; Isaiah 53:7; 1 Peter 1:18–19). Victory has been achieved through sacrifice, thus the heavenly cohort cried out, "Worthy is the Lamb that was slain to receive power and riches . . . " (Revelation 5:9).

Like John 7:53 — 8:11 (the woman caught in adultery), John 21 is a later addition to the fourth Gospel. Originally, the Gospel ended with the narrator's parting comments: "Now Jesus did many other signs in the presence of his disciples that are not written in this book" (John 20:30). Scholars propose that by the end of the first century, heretical influences had infiltrated part of the Johannine community. John 21 counters that influence, firmly aligning the community with emerging orthodoxy as symbolized by Peter. Jesus' repeated question, "Peter, do you love me?" and Peter's response atoned for Peter's three denials. The scene also uses Johannine imagery (shepherd/sheep, John 10:2, 11–16, 27) and vocabulary (love, John 13:34–35, 14:15, 21, 23, etc,) to establish Peter as the legitimate leader of the community.

✤ Reflecting on the Word

The tender dialogue between Jesus and Peter is a favorite of mine. It is the exchange two dear friends can have after one has deeply hurt the other and wonders if things can be the same. Maybe you've had a similar experience? Jesus begins: "Simon, son of John do you love me more than these?" Peter answers, "Yes, Lord, you know that I love you." Jesus asks Peter to care for his lambs. When asked a third time Peter is upset. In the original language the word for love is changed. Jesus asks for the total sacrificial love of close friends. Peter's answer reflects the love between siblings. Jesus meets Peter there, trusting that the sacrificial love originally asked for will return. Jesus' description of Peter's actions when he is older makes this clear.

In the first reading we see Peter's willingness to sacrifice. Newly out of prison, Peter proclaims Jesus even when that could mean return to prison and death. In late 2014, ISIS beheaded four children because they would not convert to Islam. Those children said, "We love Yeshua (Jesus). We have always loved Yeshua." They witnessed to sacrificial love as modern Holy Innocents.

We might not be asked to give ourselves in physical death. I'm not sure I'd have the strength to do so. But we are asked to love Jesus totally, to feed others with forgiveness, pay attention to others' needs and "smell like the sheep," as Pope Francis often asks. We are asked to live unconditional love of God by how we try to love others. The measure of our love is to love without measure, like Jesus, Peter, and the other disciples. Love and give blessing and honor to the Risen Lamb of God forever. Amen.

✤ Consider/Discuss

- How do you love Jesus, as a brother or with the sacrificial love of spouses or best friends?
- Name the ways you feed Jesus' lambs and sheep in the daily-ness of life.

✤ Living and Praying with the Word

Loving God, you gave yourself to us totally by becoming human. Jesus gave himself totally to us and to you by his death on the cross. You raised him from death. Raise us up and help us to love you totally by the ways in which we love our sisters and brothers.

April 17, 2016

FOURTH SUNDAY OF EASTER

Today's Focus: Whose Voice Do You Know?

We can often recognize those closest to us—even without seeing them—just by hearing them speak.

FIRST READING
Acts 13:14, 43–52

Paul and Barnabas continued on from Perga and reached Antioch in Pisidia. On the sabbath they entered the synagogue and took their seats. Many Jews and worshipers who were converts to Judaism followed Paul and Barnabas, who spoke to them and urged them to remain faithful to the grace of God.

On the following sabbath almost the whole city gathered to hear the word of the Lord. When the Jews saw the crowds, they were filled with jealousy and with violent abuse contradicted what Paul said. Both Paul and Barnabas spoke out boldly and said, "It was necessary that the word of God be spoken to you first, but since you reject it and condemn yourselves as unworthy of eternal life, we now turn to the Gentiles. For so the Lord has commanded us,
I have made you a light to the Gentiles,
that you may be an instrument of salvation
to the ends of the earth."

The Gentiles were delighted when they heard this and glorified the word of the Lord. All who were destined for eternal life came to believe, and the word of the Lord continued to spread through the whole region. The Jews, however, incited the women of prominence who were worshipers and the leading men of the city, stirred up a persecution against Paul and Barnabas, and expelled them from their territory. So they shook the dust from their feet in protest against them, and went to Iconium. The disciples were filled with joy and the Holy Spirit.

PSALM RESPONSE
Psalm 100:3c

We are his people, the sheep of his flock.

SECOND READING
Revelation 7:9, 14b–17

I, John, had a vision of a great multitude, which no one could count, from every nation, race, people, and tongue. They stood before the throne and before the Lamb, wearing white robes and holding palm branches in their hands.

Then one of the elders said to me, "These are the ones who have survived the time of great distress; they have washed their robes and made them white in the blood of the Lamb.

"For this reason they stand before God's throne
and worship him day and night in his temple.
The one who sits on the throne will shelter them.
They will not hunger or thirst anymore,
nor will the sun or any heat strike them.
For the Lamb who is in the center of the throne
will shepherd them
and lead them to springs of life-giving water,
and God will wipe away every tear from their eyes."

GOSPEL Jesus said: "My sheep hear my voice; I know them, and they follow
John 10:27–30 me. I give them eternal life, and they shall never perish. No one
can take them out of my hand. My Father, who has given them to
me, is greater than all, and no one can take them out of the Father's
hand. The Father and I are one."

❖ Understanding the Word

Scholars note the complicated portrait of the Jews in the Acts of the Apostles.
The Sanhedrin seeks to destroy the apostles (Acts 5:33), oversees the stoning of
Stephen (Acs 6:12), and brings charges against Paul (Acts 22:30). Some Jews of the
Diaspora (those living outside of Israel) stir up crowds against Paul and Barnabas,
as we see in today's first reading. In Thessalonica, the Jews will instigate a mob to
storm the house where Paul is staying (Acts 17:5) and then chase Paul out of the
nearby town of Beroea (Acts 17:13). However, some do come to belief, chiefly the
apostles and deacons and disciples of Jerusalem. "Fair-minded" Jews in Beroea
receive the word in all willingness (Act 17:11). And in the last scene, Paul is in
custody in Rome, still preaching the word first to the Jews (Acts 28:17).

The second reading describes part of John's vision of those who had suffered
persecution, who "have washed their robes and made them white in the blood of
the Lamb" (Revelation 7:14). The multitude, representing people of every nation,
carry palm branches as a sign of their victory over death (Revelation 7:9). The "great
distress" (Revelation 7:14) may refer to the tyranny and torture of Christians under
Nero (54–68 AD) or the persecution of Christians who refused to engage in the
imperial cult under Domitian (81–96 AD). Since Rome is referred to as "Babylon"
in Revelation, a term used for Rome after the destruction of the Jewish temple in
70 AD, the later persecution may be the "great distress" of which Revelation speaks.

Today's Gospel reading comes from an interesting chapter in John's Gospel. Jesus
continues his attack on the Pharisees (John 9:40–41) through parabolic language
(though John prefers "figure of speech" [John 10:6] rather than the word "parable" as
used by the Synoptic writers). Jesus compares the Pharisees to "hired hands" who
leave the sheep unattended when the wolf comes (John 10:12). Jesus, on the other
hand, is the "good shepherd who lays down his life for the sheep" (John 10:11). In
the brief pericope for today, Jesus stresses the intimacy that the shepherd and the
sheep share—"I know them" (John 10:27), "No one can take them out of my hand"
(John 10:28), and the intimacy that Jesus shares with the Father—"the Father and
I are one" (John 10:30). This relationship among disciples (sheep), Jesus, and God
will be made explicit in John 14:23: "Whoever loves me will keep my word and my
Father will love him, and we will come to him and make our dwelling with him."

I once visited a parish where I'd served as director of music for eight years. After the morning Mass, while talking with a parishioner, I broke into laughter. The principal came from her office and said: "I heard your laugh and knew you were back." When we have been close to others, we know their voices, laughs, and presence and do what we can to reconnect. Such was the intimacy Jesus describes in today's Gospel. Such is the intimacy Jesus seeks with all who believe in him.

The Jewish leaders in Antioch were not as inclusive in how they understood God's love as Paul and Barnabas were. They could not or would not accept that Christ was a light to the Gentiles and offered salvation to all. Because they narrowly defined who belonged and who did not, they could not or would not accept people who heard and followed Jesus' voice outside their narrow definition. They had Paul and Barnabas expelled because the leaders were not ready to believe that God could call anyone other than their own kind.

This has been true throughout history. Our narrow definition of who can hear the voice of God, Christ, or the Spirit has persecuted people who believe differently than we do. We start crusades and holocausts, build walls, and even kill those who refuse to convert to a certain faith. The Body of Christ has been divided by narrow definitions of "truth." God's love is much more inclusive. John's vision pictures a great multitude from every nation, race, people, and tongue before God's throne. We might be surprised by who stands next to us before the throne of the Lamb because they knew him intimately, heard his voice, and followed. If God is that welcoming, can we be any less?

✤ Consider/Discuss

- Where have you heard Jesus' voice or seen signs of the Spirit of God and were surprised?
- How can we honor and express our faith in ways that also respect how others understand God?

✤ Living and Praying with the Word

God, our shepherd, open our ears to recognize your voice and follow Jesus, the Good Shepherd. Open our eyes to see you where we least expect.

April 24, 2016

FIFTH SUNDAY OF EASTER

Today's Focus: The Where and What of Love

The life and ministry of Jesus is one of complete, self-giving love, extended always and everywhere. We give witness to the Resurrection when we love as he did.

FIRST READING
Acts 14:21–27

After Paul and Barnabas had proclaimed the good news to that city and made a considerable number of disciples, they returned to Lystra and to Iconium and to Antioch. They strengthened the spirits of the disciples and exhorted them to persevere in the faith, saying, "It is necessary for us to undergo many hardships to enter the kingdom of God." They appointed elders for them in each church and, with prayer and fasting, commended them to the Lord in whom they had put their faith. Then they traveled through Pisidia and reached Pamphylia. After proclaiming the word at Perga they went down to Attalia. From there they sailed to Antioch, where they had been commended to the grace of God for the work they had now accomplished. And when they arrived, they called the church together and reported what God had done with them and how he had opened the door of faith to the Gentiles.

PSALM RESPONSE
Psalm 145:1

I will praise your name for ever, my king and my God.

SECOND READING
Revelation 21: 1–5a

Then I, John, saw a new heaven and a new earth. The former heaven and the former earth had passed away, and the sea was no more. I also saw the holy city, a new Jerusalem, coming down out of heaven from God, prepared as a bride adorned for her husband. I heard a loud voice from the throne saying, "Behold, God's dwelling is with the human race. He will dwell with them and they will be his people and God himself will always be with them as their God. He will wipe every tear from their eyes, and there shall be no more death or mourning, wailing or pain, for the old order has passed away."

The One who sat on the throne said, "Behold, I make all things new."

GOSPEL
John 13: 31–33a, 34–35

When Judas had left them, Jesus said, "Now is the Son of Man glorified, and God is glorified in him. If God is glorified in him, God will also glorify him in himself, and God will glorify him at once. My children, I will be with you only a little while longer. I give you a new commandment: love one another. As I have loved you, so you also should love one another. This is how all will know that you are my disciples, if you have love for one another."

The first reading from Acts, describes the end of Paul and Barnabas' first missionary journey. Along with John Mark, the team left Antioch (Acts 13:3), and traveled to Cyprus (Acts 13:4–12) and on to Pamphylia (Acts 13:13) before venturing into the mountainous areas of Pisidia (Acts 13:14). At each stop, Paul and Barnabas begin in the synagogue (Acts 13:15; 14:1), where Gentile "God-fearers" are part of the assembly. Scholars debate whether "god-fearer" was a specific title for a particular level of membership in the Jewish faith or simply Luke's way of designating faithful Gentiles attracted to Judaism. These God-fearers respond to the message of Paul and Barnabas and come to believe (Acts 13:48; 14:1). God "had opened the door of faith to the Gentiles" (Acts 14:27), but it would take the Council of Jerusalem to figure out exactly how these Gentiles would be incorporated into the faith (Acts 15).

The various visions beheld by John on Patmos tell the story of the final days, culminating in the glorious vision of a new creation. In apocalyptic eschatology (study of the end-times), the final battle unseats Satan and his power for all eternity and God's reign is experienced in its fullness. That fullness is described in today's second reading as the creation of a new heaven and a new earth. "God's dwelling is with the human race . . . God himself will always be with them" (Revelation 21:3). The old order of suffering, persecution, and death will cease, for God has announced, "Behold, I make all things new" (Revelation 21:5).

In the Gospel of John, the actions of Judas are presented as motivated not by his greed but by the desires of the devil (John 13:2). When Judas takes the morsel from Jesus, Satan enters him (John 13:27). But these evil machinations only serve to further the plan of God. Throughout the Gospel, Jesus has remarked that his hour of glory had not yet come (John 2:4; 7:30; 8:20), but with Judas' action, Jesus announces, "Now is the Son of Man glorified" (John 13:31). As Jesus prepares for his glorification, he leaves his disciples with a new commandment: "love one another. As I have loved you, so you also should love one another" (John 13:34). Jesus will exemplify what that love looks like—"No one has greater love than this, to lay down one's life for one's friends" (John 15:13)—and thus his glorification will be complete.

✤ Reflecting on the Word

Jesus' command is to love one another, as he has loved us (John 13:34b). In the musical *Oliver* a song asks, "Where is love?" We might rephrase that to "What is love?" In the context of today's Gospel, John's account of the Last Supper, love is living as Jesus lived by giving oneself totally. Jesus washed feet, entered into his passion and gave himself to God and us totally by dying on the cross. Love entails sacrifice, giving self totally to another.

Anyone who has loved another person deeply knows this kind of love: spouses willing to put a career on hold so that the other can follow a dream; parents sitting up all night with a sick child to bring comfort and relief; children changing their way of living to be with a parent in need. What would you add to this list? Sacrificial love tells people we are Jesus' disciples.

Sacrificial love also ushers in the new heaven and new earth, our reading from Revelation announces. We will know that God dwells among us and frees us from the effects of pain and suffering, mourning and death, when we can find love in their midst and respond to evil with love. On September 11, 2014, Pope Francis said we must be a church that teaches mercy by facing hatred with love, violence with forgiveness, and weapons with prayer. That's how we give birth to a new earth and live, "Thy kingdom come. Thy will be done."

Where is love? In you and me when we obey Jesus' command. What is love? The total gift of self to God and one another, nothing more and nothing less.

❖ Consider/Discuss

- Give examples of how you live Jesus' command to love each day.
- What does sacrifice mean to you?

❖ Living and Praying with the Word

God of love, you gave yourself to us by taking on our human flesh and limitations, excepting sin. Help us follow Jesus' command to give ourselves totally to you by the ways we love sacrificially.

May 1, 2016

SIXTH SUNDAY OF EASTER

Today's Focus: In Thought, Word, and Deed

We "speak" in ways other than words: our thoughts form us and speak through our actions; our actions show others if the words we speak are really true.

FIRST READING
Acts 15:1–2, 22–29

Some who had come down from Judea were instructing the brothers, "Unless you are circumcised according to the Mosaic practice, you cannot be saved." Because there arose no little dissension and debate by Paul and Barnabas with them, it was decided that Paul, Barnabas, and some of the others should go up to Jerusalem to the apostles and elders about this question.

The apostles and elders, in agreement with the whole church, decided to choose representatives and to send them to Antioch with Paul and Barnabas. The ones chosen were Judas, who was called Barsabbas, and Silas, leaders among the brothers. This is the letter delivered by them:

"The apostles and the elders, your brothers, to the brothers in Antioch, Syria, and Cilicia of Gentile origin: greetings. Since we have heard that some of our number who went out without any mandate from us have upset you with their teachings and disturbed your peace of mind, we have with one accord decided to choose representatives and to send them to you along with our beloved Barnabas and Paul, who have dedicated their lives to the name of our Lord Jesus Christ. So we are sending Judas and Silas who will also convey this same message by word of mouth: 'It is the decision of the Holy Spirit and of us not to place on you any burden beyond these necessities, namely, to abstain from meat sacrificed to idols, from blood, from meats of strangled animals, and from unlawful marriage. If you keep free of these, you will be doing what is right. Farewell.' "

PSALM RESPONSE
Psalm 67:4

O God, let all the nations praise you!

SECOND READING
Revelation 21: 10–14, 22–23 The angel took me in spirit to a great, high mountain and showed me the holy city Jerusalem coming down out of heaven from God. It gleamed with the splendor of God. Its radiance was like that of a precious stone, like jasper, clear as crystal. It had a massive, high wall, with twelve gates where twelve angels were stationed and on which names were inscribed, the names of the twelve tribes of the Israelites. There were three gates facing east, three north, three south, and three west. The wall of the city had twelve courses of stones as its foundation, on which were inscribed the twelve names of the twelve apostles of the Lamb.

I saw no temple in the city for its temple is the Lord God almighty and the Lamb. The city had no need of sun or moon to shine on it, for the glory of God gave it light, and its lamp was the Lamb.

GOSPEL
John 14:23–29 Jesus said to his disciples: "Whoever loves me will keep my word, and my Father will love him, and we will come to him and make our dwelling with him. Whoever does not love me does not keep my words; yet the word you hear is not mine but that of the Father who sent me.

"I have told you this while I am with you. The Advocate, the Holy Spirit, whom the Father will send in my name, will teach you everything and remind you of all that I told you. Peace I leave with you; my peace I give to you. Not as the world gives do I give it to you. Do not let your hearts be troubled or afraid. You heard me tell you, 'I am going away and I will come back to you.' If you loved me, you would rejoice that I am going to the Father; for the Father is greater than I. And now I have told you this before it happens, so that when it happens you may believe."

❖ Understanding the Word

The first reading describes the authoritative letter composed by the Jerusalem church on the question of the admission of the Gentiles into the Christian Way (Luke's preferred term for believers). All the laws followed by the Jews were not to be forced upon the Gentile believers. They need only abstain from idol meat, from blood, meat of strangled animals, and unlawful marriage (Acts 15:29). These restrictions are absent from the Jerusalem Council described in Galatians 2:1–10, where no restrictions were placed on the Gentiles. Luke may have conflated two different events, a council that dealt with questions of circumcision and a decree concerning dietary laws for Gentiles. Acts 15 thus serves as the official approbation that the Way is open to Gentile believers.

Much of the imagery found in the second reading is borrowed from Ezekiel's vision of the new Jerusalem (Ezekiel 40 — 48). Traditionally, the remnant of the faithful would be gathered in Jerusalem to await the messianic age (Micah 4:6–8). In today's reading, that wait is ended. Jerusalem is presented as a bride of the Lamb (Revelation 21:9) and symbolizes the church. The wall surrounding the city consists of twelve courses of stones, representing the apostles, the foundation for the church. The seer describes a city shaped like a giant cube (Revelation 21:15–17), a symbol of perfection (1 Kings 6:19–20), that needs neither sun or moon, for the glory of God illuminates it.

In the Gospel reading, Jesus describes the conditions and benefits of relationship with him. First, those who love him keep his word. As a result, they dwell with Jesus and his Father (John 14:23). The Father will send an Advocate, the Holy Spirit in the name of Jesus to teach and direct the disciples in Jesus' absence (John 14:26). Finally, Jesus promises his peace to sustain and comfort the community (John 14:27). The lengthy discourses in John Chapters 14 — 16 read like a Last Will and Testament in which Jesus steels his beloved disciples for his coming departure, so that having been told, they might believe (John 14:29).

✤ Reflecting on the Word

Actions speak louder than words. Loving Jesus involves living his words. Living makes loving clear. My mother used to say, "Don't tell me you love me, clean the toilet." In other words, to show my love for Christ, the Church, and other people I must ask, "Have I *shown* them that I love them?"

We often need reminders to do what is right and act on what we believe. We need advocates who support us publicly in word and deed. At the height of the clergy sexual abuse crisis, I preached at a parish where a priest friend told his parishioners he was leaving because of a credible accusation. That same weekend a spiritual confidant informed me that my presence helped her confront her abuser. Another friend preached in a diocese where he helped people deal with accusations against their bishop. Advocacy takes many forms and can be difficult.

Paul and Barnabas advocated on behalf of Gentiles called follow Christ. They spoke on their behalf to the elders in Jerusalem, where discussion and prayer resulted in declaring that no burden ought to be placed on Gentile Christians beyond the necessities heard in today's first reading. If you've been to a parish or city council meeting, you know how heated discussions can become because people believe strongly in our opinions. It took the Advocate, the Holy Spirit, to help define these basics and invite the community to find peace. Speaking truth in love, being an advocate, listening to the Holy Spirit, living Christ's commandments affirm and challenge us. If we let the light of the Lamb of God be our lamp and listen to the Advocate, we will love in word and deed. We will clean the proverbial toilet.

✤ Consider/Discuss

- How do you live Jesus' words in your life?
- Can you describe times when you have been an advocate for someone or for God?

✤ Living and Praying with the Word

Come, Holy Spirit, be our Advocate. Remind us about Jesus' words and actions so that we can live the Christian Way today and give glory to God and to the Lamb.

May 5 or 8, 2016

THE ASCENSION OF THE LORD

Today's Focus: Where Are You Looking?

When we follow the angels' advice and stop looking only heavenward to see Christ, we can be amazed at how many places the presence of the Spirit is revealed to us.

FIRST READING
Acts 1:1–11

In the first book, Theophilus, I dealt with all that Jesus did and taught until the day he was taken up, after giving instructions through the Holy Spirit to the apostles whom he had chosen. He presented himself alive to them by many proofs after he had suffered, appearing to them during forty days and speaking about the kingdom of God. While meeting with them, he enjoined them not to depart from Jerusalem, but to wait for "the promise of the Father about which you have heard me speak; for John baptized with water, but in a few days you will be baptized with the Holy Spirit."

When they had gathered together they asked him, "Lord, are you at this time going to restore the kingdom to Israel?" He answered them, "It is not for you to know the times or seasons that the Father has established by his own authority. But you will receive power when the Holy Spirit comes upon you, and you will be my witnesses in Jerusalem, throughout Judea and Samaria, and to the ends of the earth." When he had said this, as they were looking on, he was lifted up, and a cloud took him from their sight. While they were looking intently at the sky as he was going, suddenly two men dressed in white garments stood beside them. They said, "Men of Galilee, why are you standing there looking at the sky? This Jesus who has been taken up from you into heaven will return in the same way as you have seen him going into heaven."

PSALM RESPONSE
Psalm 47:6

God mounts his throne to shouts of joy: a blare of trumpets for the Lord.

SECOND READING
Hebrews 9: 24–28; 10:19–23

Christ did not enter into a sanctuary made by hands, a copy of the true one, but heaven itself, that he might now appear before God on our behalf. Not that he might offer himself repeatedly, as the high priest enters each year into the sanctuary with blood that is not his own; if that were so, he would have had to suffer repeatedly from the foundation of the world. But now once for all he has appeared at the end of the ages to take away sin by his sacrifice. Just as it is appointed that men and women die once, and after this the judgment, so also Christ, offered once to take away the sins of many, will appear a second time, not to take away sin but to bring salvation to those who eagerly await him.

Therefore, brothers and sisters, since through the blood of Jesus we have confidence of entrance into the sanctuary by the new and living way he opened for us through the veil, that is, his flesh, and since we have "a great priest over the house of God," let us approach with a sincere heart and in absolute trust, with our hearts sprinkled clean from an evil conscience and our bodies washed in pure water. Let us hold unwaveringly to our confession that gives us hope, for he who made the promise is trustworthy.

GOSPEL
Luke 24:46–53

Jesus said to his disciples: "Thus it is written that the Christ would suffer and rise from the dead on the third day and that repentance, for the forgiveness of sins, would be preached in his name to all the nations, beginning from Jerusalem. You are witnesses of these things. And behold I am sending the promise of my Father upon you; but stay in the city until you are clothed with power from on high."

Then he led them out as far as Bethany, raised his hands, and blessed them. As he blessed them he parted from them and was taken up to heaven. They did him homage and then returned to Jerusalem with great joy, and they were continually in the temple praising God.

Today's first reading includes the prologue of the Acts of the Apostles, in which the reader learns that this is not the first book by this author. Theophilus is reminded that the "first book"—which we know as the Gospel of Luke—described all that Jesus did and taught until he was taken up. After the prologue, the narrative begins. The disciples ask Jesus if he is now going to restore the rule of Israel, which was an act expected of the Messiah. But Jesus defers that decision to the Father. Rather, the disciples are to await the Holy Spirit and then become witnesses to the ends of the earth. Shortly after Jesus' commission, he is lifted up into a cloud and taken from their sight. The resurrected Jesus will make no more appearance in the Acts of the Apostles.

Today's second reading draws from Old Testament images of the sanctuary and the sacrifices offered by the high priest. Christ is the true high priest who enters into the sanctuary in heaven (Hebrews 9:24). Whereas the priest had to offer sacrifice repeatedly, Christ, by his one sacrifice, has removed sin, ushering in the beginning of the end (Hebrews 9:26). Christ will return (*parousia*) and bring the fullness of salvation (Hebrews 9:28). Entrance to the sanctuary had once been limited to the high priests; now by the blood of Jesus, all believers who possess a "sincere heart and in absolute trust" can confidently approach the sanctuary (Hebrews 10:22).

The setting for today's first reading and Gospel reading is Jerusalem. In fact, if we were to read chronologically as the author of Luke-Acts had intended, we would start with the Gospel and then turn to Acts. In the Gospel, Jesus has just appeared to the disciples in Jerusalem. After assuring them that he is not a ghost (Luke 24:37), he then "opened their minds to understand the scriptures" (Luke 24:45). Our Gospel begins with Jesus now interpreting the Christ event through the lens of those scriptures. Jesus concludes his teaching by assuring the disciples that he is "sending the promise of my Father upon you" (Luke 24:49)—this promise will be fulfilled in Acts 2 with the coming of the Holy Spirit. After blessing them, Jesus is taken up to heaven. Matthew places the Ascension in Galilee, but for Luke, Jerusalem is the symbolic center of Jewish faith, and the first place in which the gospel is to be preached (Luke 24:47).

✦ Reflecting on the Word

A principle that seems to guide today's readings is that good things come in twos. Twos fill today's readings. Two angels appear and ask, "Why are you standing there looking at the sky?" Recall that Luke's account of the Resurrection has two angels ask "Why do you seek the living one among the dead?" We read two works attributed to Luke, the Acts of the Apostles and Luke's Gospel. We hear two different descriptions for the Ascension. The Letter to the Hebrews talks about Christ's first appearance and his return. Good things come in twos.

Two angels could simply reflect that two sets of eyes are better witnesses than one. They offer important advice: "Look for Christ among the living." "Look for Jesus in your midst." Two accounts of the Ascension invite us to look beyond physical details and mere appearance to find its deeper meaning. Christ is not limited by time or space. He sends the power of the Holy Spirit upon us to be his witnesses in all times and places, whether in Jerusalem—the center of the Jewish faith—or Bethany— outside that center. We receive power to praise God and witness the joy of the gospel. At all times the Spirit helps us look beyond appearances to see the heart, deepen trust in God's promise, and live with a clear conscience. That makes us ready for Christ's return whenever he reappears.

As we prepare to celebrate Pentecost, recall how you know Christ's presence in your life. Where do you look for him? Among the dead or the living? Only in heaven or here on earth? Only in the center of faith or in all creation? Take time to refresh the life of the Spirit that has been given you. Then witness your faith like angels, disciples, and believers throughout the ages.

❖ Consider/Discuss

- Where do you look for the presence of Christ?
- How do you give witness to the power of the Spirit in your life?

❖ Living and Praying with the Word

Open my eyes, Lord, to look for your presence within and around me. Refresh the power of your Holy Spirit so that I can be your messenger and witness that you are with us each and every day.

May 8, 2016

SEVENTH SUNDAY OF EASTER

Today's Focus: Oneness

Jesus prays that his followers may be one with him as he is one with the Father. The first step in attaining that oneness is for us to make Jesus' prayer our own.

FIRST READING
Acts 7:55–60

Stephen, filled with the Holy Spirit, looked up intently to heaven and saw the glory of God and Jesus standing at the right hand of God, and Stephen said, "Behold, I see the heavens opened and the Son of Man standing at the right hand of God." But they cried out in a loud voice, covered their ears, and rushed upon him together. They threw him out of the city, and began to stone him. The witnesses laid down their cloaks at the feet of a young man named Saul. As they were stoning Stephen, he called out, "Lord Jesus, receive my spirit." Then he fell to his knees and cried out in a loud voice, "Lord, do not hold this sin against them"; and when he said this, he fell asleep.

PSALM RESPONSE
Psalm 97:1a, 9a

The Lord is king, the most high over all the earth.

SECOND READING
Revelation 22: 12–14, 16–17, 20

I, John, heard a voice saying to me: "Behold, I am coming soon. I bring with me the recompense I will give to each according to his deeds. I am the Alpha and the Omega, the first and the last, the beginning and the end."

Blessed are they who wash their robes so as to have the right to the tree of life and enter the city through its gates.

"I, Jesus, sent my angel to give you this testimony for the churches. I am the root and offspring of David, the bright morning star."

The Spirit and the bride say, "Come." Let the hearer say, "Come." Let the one who thirsts come forward, and the one who wants it receive the gift of life-giving water.

The one who gives this testimony says, "Yes, I am coming soon." Amen! Come, Lord Jesus!

GOSPEL
John 17:20–26

Lifting up his eyes to heaven, Jesus prayed, saying: "Holy Father, I pray not only for them, but also for those who will believe in me through their word, so that they may all be one, as you, Father, are in me and I in you, that they also may be in us, that the world may believe that you sent me. And I have given them the glory you gave me, so that they may be one, as we are one, I in them and you in me, that they may be brought to perfection as one, that the world may know that you sent me, and that you loved them even as you loved me. Father, they are your gift to me. I wish that where I am they also may be with me, that they may see my glory that you gave me, because you loved me before the foundation of the world. Righteous Father, the world also does not know you, but I know you, and they know that you sent me. I made known to them your name and I will make it known, that the love with which you loved me may be in them and I in them."

❖ Understanding the Word

In our first reading, we are introduced to Stephen, one of the newly elected Greek-speaking Jews who will minister to the needs of the community (Acts 6:5). Stephen is identified as full of grace and power, one who did great wonders and signs among the people (Acts 6:8)—a description reminiscent of Jesus in Luke's Gospel. And like Jesus, Stephen's speech provokes the ire of some of the religious authorities. He is brought before the Jewish Council, the Sanhedrin, where his face is described as being like than of an angel (Acts 6:15). He stands as an orator and presents his case (Acts 7:2–53), which only enrages his hearers, who stone him (Acts 7:58). Stephen becomes the first martyr for the faith. In Acts, his martyrdom will be followed by that of James, the brother of John (Acts 12:2). Acts will close with Paul, awaiting martyrdom in Rome (Acts 28:16).

The book of Revelation closes much as it opened—with a series of warnings and exhortations. Revelation 1:1–3 introduces the reader to the revelation of Jesus Christ concerning what would be coming. Those who read the revelation and heed it are blessed, for the appointed time is near. In Revelation 22:12–14, Jesus promises that he is coming soon and will judge each according to their deeds. In apocalyptic eschatology, the final judgment was the last stage before the Kingdom of God would be complete. Today's reading from Revelation reminds us that Jesus' promise—"Yes, I am coming soon"—is yet to be fulfilled! The Gospel of John does not include the "Lord's Prayer" as found in the Synoptics; however, Chapter 17 provides an intimate glimpse into Jesus' conversation with his Father. The prayer has a hymn-like quality and may have originally been found in a liturgical context. The use of the divine name and glorification of the Father in John 17:1, 11–12 is similar to that found in Matthew 6:9 and Luke 11:2 6:9. And the request to be delivered from evil is found in both John 17:15 and Matthew 6:13. The prayer itself can be divided into three units. In vv. 1–8, Jesus asks for glory. In vv. 9–19, Jesus prays for his disciples. In the final unit, which is read today, Jesus prays for those who believe through the disciples' word.

Jesus prays that the disciples who hear his prayer, and we who will come after, may be one and know that the Father sent him. Jesus is one with the Father. We are to be one with Jesus. Jesus shares the love the Father has for him with us so that when people see us, they see him.

To be one with another does not mean being a mold or carbon copy of someone. Union invites us to model our lives after another in our own unique way by following their example. St. Francis de Sales called this unidiversity, oneness amidst difference. We see an example of unidiversity in the account of Stephen's martyrdom. He modeled his life after Jesus, so much so that his words and witness outraged the religious leaders as Jesus' life had. Even in death his words are similar to Jesus' words on the cross: "Receive my spirit" and "do not hold this sin against them." However, Jesus addressed his words to the Father. Stephen addresses his words to Jesus. They are united in life and death, yet each was his own unique person.

At baptism we promised to live Jesus and model our lives on his. We promised to live his commandments so that the world could know him. One with Christ, each of us has unique gifts for living Jesus. We will receive recompense from the Lord Jesus according to our deeds. Do your deeds model Jesus Christ? In what unique ways do others know that you are one with him? Give God the glory by living Jesus clearly so that all may be one.

✦ Consider/Discuss

- Describe ways that you model your life on the life, death, and resurrection of Jesus Christ.
- Can you name a time when you were sure that you and Jesus are one? How did you know?

✦ Living and Praying with the Word

Father, fill me with the same Spirit that you and Jesus share so that it is clear to all that he is the model and center of my life.

May 15, 2016

PENTECOST

Today's Focus: Children in the Spirit

The Holy Spirit continues to bind us in love to the Father and Son as beloved children. The Spirit also fills us and sends us forth to give witness to that love.

FIRST READING
Acts 2:1–11

When the time for Pentecost was fulfilled, they were all in one place together. And suddenly there came from the sky a noise like a strong driving wind, and it filled the entire house in which they were. Then there appeared to them tongues as of fire, which parted and came to rest on each one of them. And they were all filled with the Holy Spirit and began to speak in different tongues, as the Spirit enabled them to proclaim.

Now there were devout Jews from every nation under heaven staying in Jerusalem. At this sound, they gathered in a large crowd, but they were confused because each one heard them speaking in his own language. They were astounded, and in amazement they asked, "Are not all these people who are speaking Galileans? Then how does each of us hear them in his native language? We are Parthians, Medes, and Elamites, inhabitants of Mesopotamia, Judea and Cappadocia, Pontus and Asia, Phrygia and Pamphylia, Egypt and the districts of Libya near Cyrene, as well as travelers from Rome, both Jews and converts to Judaism, Cretans and Arabs, yet we hear them speaking in our own tongues of the mighty acts of God."

PSALM RESPONSE
Psalm 104:30

Lord, send out your Spirit, and renew the face of the earth.

SECOND READING
1 Corinthians 12:3b–7, 12–13

Brothers and sisters: No one can say, "Jesus is Lord," except by the Holy Spirit. There are different kinds of spiritual gifts but the same Spirit; there are different forms of service but the same Lord; there are different workings but the same God who produces all of them in everyone. To each individual the manifestation of the Spirit is given for some benefit.

As a body is one though it has many parts, and all the parts of the body, though many, are one body, so also Christ. For in one Spirit we were all baptized into one body, whether Jews or Greeks, slaves or free persons, and we were all given to drink of one Spirit.

– or –

Romans 8:8–17 Brothers and sisters: Those who are in the flesh cannot please God. But you are not in the flesh; on the contrary, you are in the spirit, if only the Spirit of God dwells in you. Whoever does not have the Spirit of Christ does not belong to him. But if Christ is in you, although the body is dead because of sin, the spirit is alive because of righteousness. If the Spirit of the one who raised Jesus from the dead dwells in you, the one who raised Christ from the dead will give life to your mortal bodies also, through his Spirit that dwells in you. Consequently, brothers and sisters, we are not debtors to the flesh, to live according to the flesh. For if you live according to the flesh, you will die, but if by the Spirit you put to death the deeds of the body, you will live.

For those who are led by the Spirit of God are sons of God. For you did not receive a spirit of slavery to fall back into fear, but you received a Spirit of adoption, through whom we cry, "Abba, Father!" The Spirit himself bears witness with our spirit that we are children of God, and if children, then heirs, heirs of God and joint heirs with Christ, if only we suffer with him so that we may also be glorified with him.

GOSPEL On the evening of that first day of the week, when the doors were
John 20:19–23 locked, where the disciples were, for fear of the Jews, Jesus came and stood in their midst and said to them, "Peace be with you." When he had said this, he showed them his hands and his side. The disciples rejoiced when they saw the Lord. Jesus said to them again, "Peace be with you. As the Father has sent me, so I send you." And when he had said this, he breathed on them and said to them, "Receive the Holy Spirit. Whose sins you forgive are forgiven them, and whose sins you retain are retained."

– or –

John 14:15–16, Jesus said to his disciples: "If you love me, you will keep my com-
23b-26 mandments. And I will ask the Father, and he will give you another Advocate to be with you always.

"Whoever loves me will keep my word, and my Father will love him, and we will come to him and make our dwelling with him. Those who do not love me do not keep my words; yet the word you hear is not mine but that of the Father who sent me.

"I have told you this while I am with you. The Advocate, the Holy Spirit whom the Father will send in my name, will teach you everything and remind you of all that I told you."

126

In the first reading, the apostles are gathered in one place during the Jewish pilgrim feast of Pentecost. Also called the Festival of Weeks, the feast celebrated the first fruits of the field and was later associated with the giving of the Law. After the coming of the Spirit, Pentecost will be celebrated as the founding of the Church. The descent of the Spirit is described as a sound—a strong, driving wind, and as a visual representation—tongues of fire, which separate and rest on all in the room. All are filled with Holy Spirit and immediately speak in foreign tongues. The commission Jesus had given—to proclaim to the ends of the earth (Acts 1:8)—can now be realized, for the disciples have the gifts of the Holy Spirit to empower them.

Earlier in the Letter to the Romans—from which our second reading is taken— Paul had written, "We were indeed buried with him through baptism into death, so that, just as Christ was raised from the dead by the glory of the Father, we too might live in newness of life" (Romans 6:4). By virtue of our baptism, the Spirit of God dwells within the believer, so that the bodily things of the world are no longer of import. Paul enumerates the benefits of this life of the Spirit. If God's spirit could raise Jesus from the dead, that same spirit will raise believers. Those led by the Spirit are children of God, since they have received a spirit of adoption. And if children, then heirs with Christ.

John's Gospel narrates the coming of the Spirit in as lightly different way than Acts of the Apostles. For John, Jesus will not leave his disciples bereft of his presence. He will ask his father to send the Advocate, the Holy Spirit (John 14:16), also described as the Spirit of truth (John 14:17) who will remain with believers though the world will not recognize it. Jesus promised he would not leave the community orphaned, but would return. The Synoptics interpret Jesus' return through the lens of eschatology (the anticipation of the end times and the final judgment). But John's community recognized that the Paraclete was the presence of the Resurrected Christ in their midst. Some scholars interpret this as "realized eschatology"—Jesus is present and experienced now. The disciples need only keep Jesus' commandments, and thus the Father would love them, and both Jesus and the Father would dwell with them (John 14:23).

✦ Reflecting on the Word

Have you seen the Holy Spirit or felt the Spirit's presence? I started music ministry at a very young age. During a Mass celebrated with some of our parishioners, I voiced my fear that I could not handle the job. One by one people affirmed that if they hadn't thought I could do the job, I would not have been hired, and that if I weren't capable the choir members would not be listening to me and improving. By the end of that liturgy I felt the Holy Spirit and was on fire for a ministry that lasted eight years in that parish and has continued to this day.

During one month's span, I have watched our parish outreach ministry prepare meals for people to take home and celebrate Thanksgiving and Christmas. I have witnessed the time and energy they put into organizing gifts for families, helping people figure out how to pay bills and find housing. I have seen the Spirit's fire in their care and activity. By paying attention to each person, these sisters and brothers speak to them in a tongue that they can understand and help them experience the mighty acts of God. The Spirit renews the face of the earth.

We were given the Holy Spirit in Baptism, sealed with the Spirit in Confirmation, and pray to become one body and spirit in Christ in the Eucharistic Prayer. We did not receive a spirit of slavery to fall back into fear, but the Spirit of adoption that gives freedom to live as children of God. When afraid, cry out for confidence. When weak, cry out for strength. Pray "Come, Holy Spirit, fill the hearts of your faithful," set me on fire for people see you today.

❖ Consider/Discuss

- How has the Holy Spirit been present in your life?
- What will it take for you to proclaim the presence of the Spirit clearly?

❖ Living and Praying with the Word

Come, Holy Spirit, heal us, bend us, melt us, and free us to make you known so that we can set the world on fire with your love.

In this segment of Ordinary Time, we celebrate two feasts: the Most Holy Trinity and the Most Holy Body and Blood of Christ. The readings for Trinity Sunday reveal the ongoing relationship evident in the Triune God. Wisdom, personified as a woman, stands as welcoming mediator between God and humanity (Proverbs 8:22–31), while Paul confirms that faith in God through Jesus Christ is strengthened by the presence of the Holy Spirit. The Gospel of John highlights the intimacy shared between God and Jesus, an intimacy to which the disciples are invited. On Corpus Christi, we remember that the use of bread and wine to symbolize covenant and relationship is rooted in ancient tradition. The encounter between the Canaanite priest and king Melchizedek and Abram, Paul's recounting the tradition of the institution of the Eucharist, and Jesus' feeding of the multitudes are readings that help us deepen our understanding of the Body and Blood of Christ.

The first readings come from a variety of Old Testament books. The prophets demonstrate God's power and authority (Tenth, Eleventh, Thirteenth, Twentieth, and Twenty-first Sundays). They also promise a new beginning (Twelfth and Fourteenth Sundays). Deuteronomy (Fifteenth Sunday) reminds the reader that the commandments of God reside in one's heart. The story of Abraham and the three visitors demonstrates how hospitality toward strangers leads to blessing (Sixteenth Sunday). Abraham's kindness is extended toward the doomed cities of Sodom and Gomorrah in the reading from the Seventeenth Sunday. Having an appropriate attitude toward life is the recommendation of Ecclesiastes (Eighteenth Sunday), Wisdom (Nineteenth Sunday), and Sirach (Twenty-second Sunday).

The second readings trace major portions of Paul's Letter to the Galatians (Tenth through Fourteenth Sundays) and the Letter to the Colossians (Fifteenth through Eighteenth Sundays). The readings for the Nineteenth through Twenty-second Sundays in Ordinary Time are taken from Hebrews, an extended sermon in letter form.

The Gospel readings for the Tenth through Twenty-second Sundays are taken from the central part of Luke. At the beginning of his public ministry, Jesus had read from the prophet Isaiah, "The Spirit of the Lord is upon me / because he has anointed me to bring glad tidings to the poor . . . to proclaim liberty to captives and recovery of sight to the blind / to let the oppressed go free" (Luke 4:18; Third Sunday). The Gospel readings for this period of Ordinary Time narrate the fulfillment of Isaiah's prophecy. Jesus raises the widow's son (Tenth Sunday) and forgives and heals (Eleventh Sunday). Along the journey to Jerusalem, Jesus outlines the rigors of discipleship (Thirteenth, Fourteenth, Sixteenth, and Eighteenth through Twentieth Sundays), the expectations of fulfilling the gospel (Fifteenth and Twenty-second Sundays), and the results of failing to do so (Twenty-first Sunday). Prayer not only brings one closer to God; prayer also directs one outward toward those in need (Seventeenth Sunday).

May 22, 2016

THE MOST HOLY TRINITY

Today's Focus: Behind Us All the Way

The Holy Trinity is bound together in a relationship of love, and that love also binds us to the Trinity. Our mission is to let that love be the bond of relationship we have with one another.

FIRST READING
Proverbs 8: 22–31

Thus says the wisdom of God:
"The Lord possessed me, the beginning of his ways,
    the forerunner of his prodigies of long ago;
from of old I was poured forth,
    at the first, before the earth.
When there were no depths I was brought forth,
    when there were no fountains or springs of water;
before the mountains were settled into place,
    before the hills, I was brought forth;
while as yet the earth and fields were not made,
    nor the first clods of the world.

"When the Lord established the heavens I was there,
    when he marked out the vault over the face of the deep;
when he made firm the skies above,
    when he fixed fast the foundations of the earth;
when he set for the sea its limit,
    so that the waters should not transgress his command;
then was I beside him as his craftsman,
    and I was his delight day by day,
playing before him all the while,
    playing on the surface of his earth;
    and I found delight in the human race."

PSALM RESPONSE
Psalm 8:2a

O Lord, our God, how wonderful your name in all the earth!

SECOND READING
Romans 5:1–5

Brothers and sisters: Therefore, since we have been justified by faith, we have peace with God through our Lord Jesus Christ, through whom we have gained access by faith to this grace in which we stand, and we boast in hope of the glory of God. Not only that, but we even boast of our afflictions, knowing that affliction produces endurance, and endurance, proven character, and proven character, hope, and hope does not disappoint, because the love of God has been poured out into our hearts through the Holy Spirit that has been given to us.

Jesus said to his disciples: "I have much more to tell you, but you cannot bear it now. But when he comes, the Spirit of truth, he will guide you to all truth. He will not speak on his own, but he will speak what he hears, and will declare to you the things that are coming. He will glorify me, because he will take from what is mine and declare it to you. Everything that the Father has is mine; for this reason I told you that he will take from what is mine and declare it to you."

✤ Understanding the Word

The book of Proverbs can be divided into two sections: Chapters 1–9 and 10–31. The latter is a collection of proverbs and mostly likely predates the first section. Chapters 1–9 are a group of extended metaphors and narrative poems personifying Wisdom, and serve as an introduction to the proverbial collection. The female presentation of Wisdom is also found in Proverbs 31:10–31, Song of Songs, Sirach 24, and Wisdom 7–9. As scholars readily note, the chief attribute of Wisdom is her relationality. She is present with God in the beginning, is the companion of God in the work of creation, and delights in the human race.

The second reading from Paul's Letter to the Romans also demonstrates the importance of relationality. Jesus Christ gives believers access to faith, which leads to grace and peace with God. But Paul recognizes that this relationship does not protect us from difficulties and sufferings. Rather, "affliction produces endurance" and encourages hope. And hope does not disappoint, since the Holy Spirit has been given as a testament to God's love. In Paul's developing theology, the death and resurrection of Jesus Christ opened the way for justification with God, which would only be fully realized when Christ returned. Until that time, the Holy Spirit serves as the conduit of God's grace.

The "Book of Glory" found in John Chapters 13–19 describes Jesus' return to God and the invitation to the disciples to join in the divine relationship. In John 14: 20, Jesus said, "I am in my Father and you are in me and I am in you." Since God has given all to the Son, and the Son freely shared it with the disciples, they now are one with God (John 14:17; 15:4, 9; 16:15). In today's reading, Jesus promises that the Spirit of Truth will continue to guide the disciples after he has departed. The Father has shared everything with the Son, and now the Son through the Spirit declares all to the disciples. Thus the Trinity of Father, Son, and Spirit is expanded to include all believers.

When I entered religious life I needed a new credit card. My religious community's letter of application said that all the resources of the community stand behind me. The letter was talking about our financial resources. I soon learned that it spoke about much more. When I broke my wrist and needed surgery to regain as much use of my hand as possible, the community supported me physically and emotionally. I am an organist. Their support made all the difference in my healing process. I regained 95 percent of my hand's function and discovered that my relationship with the community was strong.

Today's solemnity and its readings speak about relationship within God and between God and us. Wisdom, with God from the beginning, plays on the earth and delights in us. Wisdom, made known as the Holy Spirit, has been poured into our hearts. Wisdom-made-visible is another name for Jesus. Everything the Father has is Jesus' and will be given us through the Spirit. Father, Son, and Spirit—one God yet three persons. Some name the Holy Spirit as the life force within the Trinity. Our readings make clear that the Spirit is also the life force connecting the Trinity with us. We sing this belief at every Mass: "Through him, and with him, and in him, O God, almighty Father, in the unity of the Holy Spirit, all glory . . . for ever and ever. Amen."

Created in the image and likeness of a God who is relationship, we are called to deepen our relationship with the God who delights in us, dwells in our hearts (even in the midst of affliction), and offers us peace. Give glory to God today. Pray and deepen your relationship with God, through Christ, in the Spirit. Invite others into this relationship by your words and witness.

✤ Consider/Discuss

- What relationships help you know the God who dwells in you?
- What real difference does belief in the Trinity make in your daily living?

✤ Living and Praying with the Word

Triune God, you invite us into relationship with you and with each other. May we be a living doxology that proclaims glory to you, Father, Son, and Spirit, now and for ever. Amen.

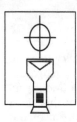

May 29, 2016

THE MOST HOLY BODY AND BLOOD OF CHRIST

Today's Focus: God Bless, Bless God

We often think of God's blessings upon us, but the table prayer of thanksgiving that Jesus handed on to us calls on us to bless God for all we have in life.

FIRST READING
Genesis 14: 18–20

In those days, Melchizedek, king of Salem, brought out bread and wine, and being a priest of God Most High, he blessed Abram with these words:
"Blessed be Abram by God Most High,
    the creator of heaven and earth;
and blessed be God Most High,
    who delivered your foes into your hand."
Then Abram gave him a tenth of everything.

PSALM RESPONSE
Psalm 110:4b

You are a priest for ever, in the line of Melchizedek.

SECOND READING
1 Corinthians 11:23–26

Brothers and sisters: I received from the Lord what I also handed on to you, that the Lord Jesus, on the night he was handed over, took bread, and, after he had given thanks, broke it and said, "This is my body that is for you. Do this in remembrance of me." In the same way also the cup, after supper, saying, "This cup is the new covenant in my blood. Do this, as often as you drink it, in remembrance of me." For as often as you eat this bread and drink the cup, you proclaim the death of the Lord until he comes.

GOSPEL
Luke 9:11b–17

Jesus spoke to the crowds about the kingdom of God, and he healed those who needed to be cured. As the day was drawing to a close, the Twelve approached him and said, "Dismiss the crowd so that they can go to the surrounding villages and farms and find lodging and provisions; for we are in a deserted place here." He said to them, "Give them some food yourselves." They replied, "Five loaves and two fish are all we have, unless we ourselves go and buy food for all these people." Now the men there numbered about five thousand. Then he said to his disciples, "Have them sit down in groups of about fifty." They did so and made them all sit down. Then taking the five loaves and the two fish, and looking up to heaven, he said the blessing over them, broke them, and gave them to the disciples to set before the crowd. They all ate and were satisfied. And when the leftover fragments were picked up, they filled twelve wicker baskets.

In the first reading, we meet a Canaanite ruler and priest. He is *Melek* (king) of *zedek* (righteousness) from Salem, likely Canaanite Jerusalem. In fact, Melchizedek is a priest of the "Most High God," and an old Canaanite cult of *el elyon* (Most High God) practiced in ancient Jerusalem. Abram receives the blessing from this stranger, and then offers him a tithe, thereby accepting the blessing. Far from disparaging the Canaanite priest and king, in verse 22 Abram unites Yahweh with "most high god." After he declines the king of Sodom's support, Abram announces, "I have sworn to the LORD, God Most High, the creator of heaven and earth" (Genesis 14:22). Here is the first time we hear of the Lord being called "the Most High God."

Paul records our earliest example of the liturgy of the Lord's Supper. After admonishing the Corinthians for their poor behavior at the celebration of the Lord's Supper (1 Corinthians 11:17–22), he then recites the tradition that he had received. The Synoptic Gospels also record the institution of the Eucharist. Paul's account is most similar to that found in the Gospel of Luke 22:19–20. In both Paul and Luke, Jesus gives thanks, acknowledges that his body will be broken for their sake, and recites the *anamnesis* formula, "Do this in remembrance of me," after the bread and after the cup. The cup is the new covenant and is taken after the meal. Matthew and Mark do not include an *anamnesis*, and the cup is part of the meal and represents not a new covenant but the blood of the covenant. Both Matthew and Mark anticipate an eschatological banquet (Matthew 26:29; Mark 14:25), absent in Paul and Luke.

All four Gospels record the miracle of the loaves and the fishes (Matthew 14:13–21; Mark 6:32–44; Luke 9:10b-18; John 6:15), and Matthew and Mark include a second multiplication for a Gentile audience (Matthew 15:32–39; Mark 8:1–10). Though the scene is often referred to as the multiplication, Jesus is not described as producing more bread (as he produced wine from water in John 2). He simply blesses what is available and then has his disciples distribute the food.

❖   Reflecting on the Word

How does God bless you? How do you bless God? To bless is to thank God for someone or something and to ask God's protection of what is blessed. Our first reading reflects this: "Blessed be Abram by God Most High . . . and blessed be God Most High." Jesus blesses God for the five loaves and two fish the Twelve provide. God's "protection" is experienced in more than enough food for the crowd. In our second reading, the earliest scriptural description of celebrating Eucharist, Jesus takes bread and wine, gives thanks (blesses God) for them, shares them and says "Do this in remembrance of me." By doing as he did we renew the covenant with God through Jesus, Jesus is present in our midst, and he offers us God's blessing.

Notice the importance of blessing or thanking God. We need an attitude of gratitude for God's providence. Gratitude must be expressed by feeding others with the living presence of Christ that we receive in Communion and adore in the Blessed Sacrament. Like Jesus, we must take what we have, give God thanks, and share our very selves with others in the name of Jesus. We offer God what we have like Abram, the Twelve, and Jesus to feed our deepest hungers.

Reflect on the gifts God has given you. Thank God for them. Use them to feed others with the presence of the Christ, in remembrance of him. That is one way we give praise to Christ (to quote today's Sequence), and proclaim the death of the Lord with the food of our lives.

✦ Consider/Discuss

- What gifts do you have that can satisfy people's hungers?
- What would be included in a "Litany of Thanksgiving" to God for you and your gifts?

✦ Living and Praying with the Word

Christ, we thank you for giving us yourself in bread and wine, become your Body and Blood. Help us be the living bread and drink you use to satisfy the hungers of our world.

June 5, 2016

TENTH SUNDAY IN ORDINARY TIME

Today's Focus: Pay Attention!

The great miracles and acts of kindness recounted in the Bible would not have been possible if people like Elijah and Jesus hadn't been paying attention. Our world needs our compassion, if we pay attention.

FIRST READING
1 Kings 17:17–24

Elijah went to Zarephath of Sidon to the house of a widow. The son of the mistress of the house fell sick, and his sickness grew more severe until he stopped breathing. So she said to Elijah, "Why have you done this to me, O man of God? Have you come to me to call attention to my guilt and to kill my son?" Elijah said to her, "Give me your son." Taking him from her lap, he carried the son to the upper room where he was staying, and put him on his bed. Elijah called out to the LORD: "O LORD, my God, will you afflict even the widow with whom I am staying by killing her son?" Then he stretched himself out upon the child three times and called out to the LORD: "O LORD, my God, let the life breath return to the body of this child." The LORD heard the prayer of Elijah; the life breath returned to the child's body and he revived. Taking the child, Elijah brought him down into the house from the upper room and gave him to his mother. Elijah said to her, "See! Your son is alive." The woman replied to Elijah, "Now indeed I know that you are a man of God. The word of the LORD comes truly from your mouth."

PSALM RESPONSE
Psalm 30:2a

I will praise you, Lord, for you have rescued me.

SECOND READING
Galatians 1:11–19

I want you to know, brothers and sisters, that the gospel preached by me is not of human origin. For I did not receive it from a human being, nor was I taught it, but it came through a revelation of Jesus Christ.

For you heard of my former way of life in Judaism, how I persecuted the church of God beyond measure and tried to destroy it, and progressed in Judaism beyond many of my contemporaries among my race, since I was even more a zealot for my ancestral traditions. But when God, who from my mother's womb had set me apart and called me through his grace, was pleased to reveal his Son to me, so that I might proclaim him to the Gentiles, I did not immediately consult flesh and blood, nor did I go up to Jerusalem to those who were apostles before me; rather, I went into Arabia and then returned to Damascus.

Then after three years I went up to Jerusalem to confer with Cephas and remained with him for fifteen days. But I did not see any other of the apostles, only James the brother of the Lord.

GOSPEL
Luke 7:11–17
Jesus journeyed to a city called Nain, and his disciples and a large crowd accompanied him. As he drew near to the gate of the city, a man who had died was being carried out, the only son of his mother, and she was a widow. A large crowd from the city was with her. When the Lord saw her, he was moved with pity for her and said to her, "Do not weep." He stepped forward and touched the coffin; at this the bearers halted, and he said, "Young man, I tell you, arise!" The dead man sat up and began to speak, and Jesus gave him to his mother. Fear seized them all, and they glorified God, exclaiming, "A great prophet has arisen in our midst," and "God has visited his people." This report about him spread through the whole of Judea and in all the surrounding region.

❖ Understanding the Word

The Elijah-Elisha cycle is a collection of stories of the two prophets woven into First and Second Kings. Elijah's name means "My God is the LORD" (when written in capital letters, the word "LORD" stands for the Tetragrammaton, the holy name of God). Elijah is presented as God's prophet and intermediary. Earlier in 1 Kings 17, Elijah had come upon the widow of Zarephath as she was about to cook her remaining food (vv. 10–12). Elijah asks that she share her food, promising that the LORD, the God of Israel, will not allow her flour or oil to run out until the drought has ended (vv.13–16). In today's first reading, God enacts an even greater miracle through Elijah. The widow's son is brought back to life. The unending supply of flour and oil had not convinced her, but the resuscitation of son leads her to acknowledge, "The word of the LORD comes truly from your mouth" (v. 24).

In the second reading, Paul describes his call in prophetic terms. Like Jeremiah, he was set apart in his mother's womb (Galatians 2:15; Jeremiah 1:5). Though he had once zealously persecuted the church of God, he was abruptly redirected by a revelation of Jesus Christ. He testifies that the gospel that he preaches is not of human origins. Where Elijah could verify his heavenly calling through miracles, Paul has only his preaching to certify his legitimacy. Much of the Letter to the Galatians is Paul's apology or defense of his apostleship, and thus his authority to preach Christ crucified to the Gentiles.

Only in the Gospel of Luke do we find the story of Jesus' raising the son of the widow of Nain. It follows the healing the centurion's servant (Luke 7:1–10) and precedes the questioning of the disciples sent by John the Baptist. The resuscitation of the widow's son parallels the story of Elijah and leads the crowds to announce, "A great prophet has arisen in our midst" (v. 22). The actions of healing the sick and lame, granting sight to the blind and hearing to the deaf, and finally raising the dead testify that Jesus is "the one who is to come" (v.19).

Have you experienced God's compassionate attention in your need? To have compassion is to *feel with* another person. Feeling with another involves paying attention. Jesus is moved with pity or compassion for a grieving widow. He raises her son to life, and gives him back to her. Elijah has compassion on his hostess, stretches himself out on her son, and asks God to return his life breath. God answers this prayer and Elijah gives him back to his mother. Attentive to the needs of two widows, Jesus and Elijah are filled with compassion and God returns life to the dead. Paul is dead to the early church, blinded by his zeal for his ancestral traditions. Jesus attends to Paul's needs and gifts, has compassion on him, and turns a persecutor into a powerful preacher of the gospel.

Elijah and Jesus paid attention to people in need. Their attentiveness gave them compassion for those people. Two widows and Paul were willing to give their lives over to God's touch. Because of that surrender to God through Elijah and Jesus, life was restored to their sons and Paul was given new life. By paying attention to God and to the other, we feel with the other, and God responds to us and through our words and deeds.

Pay attention to what is going on in your life and in the world around you. Throw yourself upon God's merciful love as Elijah threw himself over the widow's son. Let God see your heart as clearly as Jesus could see that of the widow of Nain. Turn to God in prayer like Paul. Through attentive compassion the Lord will visit his people today.

✤ Consider/Discuss

- In what ways have you felt God's compassion in your life?
- How does God visit other people through you?

✤ *Living and Praying with the Word*

Compassionate God, thank you for visiting us through prophets like Elijah, preachers like Paul, and most of all through your Son, Jesus Christ. Open our eyes to the needs of all, that you might continue to give life through us.

June 12, 2016

ELEVENTH SUNDAY IN ORDINARY TIME

Today's Focus: Forgiven, Not Perfect

In the Lord's Prayer we ask God to forgive us as we forgive others. After we have knelt at Jesus' feet like the unnamed woman in Luke, asking pardon, are we ready to extend pardon to those who have wronged us?

FIRST READING
2 Samuel 12: 7–10, 13

Nathan said to David: "Thus says the LORD God of Israel: 'I anointed you king of Israel. I rescued you from the hand of Saul. I gave you your lord's house and your lord's wives for your own. I gave you the house of Israel and of Judah. And if this were not enough, I could count up for you still more. Why have you spurned the Lord and done evil in his sight? You have cut down Uriah the Hittite with the sword; you took his wife as your own, and him you killed with the sword of the Ammonites. Now, therefore, the sword shall never depart from your house, because you have despised me and have taken the wife of Uriah to be your wife.' " Then David said to Nathan, "I have sinned against the LORD." Nathan answered David: "The LORD on his part has forgiven your sin: you shall not die."

PSALM RESPONSE
Psalm 32:5c

Lord, forgive the wrong I have done.

SECOND READING
Galatians 2:16, 19–21

Brothers and sisters: We who know that a person is not justified by works of the law but through faith in Jesus Christ, even we have believed in Christ Jesus that we may be justified by faith in Christ and not by works of the law, because by works of the law no one will be justified. For through the law I died to the law, that I might live for God. I have been crucified with Christ; yet I live, no longer I, but Christ lives in me; insofar as I now live in the flesh, I live by faith in the Son of God who has loved me and given himself up for me. I do not nullify the grace of God; for if justification comes through the law, then Christ died for nothing.

In the shorter form of the reading, the passage in brackets is omitted.

GOSPEL
Luke 7:36 — 8:3
or 7:36–50

A Pharisee invited Jesus to dine with him, and he entered the Pharisee's house and reclined at table. Now there was a sinful woman in the city who learned that he was at table in the house of the Pharisee. Bringing an alabaster flask of ointment, she stood behind him at his feet weeping and began to bathe his feet with her tears. Then she wiped them with her hair, kissed them, and anointed them with the ointment. When the Pharisee who had invited him saw this he said to himself, "If this man were a prophet, he would know who and what sort of woman this is who is touching him, that she is a sinner." Jesus said to him in reply, "Simon, I have something to say to you." "Tell me, teacher," he said. "Two people were in debt to a certain creditor; one owed five hundred days' wages and the other owed fifty. Since they were unable to repay the debt, he forgave it for both. Which of them will love him more?" Simon said in reply, "The one, I suppose, whose larger debt was forgiven." He said to him, "You have judged rightly."

Then he turned to the woman and said to Simon, "Do you see this woman? When I entered your house, you did not give me water for my feet, but she has bathed them with her tears and wiped them with her hair. You did not give me a kiss, but she has not ceased kissing my feet since the time I entered. You did not anoint my head with oil, but she anointed my feet with ointment. So I tell you, her many sins have been forgiven because she has shown great love. But the one to whom little is forgiven, loves little." He said to her, "Your sins are forgiven." The others at table said to themselves, "Who is this who even forgives sins?" But he said to the woman, "Your faith has saved you; go in peace."

[Afterward he journeyed from one town and village to another, preaching and proclaiming the good news of the kingdom of God. Accompanying him were the Twelve and some women who had been cured of evil spirits and infirmities, Mary, called Magdalene, from whom seven demons had gone out, Joanna, the wife of Herod's steward Chuza, Susanna, and many others who provided for them out of their resources.]

❖ Understanding the Word

As Second Samuel depicts it, the role of the prophet was a particularly precarious one. Nathan is to speak as God's mouthpiece to a king who has failed greatly. To cover up his adulterous affair with Bathsheba, the wife of Uriah the Hittite, David has the faithful soldier killed in battle (2 Samuel 11). Through a parable, Nathan confronts the king, who acknowledges his guilt (2 Samuel 12:7–13). God forgives David and spares his life, but not the life of the unborn child of the adulterous affair (2 Samuel 12:14). The second child born of David and Bathsheba will be Solomon, whom the Lord loved (2 Samuel 12:25).

140

In the second reading, Paul reminds the Galatian Christians that by virtue of their baptism into Christ (Galatians 3:28), they are no longer bound to the law. The root of the dissension in the region appears to be Jewish Christian missionaries who advocate circumcision and works of the law (following the dictates of the Torah). The terms "just," "justify," and "righteousness" share the same Greek root, *dikaios*. God's justice/righteousness cannot be obtained by individual effort. Nonetheless, the Israelites were commanded to strive to be just as God was just. The Law provided the parameters by which the faithful Israelite was to pursue righteousness. By Christ's death and resurrection, the law is no longer needed, for the believer has been "crucified with Christ" (Galatians 2:19).

The Gospel passage requires careful and attentive reading. First, the story of the woman who anoints Jesus is told in slightly different ways in the other Gospels. Luke places the story during the Galilean ministry of Jesus, while Mathew, Mark, and John set the encounter in Bethany during Jesus' time in Jerusalem (Matthew 26:6–13; Mark 14:3–9; John 12:1–8). Immediately after the anointing episode, Luke recounts that several women traveled with Jesus and "provided for them out of their resources" (Luke 8:3). In other words, these women bankrolled the itinerant preaching ministry of Jesus and the disciples. Because of the proximity of the anointing episode with the depiction of the women who accompany Jesus, the woman known in the city to be a sinner was conflated with Mary Magdalene. However, Luke clearly distinguishes the episodes, so the later depictions of Mary Magdalene as a sinner (i.e., a prostitute) are inaccurate.

❖ Reflecting on the Word

Have you seen the bumper sticker "Christians aren't perfect, they're forgiven"? Jesus' death and resurrection have opened the door to God's forgiveness, whether our sin is great or small. Yet, we spend so much time living as if we are unforgiveable. What a difference it makes to admit that we are sinners, turn to God, name our sin, and receive that mercy.

The Pharisee presumes that Jesus does not know the woman is a sinner, making her faithless. But Jesus is well aware that she is a sinner and a woman with great faith. If only the Pharisee could see her and himself as Jesus does, he'd have seen her faith and how God's mercy can transform us all. He was a sinner. He broke the Law by not showing Jesus its required hospitality, but the woman shows Jesus hospitality. David, God's anointed king, presumes to be above God's commandments and suffers the consequences for that presumption. Because he admits his sin, he experiences God's great mercy.

We spend too much time trying to live like angels, rather than the human beings that we are. We all sin and need to say, "I have sinned against the LORD." Our tears wash Jesus' feet, inviting his mercy to anoint us. The unnamed woman models the faith and hospitality being Christian entails. "Sometimes we are saddened by the weight of our sins. May we not be discouraged. Christ has come to lift this burden and give us peace," says Pope Francis.

Since Christ has done that for us, how can we not do the same for one another? Remember, Christians are forgiven and forgiving.

✤ Consider/Discuss

- Name a time when you have experienced God's forgiveness as clearly as did the woman in today's Gospel.
- What helps you accept God's mercy and share it with others?

✤ Living and Praying with the Word

My God, my mercy, I have sinned against you. Fill me with your love today, that I might anoint those I meet with the same gift of mercy that you pour over me.

June 19, 2016

TWELFTH SUNDAY IN ORDINARY TIME

Today's Focus: Who?

Jesus asked his followers who they thought he was, well before he offered any self-explanation. Can others see who we are—and who lives in us—without our having to offer them an explanation?

FIRST READING
Zechariah 12: 10–11; 13:1

Thus says the LORD: I will pour out on the house of David and on the inhabitants of Jerusalem a spirit of grace and petition; and they shall look on him whom they have pierced, and they shall mourn for him as one mourns for an only son, and they shall grieve over him as one grieves over a firstborn.

On that day the mourning in Jerusalem shall be as great as the mourning of Hadadrimmon in the plain of Megiddo.

On that day there shall be open to the house of David and to the inhabitants of Jerusalem, a fountain to purify from sin and uncleanness.

PSALM RESPONSE
Psalm 63:2b

My soul is thirsting for you, O Lord my God.

SECOND READING
Galatians 3: 26–29

Brothers and sisters: Through faith you are all children of God in Christ Jesus. For all of you who were baptized into Christ have clothed yourselves with Christ. There is neither Jew nor Greek, there is neither slave nor free person, there is not male and female; for you are all one in Christ Jesus. And if you belong to Christ, then you are Abraham's descendant, heirs according to the promise.

GOSPEL
Luke 9:18–24

Once when Jesus was praying in solitude, and the disciples were with him, he asked them, "Who do the crowds say that I am?" They said in reply, "John the Baptist; others, Elijah; still others, 'One of the ancient prophets has arisen.' " Then he said to them, "But who do you say that I am?" Peter said in reply, "The Christ of God." He rebuked them and directed them not to tell this to anyone.

He said, "The Son of Man must suffer greatly and be rejected by the elders, the chief priests, and the scribes, and be killed and on the third day be raised."

Then he said to all, "If anyone wishes to come after me, he must deny himself and take up his cross daily and follow me. For whoever wishes to save his life will lose it, but whoever loses his life for my sake will save it."

The reading from the prophet Zechariah depicts the coming blessings of the messianic age, when the house of David and all of Jerusalem will receive a spirit of grace and petition. The unnamed person whom they have just pierced is not identified, but is reminiscent of the suffering servant imagery from Second Isaiah. Other scholars suggest that it may refer to the death of King Josiah, who died on the plains of Megiddo (Zechariah 12:11). The book of Zechariah is actually a collection of oracles from several prophets written over time. Chapters 1–8 belong to the period of Zechariah, a contemporary of Haggai. Chapters 9–14 are considered "Deutero-Zechariah", perhaps composed as early as the fourth century B.C. or as late as the Maccabean period.

Paul interprets baptism not only as a gateway into the Christian faith, but also as an experience through which baptized believers clothe themselves with Christ (Galatians 3:27). The distinctions that once set people apart are no longer operative. To emphasize this, Paul states that the three polarities of race (Jew or Gentile), status (free or slave), and gender (male or female) no longer exist for the baptized in Christ. All are children of God (Galatians 3:27).

All three of the Synoptic Gospels record Jesus' question to his disciples: "Who do you say that I am?" (Matthew 16;13–20; Mark 8:27–30; Luke 9:18–21). Peter answers, "The Christ of God." Jesus' response seems abrupt: "He rebuked them and directed them not to tell this to anyone" (Luke 9:21). The Christ whom the disciples are expecting likely looked much different than the Son of Man whom Jesus then describes as one who "must suffer greatly" (Luke 9:22). Early Christian reflection came to understand the death of Jesus in light of the suffering servant imagery from Second Isaiah and perhaps Zechariah. Though the three evangelists portray the scene slightly differently, they follow up Jesus' question—"Who do you say that I am?"—with the first announcement of his passion and the conditions of discipleship, suggesting that those who follow "the Christ of God" may likewise suffer greatly.

✦ Reflecting on the Word

How do you answer Jesus' question, "Who do you say that I am?" Our answers are known more by how we live than by words alone. So I ask, "Who do people say that you are?" Do they see Christ clearly enough to answer, "One of the baptized" or "Someone clothed with Christ"? Can people see that we take up our cross to live the values of the gospel, even when that puts us at odds with the world, the Church, family, or friends?

Last year marked the fiftieth anniversary of the March on Selma. In Martin Luther King and those who joined him there, people saw believers willing to put their lives on the line for the sake of their faith and for their sisters and brothers. Pope Francis has beautified Archbishop Óscar Romero. His life proclaimed the gospel so clearly that he was a threat to the Salvadoran leaders. It cost him his life. Neither man looked for these causes. They chose to accept them, like Jesus, who ushered in messianic age. We continue living its values by losing ourselves in Jesus and his message so that others might experience God's merciful, unconditional love.

When our lives proclaim that we are clothed in Christ, others cannot doubt that we are the baptized who take up our cross daily, no matter the cost. St. Francis de Sales taught that if we accept the troubles, afflictions, and contradictions of life we imitate Jesus, who did not choose his cross but accepted it in obedience to make God's ways known. Live Jesus. Take up your cross. Make clear that you are a Christian, a Christ-bearer, clothed with Christ each and every day.

❖ Consider/Discuss

- Name the ways in which you believe you clearly live Jesus.
- What cross(es) do you bear and how do you carry them?

❖ Living and Praying with the Word

O God, at baptism we were clothed with Christ and told to keep his light burning brightly. Help us wear Christ so well that people see him in us and experience the freedom and love you promise.

June 26, 2016

THIRTEENTH SUNDAY IN ORDINARY TIME

Today's Focus: No Turning Back

Even though we don't always grasp the ways that discipleship guides our life, we can only keep going forward, following Christ.

FIRST READING
1 Kings 19:16b, 19–21

The LORD said to Elijah: "You shall anoint Elisha, son of Shaphat of Abel-meholah, as prophet to succeed you."

Elijah set out and came upon Elisha, son of Shaphat, as he was plowing with twelve yoke of oxen; he was following the twelfth. Elijah went over to him and threw his cloak over him. Elisha left the oxen, ran after Elijah, and said, "Please, let me kiss my father and mother goodbye, and I will follow you." Elijah answered, "Go back! Have I done anything to you?" Elisha left him, and taking the yoke of oxen, slaughtered them; he used the plowing equipment for fuel to boil their flesh, and gave it to his people to eat. Then Elisha left and followed Elijah as his attendant.

PSALM RESPONSE
Psalm 16:5a

You are my inheritance, O Lord.

SECOND READING
Galatians 5:1, 13–18

Brothers and sisters: For freedom Christ set us free; so stand firm and do not submit again to the yoke of slavery.

For you were called for freedom, brothers and sisters. But do not use this freedom as an opportunity for the flesh; rather, serve one another through love. For the whole law is fulfilled in one statement, namely, *You shall love your neighbor as yourself.* But if you go on biting and devouring one another, beware that you are not consumed by one another.

I say, then: live by the Spirit and you will certainly not gratify the desire of the flesh. For the flesh has desires against the Spirit, and the Spirit against the flesh; these are opposed to each other, so that you may not do what you want. But if you are guided by the Spirit, you are not under the law.

GOSPEL
Luke 9:51–62
When the days for Jesus' being taken up were fulfilled, he resolutely determined to journey to Jerusalem, and he sent messengers ahead of him. On the way they entered a Samaritan village to prepare for his reception there, but they would not welcome him because the destination of his journey was Jerusalem. When the disciples James and John saw this they asked, "Lord, do you want us to call down fire from heaven to consume them?" Jesus turned and rebuked them, and they journeyed to another village.

As they were proceeding on their journey someone said to him, "I will follow you wherever you go." Jesus answered him, "Foxes have dens and birds of the sky have nests, but the Son of Man has nowhere to rest his head."

And to another he said, "Follow me." But he replied, "Lord, let me go first and bury my father." But he answered him, "Let the dead bury their dead. But you, go and proclaim the kingdom of God." And another said, "I will follow you, Lord, but first let me say farewell to my family at home." To him Jesus said, "No one who sets a hand to the plow and looks to what was left behind is fit for the kingdom of God."

✥ Understanding the Word

In the first reading, Elisha, son of Shaphat, is plowing a field when the prophet Elijah throws his cloak over him, symbolizing the sharing of Elijah's prophetic office. Elisha will be present when Elijah is taken up to heaven and is given a double portion of his prophetic spirit (2 Kings 2:1–18). In response to the initial prophetic invitation, Elisha wishes first to bid farewell to his family. However, Elijah's rebuke ("Go back!") spurs Elisha to a complete commitment. He slaughters the oxen, burns the plow, and feeds the people. The absolute destruction of his former way of life symbolizes his obedience to his prophetic call.

In the second reading, Paul continues his chastisement of the Galatians by reminding them of their freedom in Christ. The boundaries that once separated people are no longer operational (3:28). The Gentile believers are freed from the law and have been given the Spirit as a guide (5:18). Paul understood that the Spirit made the power of the death and resurrection of Christ a present reality. The fruits of the Spirit are not virtues but manifestations of divine redemption; therefore, the Galatians are to "live by the Spirit" (5:16).

Luke depicts Jesus' journey to Jerusalem as a "fulfillment" of his destiny. Our translation reads, "he resolutely determined to journey to Jerusalem." The Greek is more literally translated, "he, himself, set his face toward Jerusalem." Jesus has turned from his ministry of teaching and preaching in Galilee (4:14 — 9:50), and now presents himself to Jerusalem, the city that kills prophets and stones those sent to it (13:34). It is no wonder that on this march to the Passion, Jesus outlines the severity of discipleship: one is homeless (9:58), separated from family (9:60), and like Elisha, cannot look back. That James and John desire revenge against the inhospitable Samaritan town suggests they have not fully understood the mission of Jesus or what discipleship will ultimately cost.

Did you notice the contrast between Jesus' attitude at the beginning of today's Gospel and that of the would-be followers near the end? Jesus "resolutely determined to journey to Jerusalem." There was no turning back from going to the place that rejected the prophets and would ultimately reject and crucify him. He was totally committed to proclaiming his Father's message, even when it meant his life. How different from the response of others to Jesus' call: "Let me go first and bury my father" or "but first let me say farewell . . . " These attitudes are not as resolute, but following Jesus asks for total commitment.

It's not that Jesus has anything against the dead or one's family. The question is, are we ready to change our lives completely? We are called to live by the Spirit and like Elisha destroy the vestiges of our former way of life. First fervor often reflects this desire for total commitment. James and John do not fully understand Jesus' teaching when they ask to call down fire on the village that rejected them. It takes time to understand fully what following Jesus entails.

We have only today to recommit ourselves to the promises we made when we first said yes to following Jesus. In the "Direction of Intention," St. Francis de Sales asks us to give God *this* day, to offer God the good we will do or accept the difficulty we might encounter today. Follow Jesus resolutely. Live your commitment to him now, not "later," not "after," not "until." His Spirit will help you face any difficulty that comes your way.

❖ Consider/Discuss

- What "but first" can keep you from resolutely following Jesus today?
- How have you grown in your understanding of what it means to "live Jesus" since you first said yes to following him?

❖ Living and Praying with the Word

Almighty God, I seek to follow your Son each and every day of my life. Help me give you this day. I offer you the good that I will do for love of Jesus. Help me accept any difficulty I might encounter for love of him, too.

July 3, 2016

FOURTEENTH SUNDAY IN ORDINARY TIME

Today's Focus: Leaving the Island

"No one is an island," says the common wisdom—as disciples, we are constantly called to leave our isolated and individual lives to bear the Good News everywhere.

FIRST
READING
Isaiah 66:
10–14c

Thus says the LORD:
Rejoice with Jerusalem and be glad because of her,
    all you who love her;
exult, exult with her,
    all you who were mourning over her!
Oh, that you may suck fully
    of the milk of her comfort,
that you may nurse with delight
    at her abundant breasts!
    For thus says the LORD:
Lo, I will spread prosperity over Jerusalem like a river,
    and the wealth of the nations like an overflowing torrent.
As nurslings, you shall be carried in her arms,
    and fondled in her lap;
as a mother comforts her child,
    so will I comfort you;
    in Jerusalem you shall find your comfort.

When you see this, your heart shall rejoice
    and your bodies flourish like the grass;
the LORD's power shall be known to his servants.

PSALM
RESPONSE
Psalm 66:1

Let all the earth cry out to God with joy.

SECOND
READING
Galatians 6:
14–18

Brothers and sisters: May I never boast except in the cross of our Lord Jesus Christ, through which the world has been crucified to me, and I to the world. For neither does circumcision mean anything, nor does uncircumcision, but only a new creation. Peace and mercy be to all who follow this rule and to the Israel of God.

From now on, let no one make troubles for me; for I bear the marks of Jesus on my body.

The grace of our Lord Jesus Christ be with your spirit, brothers and sisters. Amen.

In the shorter form of the reading, the passage in brackets is omitted.

GOSPEL
Luke 10:1–12,
17–20 or 10:1–9

At that time the Lord appointed seventy-two others whom he sent ahead of him in pairs to every town and place he intended to visit. He said to them, "The harvest is abundant but the laborers are few; so ask the master of the harvest to send out laborers for his harvest. Go on your way; behold, I am sending you like lambs among wolves. Carry no money bag, no sack, no sandals; and greet no one along the way. Into whatever house you enter, first say, 'Peace to this household.' If a peaceful person lives there, your peace will rest on him; but if not, it will return to you. Stay in the same house and eat and drink what is offered to you, for the laborer deserves his payment. Do not move about from one house to another. Whatever town you enter and they welcome you, eat what is set before you, cure the sick in it and say to them, 'The kingdom of God is at hand for you.' [Whatever town you enter and they do not receive you, go out into the streets and say, 'The dust of your town that clings to our feet, even that we shake off against you.' Yet know this: the kingdom of God is at hand. I tell you, it will be more tolerable for Sodom on that day than for that town."

The seventy-two returned rejoicing, and said, "Lord, even the demons are subject to us because of your name." Jesus said, "I have observed Satan fall like lightning from the sky. Behold, I have given you the power to 'tread upon serpents' and scorpions and upon the full force of the enemy and nothing will harm you. Nevertheless, do not rejoice because the spirits are subject to you, but rejoice because your names are written in heaven."]

❖❖ Understanding the Word

Jerusalem will give birth to a new people, announces the prophet in the first reading. Even before labor begins and without pain, the child arrives (v. 7). A nation will be born in a single moment (v. 8). The prophet whose oracles fill Chapters 56–66 takes up the message of Second Isaiah but brings his own unique concerns, such as the inclusion of the Gentiles (v. 21). The vision of a joyful and prosperous Jerusalem nursing a new people is expanded and will include all nations of every language (v. 18).

The foundation of Paul's theology is the Cross of Christ, which represents the whole of Christ's death, burial, and resurrection (1 Corinthians 15:3–4). As Paul concludes his Letter to the Galatians, he counters his rivals' claims that he is boasting of himself. Rather, it is Christ's cross that is the subject of his boast. In his defense of his apostleship, Paul has continually demonstrated that though he may have become an apostle abnormally (1 Corinthians 15:8), nonetheless, he suffers fully for the gospel, even bearing the marks of Jesus on his body (Galatians 6:17).

Only the Gospel of Luke includes the narrative of the sending of the seventy-two disciples to prepare the way for Jesus. (Some manuscripts read "seventy" while others say "seventy-two.") In Luke 9:1–6, the Twelve had been commissioned and given similar instructions: no money bag, no sandals, and stay wherever you are welcomed. But whereas the Twelve are sent to proclaim the kingdom of God and to heal the sick (9:2, 6), the seventy-two appear to be Jesus' advance team (10:1). However, in 10:9, their mission is broadened, and they are told to cure the sick and to say, "The kingdom of God is at hand for you." The report of the seventy-two upon their return suggests that they were as successful as the Twelve (9:10). Jesus' additional commission foreshadows the work of the disciples after Pentecost, which will be narrated in Luke' second volume, Acts of the Apostles.

✤ Reflecting on the Word

The seventy-two are sent totally dependent upon God and mutually dependent upon others, carrying only their experience of Jesus and the power to heal. If rejected, they are to shake the dust off their feet but still announce that God's kingdom is at hand. Some say this means that if the message will be received, it will happen when people are ready. When they return, they learn to boast not in themselves, but that their "names are written in heaven." Their boast is God and the only-begotten Son, Jesus Christ.

Pope Francis reminds us that as Church we are to proclaim the good news of Jesus, "so that faith in him might spread to every corner of the earth" (Evangelii Gaudium, 19). We are missionaries whose lives proclaim the joy of the gospel. We are dependent upon God for everything: faith, talents, the ability to develop our talents, and life. We are mutually dependent upon one another. No one is an island, even in our highly individualistic society. When sick, I need someone to help me. When in need, people turn to others for assistance. God's comfort is known by how we accept our mission to live the gospel and share the gifts God has given us.

We can invite others to God's kingdom but we are not in control of how people respond. As St. Francis de Sales taught, do all through love, nothing through fear or force. Take time to deepen your union with God in prayer. Give thanks for God's gift of life and the gifts you've been given. Ask for help where you are in need. Turn to the Body of Christ to fill in the gifts you lack. Now go and proclaim the gospel one person, one day, one moment at a time.

✤ Consider/Discuss

- How do you proclaim the good news of Jesus Christ in your daily living?
- What nourishes your relationship with God to be able to proclaim the gospel?

✤ Living and Praying with the Word

Loving God, nurse me with the food of your love and mercy, so that strengthened by you, I can proclaim the gospel of your Son, Jesus, whose cross I bear and whose message I live.

July 10, 2016

FIFTEENTH SUNDAY IN ORDINARY TIME

Today's Focus: Scattered Categories

Life often seems simpler when we put others into pigeonholes or categories that help us de-humanize them. But when we view them as a neighbor, or as a brother or sister in Christ, it is easier to act as a follower of Christ.

FIRST READING
Deuteronomy 30:10–14

Moses said to the people: "If only you would heed the voice of the LORD, your God, and keep his commandments and statutes that are written in this book of the law, when you return to the LORD, your God, with all your heart and all your soul.

"For this command that I enjoin on you today is not too mysterious and remote for you. It is not up in the sky, that you should say, 'Who will go up in the sky to get it for us and tell us of it, that we may carry it out?' Nor is it across the sea, that you should say, 'Who will cross the sea to get it for us and tell us of it, that we may carry it out?' No, it is something very near to you, already in your mouths and in your hearts; you have only to carry it out."

PSALM RESPONSE
Psalm 69:33

Turn to the Lord in your need, and you will live.

SECOND READING
Colossians 1: 15–20

Christ Jesus is the image of the invisible God,
    the firstborn of all creation.
For in him were created all things in heaven and on earth,
    the visible and the invisible,
        whether thrones or dominions or principalities or powers;
    all things were created through him and for him.
He is before all things,
    and in him all things hold together.
He is the head of the body, the church.
He is the beginning, the firstborn from the dead,
    that in all things he himself might be preeminent.
For in him all the fullness was pleased to dwell,
    and through him to reconcile all things for him,
    making peace by the blood of his cross
    through him, whether those on earth or those in heaven.

GOSPEL
Luke 10:25–37

There was a scholar of the law who stood up to test Jesus and said, "Teacher, what must I do to inherit eternal life?" Jesus said to him, "What is written in the law? How do you read it?" He said in reply,

You shall love the Lord, your God,
with all your heart,
with all your being,
with all your strength,
and with all your mind,
and your neighbor as yourself.

He replied to him, "You have answered correctly; do this and you will live."

But because he wished to justify himself, he said to Jesus, "And who is my neighbor?" Jesus replied, "A man fell victim to robbers as he went down from Jerusalem to Jericho. They stripped and beat him and went off leaving him half-dead. A priest happened to be going down that road, but when he saw him, he passed by on the opposite side. Likewise a Levite came to the place, and when he saw him, he passed by on the opposite side. But a Samaritan traveler who came upon him was moved with compassion at the sight. He approached the victim, poured oil and wine over his wounds and bandaged them. Then he lifted him up on his own animal, took him to an inn, and cared for him. The next day he took out two silver coins and gave them to the innkeeper with the instruction, 'Take care of him. If you spend more than what I have given you, I shall repay you on my way back.' Which of these three, in your opinion, was neighbor to the robbers' victim?" He answered, "The one who treated him with mercy." Jesus said to him, "Go and do likewise."

❖ Understanding the Word

The first reading is taken from the third section of Deuteronomy, in which Moses offers an extended address to the people (29:1 — 33:29) after having revealed the words of the covenant (4:44 — 28:69). The people are called together (29:1) in order to ratify the covenant that they have just received (29:11). In our reading, Moses emphasizes that the people are to respond to the law with their whole heart and being. The "command" is not distant or difficult to understand, as it has already been recited ("in your mouths," v. 14) and internalized ("in your hearts," v. 14). Israel has merely to obey and the blessings of God (land and progeny) will be theirs (v. 15).

The reading from Colossians is a Christological hymn evoking images from Wisdom literature (Wisdom 7:26; Proverbs 8:22; Sirach 24:9, etc.). In vv. 9–13, the believers are exhorted to lead a life worthy of the Lord. In our reading, vv. 15–20 describe the identity of this Lord and his effect. He is preeminent, and by his blood on the cross, he has effected reconciliation and peace. Following in vv. 21–23, the believers are reminded that we have been reconciled by his death if we continue in faith.

Though the Samaritan towns refuse to offer Jesus hospitality (Luke 9:52–53; Thirteenth Sunday), Jesus nonetheless uses a parable about a Samaritan as the example of truly fulfilling the law and therefore assuring oneself of eternal life. The priest and Levite may have avoided the wounded man out of concerns for ritual purity. The Samaritan would have no such limitation. He is described as responding out of compassion (v. 33). He not only attends to the immediate needs, but also goes a step further and pays for his continued care. In Luke, Jesus expects exemplary ethical behavior from his disciples.

✤ Reflecting on the Word

Moses tells the people that God's command is already in their mouths and hearts. The way Jesus treats the scholar reflects this. He asks how he reads the law. The scholar knew what to do. Then Jesus ups the ante with his response to the question, "Who is my neighbor?" Jesus makes clear that the Samaritan, who treated the person with mercy, was the neighbor. The enemy was the neighbor. Why did the scholar ask the question? We don't know. We do know that Jesus asks him to stretch his definition of neighbor and see as God does. Even one's enemy is neighbor, for we are all children of God. Someone from the towns who refused Jesus hospitality models a faithful response.

A retired Marine once told me he was trained never to think of an enemy as a person. Only by putting someone in a category—enemy, opponent, evil, or threat—can we consider dismissing and mistreating other people. When we see the other as human and like us, mistreatment becomes more difficult. That's why it is difficult to eat or pray with someone who has hurt us. The tension becomes too much, so we leave or try to reconcile. Our hearts know that we are more alike than unlike.

Christ came to reconcile all things in himself, making peace by the blood of his cross. He embraced what was death-dealing and found life. Signing ourselves with the cross reminds us that God's way, difficult as it can be, is as near as our mouths and hearts. That act invites us to see all people as human, as neighbor. Show others the mercy that God has given us and love both God and neighbor.

✤ Consider/Discuss

- How would you answer the question, "Who is my neighbor?"
- What keeps you from seeing someone who has hurt you or done evil as a human being and child of God?

✤ Living and Praying with the Word

God, our mercy, your compassion toward us is pure gift. Help me see others as you do to find ways of healing where there is brokenness and reconciliation where there is rupture. Help me to take the small but steady steps that the death and resurrection of Jesus invite.

SIXTEENTH SUNDAY IN ORDINARY TIME

Today's Focus: Be Who You Are

In Mary and Martha, we see a microcosm of the Church: we each have distinct abilities and need to put them at the service of Christ and others.

FIRST READING
Genesis 18: 1–10a

The LORD appeared to Abraham by the terebinth of Mamre, as he sat in the entrance of his tent, while the day was growing hot. Looking up, Abraham saw three men standing nearby. When he saw them, he ran from the entrance of the tent to greet them; and bowing to the ground, he said: "Sir, if I may ask you this favor, please do not go on past your servant. Let some water be brought, that you may bathe your feet, and then rest yourselves under the tree. Now that you have come this close to your servant, let me bring you a little food, that you may refresh yourselves; and afterward you may go on your way." The men replied, "Very well, do as you have said."

Abraham hastened into the tent and told Sarah, "Quick, three measures of fine flour! Knead it and make rolls." He ran to the herd, picked out a tender, choice steer, and gave it to a servant, who quickly prepared it. Then Abraham got some curds and milk, as well as the steer that had been prepared, and set these before the three men; and he waited on them under the tree while they ate.

They asked Abraham, "Where is your wife Sarah?" He replied, "There in the tent." One of them said, "I will surely return to you about this time next year, and Sarah will then have a son."

PSALM RESPONSE
Psalm 15:1a

He who does justice will live in the presence of the Lord.

SECOND READING
Colossians 1: 24–28

Brothers and sisters: Now I rejoice in my sufferings for your sake, and in my flesh I am filling up what is lacking in the afflictions of Christ on behalf of his body, which is the church, of which I am a minister in accordance with God's stewardship given to me to bring to completion for you the word of God, the mystery hidden from ages and from generations past. But now it has been manifested to his holy ones, to whom God chose to make known the riches of the glory of this mystery among the Gentiles; it is Christ in you, the hope for glory. It is he whom we proclaim, admonishing everyone and teaching everyone with all wisdom, that we may present everyone perfect in Christ.

Jesus entered a village where a woman whose name was Martha welcomed him. She had a sister named Mary who sat beside the Lord at his feet listening to him speak. Martha, burdened with much serving, came to him and said, "Lord, do you not care that my sister has left me by myself to do the serving? Tell her to help me." The Lord said to her in reply, "Martha, Martha, you are anxious and worried about many things. There is need of only one thing. Mary has chosen the better part and it will not be taken from her."

❖ Understanding the Word

Abraham's encounter with the three strangers is often described as evidence of the patriarch's kindness. But nomadic people (then and now) hold a particular code of desert hospitality that requires one to offer food, water, and shelter to strangers. Lot will also offer hospitality to two of the three (Genesis. 19:1–4), and Laban will similarly welcome Jacob (Genesis 24:28–32). Failure to abide by these rules could have dire consequences for the stranger, and as seen in Judges 8:4–17, for those who are inhospitable. Once the stranger accepted the hospitality, he or she was now under the protection of the host (Genesis 19:8; Judges 19:23). The strength of the ethic of hospitality is evident in the New Testament as well. Hebrew 13:2 warns: Do not neglect hospitality, since through such actions, some have unknowingly entertained angels. The author of Hebrews has Genesis 18 in mind.

The Letter to the Colossians was a circular letter written in the name of Paul but a generation after the apostle's martyrdom. After the believers of Colossae had read the letter, they were to send it on to the church at Laodicea (Colossians 4:16). In today's reading, the author in the name of Paul makes an astounding assertion: "in my flesh I am filling up what is lacking in the afflictions of Christ" (Colossians 1:24). Perhaps the author means this in an apocalyptic sense—the suffering that must be endured before Christ's return. Or it may presume that the mystical union that Paul shared with Christ (2 Corinthians 12:1–4) allowed him to call his own sufferings the afflictions of Christ.

Much ink has been spilled over this brief encounter of Jesus, Martha, and Mary. Luke has been heralded for including many stories about women (Mary, Elizabeth, Anna, Simon's mother-in-law, the widow of Nain, Mary of Magdala, Joanna, Susanna, etc.). But outside the infancy narratives, the only time a woman speaks, as Martha does in this Gospel reading, she is effectively silenced. Some scholars propose that Luke may have been subtly redirecting the women leaders of his community toward a stance of "listening" and away from public speaking.

What does hospitality require? When I invite someone for dinner, I need to provide food and drink (or at least order a pizza) and be present to my guest, attentive to her or his needs. The combination of Martha and Mary's gifts does just that. Mary sits at the feet of Jesus, listening and attentive to their guest. Martha busily provides food and drink. Some scholars say that Mary chose the better part because she accepted her role in providing hospitality, while Martha wanted Jesus to have Mary change and take on Martha's role. Knowing and accepting our own gifts and those of others is how we choose the better part.

Abraham and Sarah also offer hospitality. In their nomadic society this was expected and not to do so could have dire consequences. They still could have chosen not to welcome the three strangers. Abraham sits with them, attentive to their needs. He also provides food for them and waits on them. Sarah, while busy in the tent, is not absent from their awareness. Asking for her, they promise to return and announce that she will have a son.

How often we try to be what we are not, or we want someone else to change to do what we are doing, rather than appreciating both their gifts and ours. St. Francis de Sales would write to his friends that they ought to be who they are, and do that well. To be who we are we must listen to God's voice, sit at Jesus' feet, and pay attention to the gifts we have or can develop. Choose the better part. Accept and appreciate those gifts and thereby welcome Christ, however he visits us.

✤ Consider/Discuss

- What are the gifts that God has given you to welcome others?
- How can you use them to thank God for those gifts and to affirm the gifts of others?

✤ *Living and Praying with the Word*

Loving God, giver of all that is good, help me to thank you today by using the gifts you have given me to welcome those people through whom you visit me.

July 24, 2016

SEVENTEENTH SUNDAY IN ORDINARY TIME

Today's Focus: Give Us This Day

In advising us to ask—seek—knock in our prayer, Jesus is reminding us that prayer always takes us out of ourselves, and places us before God.

FIRST READING
Genesis 18: 20–32

In those days, the LORD said: "The outcry against Sodom and Gomorrah is so great, and their sin so grave, that I must go down and see whether or not their actions fully correspond to the cry against them that comes to me. I mean to find out."

While Abraham's visitors walked on farther toward Sodom, the LORD remained standing before Abraham. Then Abraham drew nearer and said: "Will you sweep away the innocent with the guilty? Suppose there were fifty innocent people in the city; would you wipe out the place, rather than spare it for the sake of the fifty innocent people within it? Far be it from you to do such a thing, to make the innocent die with the guilty so that the innocent and the guilty would be treated alike! Should not the judge of all the world act with justice?" The LORD replied, "If I find fifty innocent people in the city of Sodom, I will spare the whole place for their sake." Abraham spoke up again: "See how I am presuming to speak to my Lord, though I am but dust and ashes! What if there are five less than fifty innocent people? Will you destroy the whole city because of those five?" He answered, "I will not destroy it, if I find forty-five there." But Abraham persisted, saying, "What if only forty are found there?" He replied, "I will forbear doing it for the sake of the forty." Then Abraham said, "Let not my Lord grow impatient if I go on. What if only thirty are found there?" He replied, "I will forbear doing it if I can find but thirty there." Still Abraham went on, "Since I have thus dared to speak to my Lord, what if there are no more than twenty?" The LORD answered, "I will not destroy it, for the sake of the twenty." But he still persisted: "Please, let not my Lord grow angry if I speak up this last time. What if there are at least ten there?" He replied, "For the sake of those ten, I will not destroy it."

PSALM RESPONSE
Psalm 138:3a

Lord, on the day I called for help, you answered me.

SECOND READING
Colossians 2: 12–14 Brothers and sisters: You were buried with him in baptism, in which you were also raised with him through faith in the power of God, who raised him from the dead. And even when you were dead in transgressions and the uncircumcision of your flesh, he brought you to life along with him, having forgiven us all our transgressions; obliterating the bond against us, with its legal claims, which was opposed to us, he also removed it from our midst, nailing it to the cross.

GOSPEL
Luke 11:1–13 Jesus was praying in a certain place, and when he had finished, one of his disciples said to him, "Lord, teach us to pray just as John taught his disciples." He said to them, "When you pray, say:
Father, hallowed be your name,
    your kingdom come.
    Give us each day our daily bread
    and forgive us our sins
    for we ourselves forgive everyone in debt to us,
    and do not subject us to the final test."

And he said to them, "Suppose one of you has a friend to whom he goes at midnight and says, 'Friend, lend me three loaves of bread, for a friend of mine has arrived at my house from a journey and I have nothing to offer him,' and he says in reply from within, 'Do not bother me; the door has already been locked and my children and I are already in bed. I cannot get up to give you anything.' I tell you, if he does not get up to give the visitor the loaves because of their friendship, he will get up to give him whatever he needs because of his persistence.

"And I tell you, ask and you will receive; seek and you will find; knock and the door will be opened to you. For everyone who asks, receives; and the one who seeks, finds; and to the one who knocks, the door will be opened. What father among you would hand his son a snake when he asks for a fish? Or hand him a scorpion when he asks for an egg? If you then, who are wicked, know how to give good gifts to your children, how much more will the Father in heaven give the Holy Spirit to those who ask him?"

❖ Understanding the Word

Today's first reading is a continuation from the eighteenth chapter of the book of Genesis. Abraham has discovered that the guests he has hosted are divine: God accompanied by two angels (v. 13). After the announcement that Sarah will bear a son, the Lord and his messengers continue their journey to Sodom. In his role as host, Abraham accompanies the three (v. 16). It is during these travels that Abraham learns of God's plan for the cities of Sodom and Gomorrah. Only Moses will argue with God (Exodus 33), as does Abraham in this scene. Holding up God's role as "judge of all the world," Abraham entreats God to act with justice (v. 25), sparing the innocent.

The reading from Colossians presents an early theology of baptism: "You were buried with him in baptism, in which you were also raised with him" (v. 12). Baptism immerses the believer in Christ's death so as to share in his resurrection. Countering the false teachers who would have the Gentile Colossians follow human tradition, the author reminds the believers that they have received the "circumcision of Christ" (v. 11), and therefore share in his fullness (v. 10). The former transgressions of the Gentiles have been obliterated, nailed to the cross of Christ (v. 14).

At the request of one of his disciples, Jesus offers instruction on prayer. He begins by explaining the proper address to God ("Father, hallowed be your name") and the acknowledgment of God's kingdom. Jesus then names what one should ask of God (daily sustenance and forgiveness). The forgiveness that we seek must first be shown to those who are in debt to us (v. 4). Here the forgiveness of debts is meant as a freedom from financial burden. Then by offering a narrative example, Jesus tells his disciples that prayer must be persistent (v. 8) and the petitioner confident that God will answer (v. 13). Luke describes Jesus at prayer at significant moments during his ministry: after his baptism (3:21), following a series of healings (5:16; 6:12), at his transfiguration (9:28), and on the cross (23:34).

✤ Reflecting on the Word

How do you pray? At times I pray as Jesus taught: your kingdom come, give us what we need, forgive us, help us forgive, do not test us. However, in all honesty, my prayer often focuses mostly on me. On other days I have the consciousness of Abraham. I am persistent in asking God to live up to the divine promise of mercy toward others. When my focus is on me, my vision narrows and I tend to give up when I don't get what I want. When my focus is on God and openness to the good that God offers, I often find God present even when the answer is not what I'd asked. A spiritual director used to remind me, "God always answers our prayers. Sometimes the answer looks different than what we ask and sometimes the answer is no."

Jesus says ask, seek, and knock. Then we will receive, find God present in every situation and doors will be opened. He doesn't say that we will receive what we asked, unless we ask for the Holy Spirit. Nor that we will find what we seek, unless we seek to do God's will. Nor that the door on which we knock will be opened unless that door is the heart of Christ. In his 2015 Lenten letter, Pope Francis asked the Church to pray to the Lord, "Make our hearts like yours." If that is our prayer, we will find God with us in every life circumstance. We will have Abraham's courage to be persistent before God. We will find God's power alive in us. Buried with Christ in baptism, we were also raised with him. Pray as he taught. Ask, seek, and knock today.

- How would you describe your prayer life to a close friend?
- Do you focus on gratifying your own will, finding and living God's will, or some of both?

✤ Living and Praying with the Word

God, our Father, we are totally dependent upon you for every breath, and you invite us into relationship with our brothers and sisters and all creation. Make our hearts one with the heart of Christ so that we might know and live your will for us and for our world.

July 31, 2016

EIGHTEENTH SUNDAY IN ORDINARY TIME

Today's Focus: In _____ I Trust

Many things tug at us for our allegiance—some healthy, some not. Ultimately, only one of these can hold first place in our lives.

FIRST READING
Ecclesiastes 1:2; 2:21–23

Vanity of vanities, says Qoheleth,
  vanity of vanities! All things are vanity!

Here is one who has labored with wisdom and knowledge and skill, and yet to another who has not labored over it, he must leave property. This also is vanity and a great misfortune. For what profit comes to man from all the toil and anxiety of heart with which he has labored under the sun? All his days sorrow and grief are his occupation; even at night his mind is not at rest. This also is vanity.

PSALM RESPONSE
Psalm 90:1

If today you hear his voice, harden not your hearts.

SECOND READING
Colossians 3: 1–5, 9–11

Brothers and sisters: If you were raised with Christ, seek what is above, where Christ is seated at the right hand of God. Think of what is above, not of what is on earth. For you have died, and your life is hidden with Christ in God. When Christ your life appears, then you too will appear with him in glory.

Put to death, then, the parts of you that are earthly: immorality, impurity, passion, evil desire, and the greed that is idolatry. Stop lying to one another, since you have taken off the old self with its practices and have put on the new self, which is being renewed, for knowledge, in the image of its creator. Here there is not Greek and Jew, circumcision and uncircumcision, barbarian, Scythian, slave, free; but Christ is all and in all.

GOSPEL
Luke 12:13–21

Someone in the crowd said to Jesus, "Teacher, tell my brother to share the inheritance with me." He replied to him, "Friend, who appointed me as your judge and arbitrator?" Then he said to the crowd, "Take care to guard against all greed, for though one may be rich, one's life does not consist of possessions."

Then he told them a parable. "There was a rich man whose land produced a bountiful harvest. He asked himself, 'What shall I do, for I do not have space to store my harvest?' And he said, 'This is what I shall do: I shall tear down my barns and build larger ones. There I shall store all my grain and other goods and I shall say to myself, "Now as for you, you have so many good things stored up for many years, rest, eat, drink, be merry!" ' But God said to him, 'You fool, this night your life will be demanded of you; and the things you have prepared, to whom will they belong?' Thus will it be for all who store up treasure for themselves but are not rich in what matters to God."

in love

The first reading is taken from the book of Ecclesiastes, part of a group of texts in our Old Testament known as Wisdom literature (Proverbs, Job, Sirach and Wisdom, together with Song of Songs and Psalms). Wisdom results from reflection on human experience and the wonders of creation in light of an underlying world order. When one walked in the ways of wisdom, the path led to appropriate social and personal order in life. Israel's unique contribution to the wisdom of the ancient Near East was its belief that the world order resulted from God. Qoheleth critiques the optimism of Wisdom. All is vanity, and our efforts futile (Ecclesiastes 1:21). The only course is to fear God and keep God's commandments, since God will judge every work (Ecclesiastes 12:13).

The writer of the Letter to the Colossians counters the "empty, seductive philosophy" of the false teachers (2:8) by reminding the church that if they believe they are raised with Christ (3:1) then their behavior should evidence that fact (3:9–10). The vices listed in 3:5, 8 are similar to those found in Romans 1:29–31 and Galatians 5:19–21. Ancient moral exhortations often used contrasting lists of virtues and vices to admonish and redirect adherents, reminding them that "you have taken off the old self with its practices and have put on the new self" (3:9–10).

The Gospel of Luke patterns itself after the Gospel of Mark and interjects additional sayings from a source that scholars call "Q." In addition to these two, Matthew and Luke have information unique to them. Much of Luke Chapter 12, from which our Gospel reading is taken, contains material only found in Luke. Verses 13–34 contrast trust in wealth with trust in God. Verses 35–48 are a collection of sayings about Jesus' instruction on the end-times. In today's reading, Jesus responds to a question about inheritance by offering a pronouncement ("Take care to guard against all greed." v. 15), followed by an illustrative parable (vv. 16–20). His conclusion—"Thus will it be for all who store up treasure . . . but are not rich in . . . God" (v. 21)—is directed at both the narrative audience (the crowd, v. 16) and Luke's own community.

✤✤ *Reflecting on the Word*

Where do you place your trust? God, money, things, a certain political party or philosophy of life, or Church, yourself, someone or something else? Jesus' parable makes clear that trusting in anyone or anything other than God will leave us empty and alone. That's the ultimate vanity of vanities. We can't buy love or happiness. Even the things we buy or in which we invest our time, money, and energy won't ultimately make us happy without a relationship with the God in whom we live, move, and have our being. We can lose everything we value and our lives can change in an instant, whether confronted with natural disasters, health crises, or the loss of loved ones, reputation, or money. At those times we have only our faith in God. Faith is bolstered by people who come to our aid. But in the end, only our relationship with God accompanies us at all times, even when we make the journey from death to eternal life.

St. Paul advised us to put to death whatever is not of God in our lives and attend to the values of Jesus that we put on in baptism. Baptism does not promise a life without tears or suffering. It promises that because we belong to Christ, we are not alone and can find hope in every situation, even pending death. One of my confrères, recently diagnosed with terminal cancer, prays to be able to embrace death as Joseph Cardinal Bernardin did, so that he will be ready when Jesus comes to take him home. Trust in God and those who lead you to God. Invest your time, money, and energy there and you will be truly rich, whatever today brings.

❖ Consider/Discuss

- What have I lost that I thought would bring me happiness but did not?
- If I knew that my life would end today, what would I change to be ready to meet God?

❖ Living and Praying with the Word

Holy God, in you we do live, move, and have our being. Allow my choices this day to express my gratitude for you and what I have or can do.

August 7, 2016

NINETEENTH SUNDAY IN ORDINARY TIME

Today's Focus: What Time's the Meeting?

In our (overly) scheduled lives we can lose sight of the fact that the most important "meeting" we will have is one that we cannot put on any schedule.

FIRST READING
Wisdom 18:6–9

The night of the passover was known beforehand to our fathers,
  that, with sure knowledge of the oaths in which they put
    their faith,
  they might have courage.
Your people awaited the salvation of the just
  and the destruction of their foes.
For when you punished our adversaries,
  in this you glorified us whom you had summoned.
For in secret the holy children of the good were offering sacrifice
  and putting into effect with one accord the divine institution.

PSALM RESPONSE
Psalm 33:12b

Blessed the people the Lord has chosen to be his own.

SECOND READING
Hebrews 11: 1–2, 8–19 or 11:1–2, 8–12

In the shorter form of the reading, the passage in brackets is omitted.

Brothers and sisters: Faith is the realization of what is hoped for and evidence of things not seen. Because of it the ancients were well attested.

By faith Abraham obeyed when he was called to go out to a place that he was to receive as an inheritance; he went out, not knowing where he was to go. By faith he sojourned in the promised land as in a foreign country, dwelling in tents with Isaac and Jacob, heirs of the same promise; for he was looking forward to the city with foundations, whose architect and maker is God. By faith he received power to generate, even though he was past the normal age—and Sarah herself was sterile—for he thought that the one who had made the promise was trustworthy. So it was that there came forth from one man, himself as good as dead, descendants as numerous as the stars in the sky and as countless as the sands on the seashore.

[All these died in faith. They did not receive what had been promised but saw it and greeted it from afar and acknowledged themselves to be strangers and aliens on earth, for those who speak thus show that they are seeking a homeland. If they had been thinking of the land from which they had come, they would have had opportunity to return. But now they desire a better homeland, a heavenly one. Therefore, God is not ashamed to be called their God, for he has prepared a city for them.

By faith Abraham, when put to the test, offered up Isaac, and he who had received the promises was ready to offer his only son, of whom it was said, "Through Isaac descendants shall bear your name." He reasoned that God was able to raise even from the dead, and he received Isaac back as a symbol.]

GOSPEL
Luke 12:32–48
or 12:35–40

In the shorter form of the reading, the passages in brackets are omitted.
Jesus said to his disciples: ["Do not be afraid any longer, little flock, for your Father is pleased to give you the kingdom. Sell your belongings and give alms. Provide money bags for yourselves that do not wear out, an inexhaustible treasure in heaven that no thief can reach nor moth destroy. For where your treasure is, there also will your heart be.]

"Gird your loins and light your lamps and be like servants who await their master's return from a wedding, ready to open immediately when he comes and knocks. Blessed are those servants whom the master finds vigilant on his arrival. Amen, I say to you, he will gird himself, have them recline at table, and proceed to wait on them. And should he come in the second or third watch and find them prepared in this way, blessed are those servants. Be sure of this: if the master of the house had known the hour when the thief was coming, he would not have let his house be broken into. You also must be prepared, for at an hour you do not expect, the Son of Man will come."

[Then Peter said, "Lord, is this parable meant for us or for everyone?" And the Lord replied, "Who, then, is the faithful and prudent steward whom the master will put in charge of his servants to distribute the food allowance at the proper time? Blessed is that servant whom his master on arrival finds doing so. Truly, I say to you, the master will put the servant in charge of all his property. But if that servant says to himself, 'My master is delayed in coming,' and begins to beat the menservants and the maidservants, to eat and drink and get drunk, then that servant's master will come on an unexpected day and at an unknown hour and will punish the servant severely and assign him a place with the unfaithful. That servant who knew his master's will but did not make preparations nor act in accord with his will shall be beaten severely; and the servant who was ignorant of his master's will but acted in a way deserving of a severe beating shall be beaten only lightly. Much will be required of the person entrusted with much, and still more will be demanded of the person entrusted with more."]

✤ Understanding the Word

The book of Wisdom is attributed to Solomon, but was likely written much later, in the first century BC, in order to strengthen the faith of Alexandrian Jews struggling against the growing tide of Hellenism (Greek cultural practices). Today's reading is taken from the final section of the book (11:2 — 19:22), which focuses on God's saving actions during the Exodus. Just as the ancestors knew the Passover was coming (v. 6, Exodus 6:8) and therefore took courage, so too should the faithful Jews of Alexandria who may have been experiencing a persecution.

In order to understand and interpret the Christ event, early Christians turned to the Jewish scriptures. The second reading is taken from Hebrews, a sermon in letter format, which recognizes that the promises to the patriarchs are fulfilled in Christ. As the author notes, "Faith is the realization of what is hoped for and evidence of things not seen" (v. 1). The patriarch Abraham is explored as a testament of fidelity. Without knowing where he was going, Abraham left his home in order to receive his inheritance (v. 8), "looking forward to the city with foundations whose architect and maker is God" (v. 10). But all these died in faith before the promise was fulfilled (v. 13).

In the Gospel reading, Jesus continues to teach the disciples the appropriate response to possessions in light of the coming reign of God. "Where your treasure is, there also will your heart be" (v. 34). Earlier Jesus had reminded them to seek the kingdom (v. 31) and now he warns about watchfulness. He alternates between pronouncements ("gird your loins and light your lamps, v. 35; "much will be required of the person entrusted with much," v. 48b) and parables of illustration (vv. 36–39, 42–48a). Early Christians expected that Jesus would return (*parousia*) very soon and fully establish God's reign on earth. As the time between the Resurrection and the return lengthened, the vigilance of believers waned.

✤ Reflecting on the Word

If your life ended tonight would you be ready to meet Jesus? Does where you invest your time, talent, and treasure make clear that living the values of Jesus is your number one priority? Or would they make clear that you value someone or something else more? Paying careful attention to how we spend our time or where we invest our emotional energy provides a good idea about an honest answer to these questions.

Sometimes the needs of those we love or our own livelihood require us to work more hours than we'd like. Sometimes the needs of those we love or our own physical or emotional needs require us to have less time for prayer or service or the activities that give us rest and refreshment. However, at other times our desire for more or our self-centeredness take time away from what is of real value in the end, living the life of faith.

Why live this or any day as if it were our last? Because it just might be. Realizing our hope to dwell with God forever in the heavenly city prepared for us requires living the values to which Jesus, the prophets, and saints gave flesh, the values that can help us be ready for the Master's return, whenever he comes.

As the reading from Wisdom proclaims, knowing the night of Passover helped our ancestors in faith have courage to journey out of Egypt into the unknown and promised land. So too, although we do not know the time or the hour we will meet Jesus, we know that he has promised to return. If he returns today, what will it take for you to be ready?

✤ Consider/Discuss

- What does where I invest my time, talent, and energy say I value most in life?
- What changes do I need to make to be ready to meet Jesus if he returns today?

✤ Living and Praying with the Word

Loving God, you have chosen us as your people. Wake us up. Shake us up. Help us evaluate our lives to live the values of your Son, Jesus, in order to be ready to meet him with joy and peace every day you give us.

TWENTIETH SUNDAY IN ORDINARY TIME

Today's Focus: Truth to Power

God's word can both comfort and challenge. Living out that word in a prophetic way can provide us with comfort—but also with times of profound challenge.

FIRST READING
Jeremiah 38: 4–6, 8–10

In those days, the princes said to the king: "Jeremiah ought to be put to death; he is demoralizing the soldiers who are left in this city, and all the people, by speaking such things to them; he is not interested in the welfare of our people, but in their ruin." King Zedekiah answered: "He is in your power"; for the king could do nothing with them. And so they took Jeremiah and threw him into the cistern of Prince Malchiah, which was in the quarters of the guard, letting him down with ropes. There was no water in the cistern, only mud, and Jeremiah sank into the mud.

Ebed-melech, a court official, went there from the palace and said to him: "My lord king, these men have been at fault in all they have done to the prophet Jeremiah, casting him into the cistern. He will die of famine on the spot, for there is no more food in the city." Then the king ordered Ebed-melech the Cushite to take three men along with him, and draw the prophet Jeremiah out of the cistern before he should die.

PSALM RESPONSE
Psalm 40:14b

Lord, come to my aid!

SECOND READING
Hebrew 12: 1–4

Brothers and sisters: Since we are surrounded by so great a cloud of witnesses, let us rid ourselves of every burden and sin that clings to us and persevere in running the race that lies before us while keeping our eyes fixed on Jesus, the leader and perfecter of faith. For the sake of the joy that lay before him he endured the cross, despising its shame, and has taken his seat at the right of the throne of God. Consider how he endured such opposition from sinners, in order that you may not grow weary and lose heart. In your struggle against sin you have not yet resisted to the point of shedding blood.

GOSPEL
Luke 12:49–53

Jesus said to his disciples: "I have come to set the earth on fire, and how I wish it were already blazing! There is a baptism with which I must be baptized, and how great is my anguish until it is accomplished! Do you think that I have come to establish peace on the earth? No, I tell you, but rather division. From now on a household of five will be divided, three against two and two against three; a father will be divided against his son and a son against his father, a mother against her daughter and a daughter against her mother, a mother-in-law against her daughter-in-law and a daughter-in-law against her mother-in-law."

❖ Understanding the Word

As the first reading describes, the lot of the prophet is a difficult one. In the book of Jeremiah, we catch a glimpse of the life of the historical prophet and hear him lamenting his call (15:10–18). Called to prophesy during the reign of King Josiah (628 BC), Jeremiah continued to preach until the destruction of Jerusalem under the Babylonians (586 BC). Opposition and violence marred his long prophetic life as today's reading attests. According to an old tradition, Jeremiah was forced to flee to Egypt, where his own people killed him.

The cloud of witnesses of which the Letter to the Hebrews speaks includes the suffering servants of God like the prophet Jeremiah. "Yet all these, though approved because of their faith, did not receive what had been promised" (Hebrews 12:39). For our part, we are to persevere in running the race, keeping focused on Jesus as the prize. As Hebrews explains, Jesus served as the ultimate witness who endured the cross in order to perfect the faith and take his seat at the right of the throne of God. The community to whom Hebrews is addressed is not suffering external persecution, but seems to be struggling against the sins of apostasy and indifference (10:23–31). The author uses Jesus' example of suffering as encouragement "in order that you may not grow weary and lose heart" (v. 3).

Jesus announces with the zeal of the prophet, "I have come to set the earth on fire, and how I wish it were already blazing!"(v. 49). And he is well aware of the cost of such preaching: "There is a baptism with which I must be baptized" (v. 50), a baptism into his death. Jesus has been directing his disciples on the proper attitude toward possessions and the need for constant watchfulness in anticipation of the coming reign of God (v. 47). But in this passage, he acknowledges that those who follow him risk even harsher difficulties—that of familial discord and rupture.

I admire people who can speak truth to power, even at the cost of reputation, life, or both. Archbishop Óscar Romero of El Salvador was such a person. He got to know the people of his archdiocese. He became aware of how abuse of power created unequal distribution of wealth and resources, and how that abused power took the lives of anyone who dared to disagree with their government. As his understanding of the gospel and his encounter with the poor and powerless in his country connected, he spoke out strongly against these abuses. He was such a threat to government leaders that he was assassinated while celebrating Mass in a hospital chapel on March 24, 1980. He suffered the same fate that Jesus did. Hoping to silence the message, the messenger was killed, to no avail. I don't know that I'd have such courage.

Jesus says that he came to set the earth on fire and establish division. Not for the sake of division, but to bring about the peace that comes only by living the way of God made known through prophets like Jeremiah, martyrs like Archbishop Romero and Sister Dorothy Stang, and leaders like Martin Luther King and Mohandas Gandhi. Jeremiah was thrown into a cistern, until Ebed-melech convinced the king to rescue him. The struggle against sin can lead to shedding our blood. Following Jesus often does not make one popular. The truth indeed will set you free, but it might make you miserable before it does. If my living Jesus' way compels me to speak the truth to bring about the kingdom he came to proclaim, I must speak it. If my only goal is to be divisive or draw attention to myself, I had best keep silent. Lord, come to my aid. Give me courage.

✤ Consider/Discuss

- When has living the gospel put me at odds with another person or them at odds with me?
- What keeps me from speaking the truth in love when I feel called to do so?

✤ Living and Praying with the Word

In the life, death, and resurrection of Jesus, you have spoken your word to us. At times it comforts. At times it challenges. At all times help me to hear your voice, and give me the courage of your Holy Spirit to live the words I hear.

August 21, 2016

TWENTY-FIRST SUNDAY IN ORDINARY TIME

Today's Focus: Lip Service or Life Service?

Jesus shows us a heavenly banquet that just might have a lot of attendees we don't expect to see: those who, by the way they lived, showed God's grace and mercy to the world around them.

FIRST READING
Isaiah 66: 18–21

Thus says the LORD: I know their works and their thoughts, and I come to gather nations of every language; they shall come and see my glory. I will set a sign among them; from them I will send fugitives to the nations: to Tarshish, Put and Lud, Mosoch, Tubal and Javan, to the distant coastlands that have never heard of my fame, or seen my glory; and they shall proclaim my glory among the nations. They shall bring all your brothers and sisters from all the nations as an offering to the LORD, on horses and in chariots, in carts, upon mules and dromedaries, to Jerusalem, my holy mountain, says the LORD, just as the Israelites bring their offering to the house of the LORD in clean vessels. Some of these I will take as priests and Levites, says the LORD.

PSALM RESPONSE
Mark 16:15

Go out to all the world and tell the Good News.

SECOND READING
Hebrews 12:5–7, 11–13

Brothers and sisters, You have forgotten the exhortation addressed to you as children:
> "My son, do not disdain the discipline of the Lord
>   or lose heart when reproved by him;
> for whom the Lord loves, he disciplines;
>   he scourges every son he acknowledges."

Endure your trials as "discipline"; God treats you as sons. For what "son" is there whom his father does not discipline? At the time, all discipline seems a cause not for joy but for pain, yet later it brings the peaceful fruit of righteousness to those who are trained by it.

So strengthen your drooping hands and your weak knees. Make straight paths for your feet, that what is lame may not be disjointed but healed.

GOSPEL Jesus passed through towns and villages, teaching as he went and
Luke 13:22–30 making his way to Jerusalem. Someone asked him, "Lord, will only a
few people be saved?" He answered them, "Strive to enter through
the narrow gate, for many, I tell you, will attempt to enter but will
not be strong enough. After the master of the house has arisen and
locked the door, then will you stand outside knocking and saying,
'Lord, open the door for us.' He will say to you in reply, 'I do not
know where you are from.' And you will say, 'We ate and drank in
your company and you taught in our streets.' Then he will say to
you, 'I do not know where you are from. Depart from me, all you
evildoers!' And there will be wailing and grinding of teeth when you
see Abraham, Isaac, and Jacob and all the prophets in the kingdom
of God and you yourselves cast out. And people will come from the
east and the west and from the north and the south and will recline
at table in the kingdom of God. For behold, some are last who will
be first, and some are first who will be last."

⁘ Understanding the Word

Third Isaiah paints a picture of redeemed Jerusalem and God as a mother comforting her child (Isaiah 66:10–13). The once rebellious people (Isaiah 65:2) are now
part of a new heaven and a new earth to which the nations stream. The exiles have
been brought home (Isaiah 66:20) and all nations worship on God's holy mountain.
Third Isaiah writes after the exiles have returned to Jerusalem, but the temple and
the city have not been fully restored. His prophecies serve to encourage and sustain the people's faith.

The writer of Hebrews shares a similar task. The original audience of this sermon
had experienced loss (10:32–34), risked apostasy (10:23–31), and desired greater
stability (11:16). The author fears that they are hardening their hearts (4:7) and
therefore presents the importance of discipline and suffering. But Christian discipline is not without effect, for it ties the faithful to Christ, who "Son though he was,
he learned obedience from what he suffered" (5:8). Discipline "brings the peaceful
fruit of righteousness to those who are trained by it" (12:11).

In the Gospel, Jesus turns from parables about the kingdom (13:13–21) to the
requirements for entrance into that kingdom. The time is shortening, and once
the door is locked, it will not be reopened (13:25). Claiming to accompany Jesus
(13:26) does not equate to true discipleship. Though set in the time of Jesus, these
sayings were understood to refer to the Jews who did not accept the message of
Jesus during Luke's day. The Gentiles ("people . . . from the east and the west . . . ")
would receive a seat at the table formerly only available to the Jews. Likely Luke's
Gentile community was particular happy to hear that "some are last who will be
first" (13:30).

Do you give lip service or life service to following Jesus and living the kingdom of God? That is, do your actions confirm your words? Saying that "We ate and drank in your company" is not enough. We strive to enter the narrow gate by doing our best to live the values of God's kingdom that Jesus showed us. Living the ways of the kingdom that Jesus' words and deeds proclaimed takes discipline. Many talk about going to the gym, taking time to practice their craft, eating in a more healthy manner, or making more time for prayer. These practices have positive effects in our lives. At other times they seem like too much, or we bite off more than we can chew rather than the amount that will help us make progress in the end. The same is true of the disciplines of faith.

Scripture tells us that God invites people from all nations, faiths, and ways of life to enter the kingdom. Practices like prayer, fasting, almsgiving, living the commandments and turning to God in need are counted among the disciplines of faith. They help us tell the good news of Jesus Christ so that others can glorify God and live on God's holy mountain. We cannot earn a place at the heavenly banquet, because faith is a gift God offers to all. We take on these faith disciplines in gratitude for that gift. Then when people see, hear, or encounter us, they see, hear, and encounter Jesus. That's the difference between life service and lip service. What discipline can I take on today so that my life and lips proclaim, "I follow Jesus Christ, the way, the truth, and the life"? Don't bite off more than you can chew. Let God help you reinforce success rather than failure.

✥ Consider/Discuss

- How do I give life service—more than mere lip service—to living the way of Jesus?
- What faith discipline can I begin to practice to help my actions reveal what my words proclaim?

✥ Living and Praying with the Word

Jesus, we desire to eat and drink in your company for all eternity. Show me the way to live so that, nourished by you, I can feed others with your all-inclusive and unconditional love.

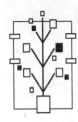

August 28, 2016

TWENTY-SECOND SUNDAY IN ORDINARY TIME

Today's Focus: The Truth of Humility

True humility is not self-deprecation, but honest self-awareness. A disciple truly aware of what it means to follow Jesus cannot help but live in humble service to others.

FIRST READING
Sirach 3:17–18, 20, 28–29

My child, conduct your affairs with humility,
    and you will be loved more than a giver of gifts.
Humble yourself the more, the greater you are,
    and you will find favor with God.
What is too sublime for you, seek not,
    into things beyond your strength search not.
The mind of a sage appreciates proverbs,
    and an attentive ear is the joy of the wise.
Water quenches a flaming fire,
    and alms atone for sins.

PSALM RESPONSE
Psalm 68:11b

God, in your goodness, you have made a home for the poor.

SECOND READING
Hebrews 12: 18–19, 22–24a

Brothers and sisters: You have not approached that which could be touched and a blazing fire and gloomy darkness and storm and a trumpet blast and a voice speaking words such that those who heard begged that no message be further addressed to them. No, you have approached Mount Zion and the city of the living God, the heavenly Jerusalem, and countless angels in festal gathering, and the assembly of the firstborn enrolled in heaven, and God the judge of all, and the spirits of the just made perfect, and Jesus, the mediator of a new covenant, and the sprinkled blood that speaks more eloquently than that of Abel.

On a sabbath Jesus went to dine at the home of one of the leading Pharisees, and the people there were observing him carefully.

He told a parable to those who had been invited, noticing how they were choosing the places of honor at the table. "When you are invited by someone to a wedding banquet, do not recline at table in the place of honor. A more distinguished guest than you may have been invited by him, and the host who invited both of you may approach you and say, 'Give your place to this man,' and then you would proceed with embarrassment to take the lowest place. Rather, when you are invited, go and take the lowest place so that when the host comes to you he may say, 'My friend, move up to a higher position.' Then you will enjoy the esteem of your companions at the table. For everyone who exalts himself will be humbled, but the one who humbles himself will be exalted." Then he said to the host who invited him, "When you hold a lunch or a dinner, do not invite your friends or your brothers or your relatives or your wealthy neighbors, in case they may invite you back and you have repayment. Rather, when you hold a banquet, invite the poor, the crippled, the lame, the blind; blessed indeed will you be because of their inability to repay you. For you will be repaid at the resurrection of the righteous."

❖ Understanding the Word

The first reading is a collection of proverbial sayings taken from the second century BC work, written by Ben Sira (50:27) and translated into Greek by his grandson. The impetus for writing seems to have been the threat of Hellenism. Greek philosophy and culture were attracting formerly religious Jews who were now forsaking their faith. By blending Israel's history and traditions with conventional wisdom, Ben Sira demonstrates that the wisdom of God is far more effective than the philosophy of the Greeks.

The covenant of Moses is contrasted with that of Christ in the second reading from Hebrews. The blazing fire and gloomy darkness and storm recall the Mountain of God (Deuteronomy 4:11) on which Moses received the Law. The manifestation of God in peals of thunder and lightning and signaled by a trumpet blast terrified the people (Exodus 19:16). In contrast, Mount Zion and the heavenly Jerusalem are presented as festive and joyful, filled with countless angels. The sprinkled blood of Christ's death "speaks more eloquently" than the murder of Abel, whose blood cried out from the soil (Genesis 4:10).

Luke's is a Gospel of reversals. Tax collectors and sinners dine with Jesus (5:30). The unjust judge fears the widow, who might strike him (18:5). The humble tax collector and not the self-righteous Pharisee is justified (18:14). And in today's reading, those whose status and wealth could assure them of the best seats at the table are told to step back, "For every one who exalts himself will be humbled, but the one who humbles himself will be exalted" (14:11). The Lucan Jesus presents us with a social ethic directed as Luke's own community. Those with means were to invite the poor, the crippled, the lame, and the blind to the table. In so doing, they would be fulfilling the words of Isaiah as Jesus had done: "The Spirit of the Lord is upon me, because he has anointed me to bring glad tidings to the poor" (Luke 4:18).

Many people have been impressed and attracted by the humility of Pope Francis. He lives in two rooms of a hotel, paid his own housing bill the day after his election, made a sandwich to feed his Swiss Guard, invites the poor to eat with him, washes prisoners' feet, installs bathrooms and showers for homeless people, and brings them in to tour the Sistine Chapel. He also calls the Mafia, the Curia, and all of us to accountability. His humility is humbling and challenging. He walks his talk and the talk of Jesus: Everyone who humbles self will be exalted.

Being humble is simply being truthful about one's gifts and one's limitations. Walking on the foot of our gifts, we thank those who affirm them and God for giving them to us along with the ability to develop them. Walking on the foot of our limitations we admit them, say "I'm sorry" when appropriate, and seek to learn from them how we might make amends. To approach Mount Zion and the city of the living God entails walking on both feet: gratitude for our gifts and honesty about our limitations and our sins.

In a world that seeks gain, notoriety, and limelight, the humility of Pope Francis is both attractive and counter-cultural. The humility of Jesus comforts and challenges us. God makes a home where we walk on both feet, the wealth of our gifts and the poverty of our weakness. God showers us with love and mercy knowing our grace and our sin. Be humble. Accept your gifts. Name your weakness. Follow the example of Pope Francis and live the way of Jesus, who humbled himself by taking on every human limitation with the exception of sin, even death.

✤ Consider/Discuss

- Do I walk on both feet of my gifts and weaknesses or limp on one?
- What keeps me from accepting others in humility as God accepts me and all earth's children?

✤ Living and Praying with the Word

Jesus, though you were in the form of God, you did not deem equality with God something to be grasped, but humbled yourself and became as we are. Free me to find you within me when affirming my gifts and forgiving my sins. Help me to be humble enough to thank you by treating others in the same way.

TWENTY-THIRD SUNDAY IN ORDINARY TIME

Today's Focus: Wise Up

Even though God's ways are not our ways, we can still search for God's wisdom as a guide for living; it will prove valuable as we strive to be faithful disciples.

FIRST READING
Wisdom 9: 13–18b

Who can know God's counsel,
    or who can conceive what the LORD intends?
For the deliberations of mortals are timid,
    and unsure are our plans.
For the corruptible body burdens the soul
    and the earthen shelter weighs down the mind
        that has many concerns.
And scarce do we guess the things on earth,
    and what is within our grasp we find with difficulty;
    but when things are in heaven, who can search them out?
Or who ever knew your counsel, except you had given wisdom
    and sent your holy spirit from on high?
And thus were the paths of those on earth made straight.

PSALM RESPONSE
Psalm 90:1

In every age, O Lord, you have been our refuge.

SECOND READING
Philemon 9–10, 12–17

I, Paul, an old man, and now also a prisoner for Christ Jesus, urge you on behalf of my child Onesimus, whose father I have become in my imprisonment; I am sending him, that is, my own heart, back to you. I should have liked to retain him for myself, so that he might serve me on your behalf in my imprisonment for the gospel, but I did not want to do anything without your consent, so that the good you do might not be forced but voluntary. Perhaps this is why he was away from you for a while, that you might have him back forever, no longer as a slave but more than a slave, a brother, beloved especially to me, but even more so to you, as a man and in the Lord. So if you regard me as a partner, welcome him as you would me.

GOSPEL
Luke 14:25–33

Great crowds were traveling with Jesus, and he turned and addressed them, "If anyone comes to me without hating his father and mother, wife and children, brothers and sisters, and even his own life, he cannot be my disciple. Whoever does not carry his own cross and come after me cannot be my disciple. Which of you wishing to construct a tower does not first sit down and calculate the cost to see if there is enough for its completion? Otherwise, after laying the foundation and finding himself unable to finish the work the onlookers should laugh at him and say, 'This one began to build but did not have the resources to finish.' Or what king marching into battle would not first sit down and decide whether with ten thousand troops he can successfully oppose another king advancing upon him with twenty thousand troops? But if not, while he is still far away, he will send a delegation to ask for peace terms. In the same way, anyone of you who does not renounce all his possessions cannot be my disciple."

✤ Understanding the Word

The book of Wisdom was likely written in Alexandria, Egypt some fifty years before the coming of Christ. Taking on the persona of Solomon, the wise king, the author of the first reading attempts to bridge his Jewish faith with the Hellenistic (Greek) society in which he lived. In today's lection, Wisdom demonstrates the limitations of human deliberations. "And scarce do we guess the things on earth" (v. 16), so the things of heaven are wholly beyond our grasp. Only the presence of the Holy Spirit sent from on high allows mortals to know the wisdom of God.

Paul's Letter to Philemon is the only extant personal correspondence in the New Testament canon. All other undisputed Pauline letters are addressed to church communities, and the pastoral epistles (First and Second Timothy and Titus) are pseudepigraphic, i.e. falsely attributed to Paul. In today's second reading, Paul demonstrates his facility with Greco-Roman rhetoric. Though seemingly returning the slave to his master (v. 12), Paul is actually forcing Philemon's hand, "so that the good you do might not be forced but voluntary" (v. 14). Paul names Onesimus as his "own heart" and later asks Philemon to "refresh my heart in Christ" (v. 20). There is little doubt that Philemon would have to capitulate to Paul's request, since Paul reminds him that "you owe me your very self" (v. 19).

The Gospel reading is taken from the journey narrative in Luke 9:51 — 19:27. Having set his face resolutely toward Jerusalem (9:51), Jesus continues to preach and teach along the way. He is preparing his disciples for what awaits them in Jerusalem, the city that kills the prophets and stones those sent to it (13:34). Today's reading features two short parables only found in Luke. Jesus announces that discipleship requires singular focus and a willingness to carry one's cross (14:26–27). The parable of building a tower (14:28–30) and the parable of the prudent king (14:31–32) suggest that discipleship also requires a realistic assessment of the costs and one's ability to complete the task.

Some people call me a "control freak" because I like to plan so that I can be ready in any situation that might arise. Planning, as Jesus notes in the parables about the tower and battle, is helpful for negotiating daily life. However, even the best human plans cannot account for every eventuality. If we pray as if all depends upon God and live as if all depends upon us, we can find God in every situation of life. Life happens and much in life is beyond our control.

God is the Creator and, as our first reading notes, we do not know the mind of God. We can use the gifts that God has given us to look for God's presence in every life situation and seek God's wisdom. Upon seeing God's presence, we need to surrender if we want to live God's will in our current reality.

St. Francis de Sales taught that taking up one's cross and following Jesus simply means accepting life as it comes to us. In this way we imitate Jesus, who did not choose his cross but accepted the one prepared for him. That's easier said than done, I know. But if we take time to unite ourselves to God in prayer each day, we will find God present even in life's difficulties. Divine wisdom will boost human wisdom so that God can prosper the work of our hands. Human planning will be informed by the wisdom of God. Even a control freak can't control everything and needs God's guidance. So, pray as if all depends upon God. It does. Live as if all depends upon you. It does. And take up your cross as Christ's disciple.

✤ Consider/Discuss

• When has planning helped you get through a difficult time in life?

• How has prayer helped you find God's presence in life's challenges?

✤ Living and Praying with the Word

In every age you are our refuge, O God. Help me seek your wisdom and presence each day, so that when those times come when you seem more absent than present, I will remember to look for you and follow your way.

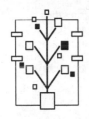

September 11, 2016

TWENTY-FOURTH SUNDAY IN ORDINARY TIME

Today's Focus: Blinded by Envy

God's love, mercy, and forgiveness are boundless. Sometimes we see this mercy extended to those we think aren't deserving and—rather than imitate God's mercy—we are blinded by jealousy.

FIRST READING
Exodus 32: 7–11, 13–14

The LORD said to Moses, "Go down at once to your people, whom you brought out of the land of Egypt, for they have become depraved. They have soon turned aside from the way I pointed out to them, making for themselves a molten calf and worshiping it, sacrificing to it and crying out, 'This is your God, O Israel, who brought you out of the land of Egypt!' I see how stiff-necked this people is," continued the LORD to Moses. "Let me alone, then, that my wrath may blaze up against them to consume them. Then I will make of you a great nation."

But Moses implored the LORD, his God, saying, "Why, O LORD, should your wrath blaze up against your own people, whom you brought out of the land of Egypt with such great power and with so strong a hand? Remember your servants Abraham, Isaac, and Israel, and how you swore to them by your own self, saying, 'I will make your descendants as numerous as the stars in the sky; and all this land that I promised, I will give your descendants as their perpetual heritage.' " So the LORD relented in the punishment he had threatened to inflict on his people.

PSALM RESPONSE
Luke 15:18

I will rise and go to my father.

SECOND READING
1 Timothy 1: 12–17

Beloved: I am grateful to him who has strengthened me, Christ Jesus our Lord, because he considered me trustworthy in appointing me to the ministry. I was once a blasphemer and a persecutor and arrogant, but I have been mercifully treated because I acted out of ignorance in my unbelief. Indeed, the grace of our Lord has been abundant, along with the faith and love that are in Christ Jesus. This saying is trustworthy and deserves full acceptance: Christ Jesus came into the world to save sinners. Of these I am the foremost. But for that reason I was mercifully treated, so that in me, as the foremost, Christ Jesus might display all his patience as an example for those who would come to believe in him for everlasting life. To the king of ages, incorruptible, invisible, the only God, honor and glory forever and ever. Amen.

GOSPEL
Luke 15:1–32 or
15:1–10

Tax collectors and sinners were all drawing near to listen to Jesus, but the Pharisees and scribes began to complain, saying, "This man welcomes sinners and eats with them." So to them he addressed this parable. "What man among you having a hundred sheep and losing one of them would not leave the ninety-nine in the desert and go after the lost one until he finds it? And when he does find it, he sets it on his shoulders with great joy and, upon his arrival home, he calls together his friends and neighbors and says to them, 'Rejoice with me because I have found my lost sheep.' I tell you, in just the same way there will be more joy in heaven over one sinner who repents than over ninety-nine righteous people who have no need of repentance.

"Or what woman having ten coins and losing one would not light a lamp and sweep the house, searching carefully until she finds it? And when she does find it, she calls together her friends and neighbors and says to them, 'Rejoice with me because I have found the coin that I lost.' In just the same way, I tell you, there will be rejoicing among the angels of God over one sinner who repents."

[Then he said, "A man had two sons, and the younger son said to his father, 'Father give me the share of your estate that should come to me.' So the father divided the property between them. After a few days, the younger son collected all his belongings and set off to a distant country where he squandered his inheritance on a life of dissipation. When he had freely spent everything, a severe famine struck that country, and he found himself in dire need. So he hired himself out to one of the local citizens who sent him to his farm to tend the swine. And he longed to eat his fill of the pods on which the swine fed, but nobody gave him any. Coming to his senses he thought, 'How many of my father's hired workers have more than enough food to eat, but here am I, dying from hunger. I shall get up and go to my father and I shall say to him, "Father, I have sinned against heaven and against you. I no longer deserve to be called your son; treat me as you would treat one of your hired workers." ' So he got up and went back to his father. While he was still a long way off, his father caught sight of him, and was filled with compassion. He ran to his son, embraced him and kissed him. His son said to him, 'Father, I have sinned against heaven and against you; I no longer deserve to be called your son.' But his father ordered his servants, 'Quickly bring the finest robe and put it on him; put a ring on his finger and sandals on his feet. Take the fattened calf and slaughter it. Then let us celebrate with a feast, because this son of mine was dead, and has come to life again; he was lost, and has been found.' Then the celebration began. Now the older son had been out in the field and, on his way back, as he neared the house, he heard the sound of music and dancing.

He called one of the servants and asked what this might mean. The servant said to him, 'Your brother has returned and your father has slaughtered the fattened calf because he has him back safe and sound.' He became angry, and when he refused to enter the house, his father came out and pleaded with him. He said to his father in reply, 'Look, all these years I served you and not once did I disobey your orders; yet you never gave me even a young goat to feast on with my friends. But when your son returns, who swallowed up your property with prostitutes, for him you slaughter the fattened calf.' He said to him, 'My son, you are here with me always; everything I have is yours. But now we must celebrate and rejoice, because your brother was dead and has come to life again; he was lost and has been found.' "]

❖ Understanding the Word

Both the first reading and Gospel speak about those who are lost. In the first reading, the wandering Hebrews have "turned aside from the way" (Exodus 32:8), and in the Gospel, a sheep, a coin, and an errant son have been temporarily lost. The incident of the golden calf signaled not Israel's apostasy (turning away from God), but Israel's fear that their leader, Moses, had left them (Exodus 32:1). The golden calf may have symbolized God's strength in the absence of Moses. Israel's error was in making an image of the divine, which was expressly forbidden (Exodus 20:4). The subsequent exchange between God and Moses demonstrates the intimacy between them (expressly stated in Exodus 33:11), and the relationship between Moses and the stiff-necked people he attempted to lead.

The second reading also reflects the mercy of God toward sinners. Though attributed to Paul and addressed to Timothy, First Timothy is a pseudepigraphic work, likely written in the early second century. It picks up themes from the undisputed Pauline Letters and develops them for a later church. In the persona of Paul, the author acknowledges his former life as "a blasphemer and a persecutor and arrogant" (1 Timothy 1:13). Throughout the pastoral epistles, the statement "This saying is trustworthy" serves to introduce a tenet of Christian faith held by the church (1 Timothy 3:1; 4:9; 2 Timothy 2:11; Titus 3:8); in this case, that Christ Jesus came to save sinners is foundational to belief.

Ironically, the "stiff-necked people" in the Gospel are not those who have sinned, but rather those who despise the sinners—the Pharisees and scribes. Chapter 15 of Luke's Gospel contains a series of "lost" parables that emphasize the magnanimity of God and are directed at the complaining religious leaders. Parables, by their very nature, do not succumb to an easy or singular interpretation; however, in general the "lost" parables tend to emphasize the paradoxical nature of God, who rejoices "over one sinner who repents rather than over ninety-nine righteous people who have no need of repentance" (Luke 15:7).

Part of today's Gospel tells the story often named "The Prodigal Son." The collection of today's readings could be named "A Merciful God and Repentant People." Our Israelite ancestors create a molten calf because they had lost faith in God's servant, Moses. Fearing that they are alone in the desert they create a concrete image of God, against the commandments. Moses reminds God to be faithful to God's promises, a way of voicing the people's repentance. God's response is to relent from punishment and show mercy.

Speaking in Paul's name, the author of First Timothy admits that he needs God's mercy. After all, he was arrogant in persecuting the early Christian community. But, he notes, "I was mercifully treated." Our merciful God not only forgave Paul, but has fed others with merciful love through Paul's preaching ever since.

The Gospel parables make clear that God rejoices more over one sinner who repents, like the "prodigal son," than any number of righteous people who think they do not need to repent. Do you believe this? How often do we—like the Pharisees, scribes, and older son—think that someone does not deserve such generous mercy? How often do we think that our sin is too great to forgive? Such narrow vision can blind us to God's mercy. As Pope Francis likes to remind us, God never tires of forgiving us.

✤ Consider/Discuss

- Name a time when you were grateful for God's mercy in your life.
- What keeps you from rejoicing over the mercy God shows to someone else?

✤ Living and Praying with the Word

God, our mercy, I can so envy the way you forgive others that I miss the merciful love with which you touch me. Open my eyes to see you today. Open my lips to proclaim your praise. Open my heart to be as compassionate to others as you are to me.

September 18, 2016

TWENTY-FIFTH SUNDAY IN ORDINARY TIME

Today's Focus: Using Wisdom Wisely

As with of God's gifts, we can use the intelligence or insight we have been given (or have gained) for our own selfish purposes. Or, in the divine image, we can use them for the benefit of others.

FIRST READING
Amos 8:4–7

Hear this, you who trample upon the needy
    and destroy the poor of the land!
"When will the new moon be over," you ask,
    "that we may sell our grain,
    and the sabbath, that we may display the wheat?
We will diminish the ephah,
    add to the shekel,
    and fix our scales for cheating!
We will buy the lowly for silver,
    and the poor for a pair of sandals;
    even the refuse of the wheat we will sell!"
The Lord has sworn by the pride of Jacob:
    Never will I forget a thing they have done!

PSALM RESPONSE
*Psalm 113:
1a, 7b*

Praise the Lord who lifts up the poor.

SECOND READING
*1 Timothy 2:
1–8*

Beloved: First of all, I ask that supplications, prayers, petitions, and thanksgivings be offered for everyone, for kings and for all in authority, that we may lead a quiet and tranquil life in all devotion and dignity. This is good and pleasing to God our savior, who wills everyone to be saved and to come to knowledge of the truth.
    For there is one God.
    There is also one mediator between God and men,
    the man Christ Jesus,
    who gave himself as ransom for all.
This was the testimony at the proper time. For this I was appointed preacher and apostle—I am speaking the truth, I am not lying—, teacher of the Gentiles in faith and truth.

It is my wish, then, that in every place the men should pray, lifting up holy hands, without anger or argument.

GOSPEL
Luke 16:1–13 or
16:10–13

Jesus said to his disciples, ["A rich man had a steward who was reported to him for squandering his property. He summoned him and said, 'What is this I hear about you? Prepare a full account of your stewardship, because you can no longer be my steward.' The steward said to himself, 'What shall I do, now that my master is taking the position of steward away from me? I am not strong enough to dig and I am ashamed to beg. I know what I shall do so that, when I am removed from the stewardship, they may welcome me into their homes.' He called in his master's debtors one by one. To the first he said, 'How much do you owe my master?' He replied, 'One hundred measures of olive oil.' He said to him, 'Here is your promissory note. Sit down and quickly write one for fifty.' Then to another the steward said, 'And you, how much do you owe?' He replied, 'One hundred kors of wheat.' The steward said to him, 'Here is your promissory note; write one for eighty.' And the master commended that dishonest steward for acting prudently.

"For the children of this world are more prudent in dealing with their own generation than are the children of light. I tell you, make friends for yourselves with dishonest wealth, so that when it fails, you will be welcomed into eternal dwellings.] The person who is trustworthy in very small matters is also trustworthy in great ones; and the person who is dishonest in very small matters is also dishonest in great ones. If, therefore, you are not trustworthy with dishonest wealth, who will trust you with true wealth? If you are not trustworthy with what belongs to another, who will give you what is yours? No servant can serve two masters. He will either hate one and love the other, or be devoted to one and despise the other. You cannot serve both God and mammon."

✤ Understanding the Word

After the death of Solomon, his kingdom was split into Israel in the north and Judah in the south. The northern kingdom of Israel, with its capital at Samaria, saw a marked increase in wealth during the reign of Jeroboam II (786–746 BC). Originally from the southern kingdom, the prophet Amos preached blistering diatribes against the wealthy citizens of Samaria for their failure to uphold the Mosaic tenets. "The Lord has sworn by the pride of Jacob: Never will I forget a thing they have done!" (Amos 8:7) Amos' prophecies would be fulfilled when the Assyrians destroyed Samaria and exiled its citizens in 721 BC.

The reading from First Timothy echoes some of the Pauline concerns for appropriate relations with civil authorities found in Romans 13. The community is to pray for kings and all those in authority and lead a quiet and tranquil life. If First Timothy is dated to the early second century, the admonition may have served to keep the Christian community safe during sporadic persecutions. Some scholars suggest that 1 Timothy 2:5, "For there is one God," contains a primitive creed based on the Jewish *Shema* (Deuteronomy 6:4–5).

Luke 16:1–13, the parable of the wily steward, has baffled scholars and pastors alike. How does an untrustworthy steward about to be fired (Luke 16:1–2) become an object of praise (Luke 16:8) and an illustration of right behavior (Luke 16:9)? A clue to interpreting this perplexing parable may be found in verse. 8. The Greek word *adikias* is often translated as "dishonest," suggesting some illegal activity on the part of the steward. A more accurate translation is "unjust" or "unrighteous," which describes the character of the steward rather than his actions. The same word appears four additional times. In verse 9, Jesus encourages his disciples to make friends of "unjust" wealth (which is temporary), so that when it is gone, they may enter into an eternal dwelling. In verse 10, Jesus announces that the person who is "unjust" is small matters will be so in larger ones. True wealth is compared to unjust wealth (Luke 16:11). Reading the steward as "unjust" or "unrighteous" in his character rather than dishonest in his actions provides a different lens with which to interpret the parable.

✤ Reflecting on the Word

Every day news reports contain stories about people who use their wisdom to take more than their fair share of the earth's goods and resources, or find ways to make more money than a person really needs, or who plot to do evil and find ways to avoid doing good. The cost of these plans is that people do not have basic needs met and care for the earth suffers. Other people use their wisdom to create new jobs, provide a living wage, treat our diverse human family justly, and care for the Creation we need for life. What a different world it would be if we put as much energy into doing justice, loving kindness, and walking humbly with God as some do into beating the system, seeking their own gain, or bullying others.

The first reading paints the picture of people only concerned with self: destroying the poor, trampling the needy, and awaiting Sabbath's end to return to unjust practices. In the Gospel Jesus praises an unjust steward for finding ways to save himself that also do good for others. Self-preservation and advancement are natural inclinations, but so are trying to right the wrongs that harm our sisters and brothers and creation, and could also harm us at the end of the day. Maybe we need to take the second reading's advice about praying for those in authority and make it a prayer for ourselves. Seek what is good and pleasing to God, who sent Jesus as mediator between all people and God. May everyone have what is needed for life, health, happiness, and a right relationship with God, one another, and all creation.

✤ Consider/Discuss

- How do I use the talents that God has given me to do good?
- Where do my desire for more and for self-preservation get in the way of my ability to treat others with biblical justice and love?

✤ Living and Praying with the Word

Bountiful God, I lift up my hands in prayer, desiring to serve you with all that I have and all that I am. Help me use your gifts to treat other people and all of creation with the same love and care that you offer us.

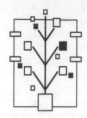

September 25, 2016

TWENTY-SIXTH SUNDAY IN ORDINARY TIME

Today's Focus: What's in a Name?

God knew and loved the homeless beggar Lazarus by name. How often do we treat the poor and homeless as though they were not real people, named, known, and loved by God?

FIRST READING
Amos 6:1a, 4–7

Thus says the LORD the God of hosts:
Woe to the complacent in Zion!
Lying upon beds of ivory,
   stretched comfortably on their couches,
they eat lambs taken from the flock,
   and calves from the stall!
Improvising to the music of the harp,
   like David, they devise their own accompaniment.
They drink wine from bowls
   and anoint themselves with the best oils;
   yet they are not made ill by the collapse of Joseph!
Therefore, now they shall be the first to go into exile,
   and their wanton revelry shall be done away with.

PSALM RESPONSE
Psalm 146:1b

Praise the Lord, my soul!

SECOND READING
1 Timothy 6: 11–16

But you, man of God, pursue righteousness, devotion, faith, love, patience, and gentleness. Compete well for the faith. Lay hold of eternal life, to which you were called when you made the noble confession in the presence of many witnesses. I charge you before God, who gives life to all things, and before Christ Jesus, who gave testimony under Pontius Pilate for the noble confession, to keep the commandment without stain or reproach until the appearance of our Lord Jesus Christ that the blessed and only ruler will make manifest at the proper time, the King of kings and Lord of lords, who alone has immortality, who dwells in unapproachable light, and whom no human being has seen or can see. To him be honor and eternal power. Amen.

GOSPEL
Luke 16:19–31

Jesus said to the Pharisees: "There was a rich man who dressed in purple garments and fine linen and dined sumptuously each day. And lying at his door was a poor man named Lazarus, covered with sores, who would gladly have eaten his fill of the scraps that fell from the rich man's table. Dogs even used to come and lick his sores. When the poor man died, he was carried away by angels to the bosom of Abraham. The rich man also died and was buried, and from the netherworld, where he was in torment, he raised his eyes and saw Abraham far off and Lazarus at his side. And he cried out, 'Father Abraham, have pity on me. Send Lazarus to dip the tip of his finger in water and cool my tongue, for I am suffering torment in these flames.' Abraham replied, 'My child, remember that you received what was good during your lifetime while Lazarus likewise received what was bad; but now he is comforted here, whereas you are tormented. Moreover, between us and you a great chasm is established to prevent anyone from crossing who might wish to go from our side to yours or from your side to ours.' He said, 'Then I beg you, father, send him to my father's house, for I have five brothers, so that he may warn them, lest they too come to this place of torment.' But Abraham replied, 'They have Moses and the prophets. Let them listen to them.' He said, 'Oh no, father Abraham, but if someone from the dead goes to them, they will repent.' Then Abraham said, 'If they will not listen to Moses and the prophets, neither will they be persuaded if someone should rise from the dead.' "

❖ Understanding the Word

The Israelite prophetic tradition arose out of the context of kingship. The prophet stood as a visible and audible reminder to the king that his primary duty was to God, not politics. The stories of Elijah and Elisha bear out the difficulty of such a task. Today's first reading is from the prophet Amos, who unlike Elijah and Elisha was not a "professional prophet." He was simply a sheep breeder in the southern kingdom of Judah. Perhaps his pastoral origins stood in stark contrast to the opulent lifestyle of the "rich and famous" of the northern kingdom. Amos warns those who stretch comfortably on beds of ivory (the ultimate in eighth-century BC luxury) will be the first sent into exile.

Right behavior is also a theme found in both the second reading and the Gospel. Writing in the name of Paul, the author of First Timothy is likely a second-generation follower of Paul who uses the letter format to offer guidelines for church order. Though the author addresses "Timothy," the plural final greeting in 1 Timothy 6:21 confirms that the letter is addressed to the entire community. The faithful are to compete well for the faith, keep the commandment, and await the *parousia* (second coming) of our Lord Jesus Christ.

The Gospel reading is taken from Chapter 16 of Luke's Gospel, which also contains the parable of the wily servant (vv. 1–8) and a series of sayings (against the Pharisees' love of money, vv. 14–15; about the law and prophets, vv. 16–17; about divorce, v. 18). The parable of the rich man and Lazarus serves as a narrative example confirming Jesus' previous sayings. Like the Pharisees who love money, the rich man enjoyed the benefits of wealth in his lifetime. At his death, he is cast into the netherworld, where he experiences the results of lifetime of ignoring the law and the prophets. Since he is now without hope, he asks that his surviving brothers be warned "lest they too come to this place of torment" (v. 28). Abraham's response foreshadows the Resurrection: "If they will not listen to Moses and the prophets, neither will they be persuaded if someone should rise from the dead" (v. 31).

✤ Reflecting on the Word

The story about the rich man and the poor man Lazarus is familiar to many of us. It is noteworthy that the poor man is named. I imagine that he was seldom called by name while begging outside the rich man's home. How many nameless men and women do we encounter on our city streets or standing on traffic islands alongside our cars? How often do we avoid eye contact or fail to show the basic respect of acknowledging another person's presence? Even if someone is "working the system," that person is still a human being, worthy of dignity and respect as our sister or brother. Even if we do not offer someone money or food or drink, we can treat another person with basic human dignity.

I read a reflection that identifies our homeless sisters and brothers as prophets who cry out to us as Amos did to the rich of his day. They remind us that those who have everything but do not care for our sisters and brothers in need "shall be the first to go into exile." Ignoring the poor could result in our experiencing the torment of the rich man in the Gospel parable. The cry of our poorer sisters and brothers reminds me of lyrics from a '60s song: "See me. Heal me. Touch me. Feel me." To "keep the commandment," as the Letter to Timothy asks, is to love God by loving our neighbor, rich or poor, named or unnamed, or . . . Jesus ate with tax collectors and sinners, people the "righteous" deemed unworthy. Like Jesus we are called to acknowledge these prophets in our midst and feed them with human dignity, sharing with them the cup of human respect and love.

✤ Consider/Discuss

- How do I treat the sister or brother who begs on our city streets?
- Who would be on my list of the "unworthy" who might actually be the prophet God is using to speak to me?

✤ Living and Praying with the Word

Almighty God, you raised Jesus from the dead. He ate with those considered least, last, and lost in his day. Help us follow his example and see your presence in every person we meet today, even the sister or brother who makes me uncomfortable.

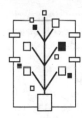

October 2, 2016

TWENTY-SEVENTH SUNDAY IN ORDINARY TIME

Today's Focus: What's in It for Me?

In our world of quick—if not instant—results or gratification, we sometimes are not able or willing to wait patiently to see what God has in store for us.

FIRST READING
Habakkuk 1: 2–3; 2:2–4

How long, O LORD? I cry for help
    but you do not listen!
I cry out to you, "Violence!"
    but you do not intervene.
Why do you let me see ruin;
    why must I look at misery?
Destruction and violence are before me;
    there is strife, and clamorous discord.
Then the LORD answered me and said:
    Write down the vision clearly upon the tablets,
    so that one can read it readily.
For the vision still has its time,
    presses on to fulfillment, and will not disappoint;
if it delays, wait for it,
    it will surely come, it will not be late.
The rash one has no integrity;
    but the just one, because of his faith, shall live.

PSALM RESPONSE
Psalm 95:8

If today you hear his voice, harden not your hearts.

SECOND READING
2 Timothy 1: 6–8, 13–14

Beloved: I remind you to stir into flame the gift of God that you have through the imposition of my hands. For God did not give us a spirit of cowardice but rather of power and love and self-control. So do not be ashamed of your testimony to our Lord, nor of me, a prisoner for his sake; but bear your share of hardship for the gospel with the strength that comes from God.

Take as your norm the sound words that you heard from me, in the faith and love that are in Christ Jesus. Guard this rich trust with the help of the Holy Spirit that dwells within us.

The apostles said to the Lord, "Increase our faith." The Lord replied, "If you have faith the size of a mustard seed, you would say to this mulberry tree, 'Be uprooted and planted in the sea,' and it would obey you.

"Who among you would say to your servant who has just come in from plowing or tending sheep in the field, 'Come here immediately and take your place at table'? Would he not rather say to him, 'Prepare something for me to eat. Put on your apron and wait on me while I eat and drink. You may eat and drink when I am finished'? Is he grateful to that servant because he did what was commanded? So should it be with you. When you have done all you have been commanded, say, 'We are unprofitable servants; we have done what we were obliged to do.' "

❖ Understanding the Word

The theme of perseverance is woven throughout today's readings. The prophet Habakkuk accuses God of turning a deaf ear to the prophet's complaint about the abuses and lack of faith among the people of Judah. In essence, God urges patience. "The vision still has its time, presses on to fulfillment, and will not disappoint; if it delays, wait for it" (v. 3). The prophet is to write down the vision that will later be proclaimed and verified upon its fulfillment. Scholars propose that Habbakkuk prophesied in Judah shortly after it had become a vassal of Assyria in 605 BC.

The second reading is taken from Second Timothy, another doubly-pseudepigraphic work purportedly written by Paul to Timothy, but long after both had died. Whereas First Timothy reads as a manual for church organization and management, Second Timothy is largely a reflection on the life and ministry of an aging Paul shortly before his death. In the mode of a last will and testament, the letter includes the passing on of a person's legacy. In today's passage, "Timothy" is reminded to "stir into a flame the gift of God" handed on to him from Paul (v. 6), and to "guard this rich trust with the help of the Holy Spirit" (v. 14).

Earlier in Luke 14:25–33 (Twenty-third Sunday in Ordinary Time), Jesus had outlined the demands of discipleship. One must abandoned one's previous life and family, realistically recognize the costs, and take up one's cross. In today's Gospel, several sayings of Jesus depict additional aspects of discipleship. The disciples ask for greater faith (v. 5), but Jesus counters that even the smallest amount of faith has miraculous effect. Jesus uses a narrative example to help the disciples better understand their role as obedient servants. Like the servant who has worked long and hard in the field, the disciple should not expect reward or acclamation. Rather, the disciples are to do what is commanded of them, recognizing that they have fulfilled their purpose. In the life of Luke's community, this story may have served to admonish the early Christians to be more faithful and obedient believers without the desire for reward.

When I invite someone to participate in Mass or join a club or volunteer for a parish or civic activity, I often hear, "What will I get out of it?" I'm glad that this is not God's question. God freely plants the seed of faith within us and offers forgiveness to all. When we accept these gifts, whether our faith seems small or great, we are simply doing what is expected of us as servants of God. A side benefit can be "getting" satisfaction for being faithful to the baptismal promise we made to live Jesus. Satisfaction can grow into an attitude of gratitude.

Habakkuk reminds us that God's time is not our time. God's vision "will surely come." It has its own time, "presses on to fulfillment, and will not disappoint." Like watching a pot of water, we cannot make it boil any faster. Nor can we make a seed planted into the ground grow any faster, even with modern technological assistance. God's vision and the seed of faith planted within us have their own time. We can tend them, nurture them, watch them, and stir into flame the gift God has given us, but we cannot force when their fulfillment will come. When we live God's vision with patience, we do what we promised at baptism. God's will has its time. So, to paraphrase St. Francis de Sales, be patient, most of all, with yourself. What will you get out of it? The satisfaction of knowing we are servants who have done what we are obliged to do, and we just might find God's vision fulfilled where we least expect.

✜ Consider/Discuss

- How do you name the obligations that are yours because you believe in Jesus Christ?
- Name where you have been impatient with yourself or with God and what has helped your patience grow.

✜ Living and Praying with the Word

Generous God, you have planted the gift of faith in our hearts. Help me trust that the faith I have will be enough whether life is easy or difficult. Stir that gift into a flame that sets the world on fire with the light of your Son, Jesus Christ.

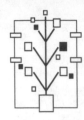

October 9, 2016

TWENTY-EIGHTH SUNDAY IN ORDINARY TIME

Today's Focus: Everyday Gratitude

It doesn't take all that much to say "thank you" to God when something extraordinary happens. But do we have the mindfulness to express our gratitude for the smaller, commonplace blessings?

FIRST READING
2 Kings 5: 14–17

Naaman went down and plunged into the Jordan seven times at the word of Elisha, the man of God. His flesh became again like the flesh of a little child, and he was clean of his leprosy.

Naaman returned with his whole retinue to the man of God. On his arrival he stood before Elisha and said, "Now I know that there is no God in all the earth, except in Israel. Please accept a gift from your servant."

Elisha replied, "As the LORD lives whom I serve, I will not take it"; and despite Naaman's urging, he still refused. Naaman said: "If you will not accept, please let me, your servant, have two mule-loads of earth, for I will no longer offer holocaust or sacrifice to any other god except to the LORD."

PSALM RESPONSE
Psalm 98:2b

The Lord has revealed to the nations his saving power.

SECOND READING
2 Timothy 2: 8–13

Beloved: Remember Jesus Christ, raised from the dead, a descendant of David: such is my gospel, for which I am suffering, even to the point of chains, like a criminal. But the word of God is not chained. Therefore, I bear with everything for the sake of those who are chosen, so that they too may obtain the salvation that is in Christ Jesus, together with eternal glory. This saying is trustworthy:
   If we have died with him
      we shall also live with him;
   if we persevere
      we shall also reign with him.
   But if we deny him
      he will deny us.
   If we are unfaithful
      he remains faithful,
      for he cannot deny himself.

GOSPEL
Luke 17:11–19 As Jesus continued his journey to Jerusalem, he traveled through Samaria and Galilee. As he was entering a village, ten lepers met him. They stood at a distance from him and raised their voices, saying, "Jesus, Master! Have pity on us!" And when he saw them, he said, "Go show yourselves to the priests." As they were going they were cleansed. And one of them, realizing he had been healed, returned, glorifying God in a loud voice; and he fell at the feet of Jesus and thanked him. He was a Samaritan. Jesus said in reply, "Ten were cleansed, were they not? Where are the other nine? Has none but this foreigner returned to give thanks to God?" Then he said to him, "Stand up and go; your faith has saved you."

❖ Understanding the Word

Within the books of First and Second Kings is a cycle of stories about the prophets, Elijah (1 Kings 17:1—19:21) and Elisha (2 Kings 2:1—13:21). Today's reading narrates the healing of the Aramean commander, Naaman, by Elisha. As Elijah's protégé, Elisha enacts miracles similar to Elijah's. Both provide an abundance of food and raise a dead child. But the curing of the leper is unique to Elisha. Like the widow of Zarephath (1 Kings 17:9) and the Shunammite woman (2 Kings 4:8–37), Naaman represents those Gentiles who recognize the power of Elisha's God. Unlike the Gentile women, Naaman makes a statement of faith: "I will no longer offer holocaust . . . to any other god except the LORD" (v. 17).

The author of Second Timothy continues to speak in the voice of Paul, encouraging the Christian community by reminding them of the gospel, for which Paul readily suffered. But Paul's sufferings were not without effect. In fact, they helped the elect achieve salvation. Verses 11–13 may have been taken from an early Christian hymn. If we die with Christ through baptism, we shall live with him, but only if we persevere and remain faithful.

In the Gospel lection, several opposites are subtly mentioned. Jesus is traveling to Jerusalem and yet he goes from Galilee through Samaritan territory. The main pilgrim route from Galilee to Jerusalem followed the Jordan Valley so as to avoid the region of Samaria. The lepers recognize him and cry out for his mercy. Jesus responds by sending them to the priests, in accordance with Leviticus 14:2–9. Along the way they are healed, but only one seems to recognize the healing. He returns and glorifies God. The punch line is not subtle: he was a Samaritan. Like Naaman in the first reading, "this foreigner returned to give thanks" (v. 18). Though Simeon had prophesied that the baby Jesus would be a light to the Gentiles (2:32), no Gentiles become believers in the gospel, though Jesus does praise their faith (also see Luke 7:9). Only after the Resurrection and coming of the Spirit will Gentiles be baptized (Acts 8, 10).

How many times during the day do you hear yourself say "Thank God!"? Whether I receive good news or discover that something is not as bad as I had expected and at times in-between, I often find myself uttering "Thank God!" And yet, I don't think I thank God often enough for a new day, the gift of life, and the ability to breathe or move and live every moment of the day. Ten people with leprosy are healed. Only one returned to thank Jesus—a Samaritan, that is, a foreigner. Were the others ungrateful? We don't know. They might have expressed their gratitude to God when they showed themselves to the priest to be readmitted to life in the community as prescribed by the law. We do know that Jesus affirms the grateful Samaritan's faith. Did he begin to follow Jesus after this experience? We don't know that either.

After Naaman, another foreigner, was healed, he not only expressed faith in Elisha's God, he also began to follow that God: "I will no longer offer holocaust or sacrifice to any other god except to the LORD." The faith that saved him led him to a new way of life. We profess faith in Jesus Christ, as does the hymn in today's second reading. Do we thank God for this faith throughout the day? Is our gratitude seen in lives that show we follow Jesus Christ? Who might surprise us by their lived faith? Pope Francis reminds us: "Jesus did not come to teach a philosophy or an ideology, but rather a way, a journey to be undertaken with him, and we learn the way as we go, by walking." Live that way and say clearly, "Thank God!"

✤ Consider/Discuss

- Make a list of the ways in which you express gratitude to God. After each item say, "Thank you, Lord."
- Whose being lifted up as an example of faith would surprise me?

✤ Living and Praying with the Word

Bountiful God, at Mass we pray that it is right and just to give you thanks. Let me begin and end each day by saying thank you, and help me live in ways that share my gratitude with those I meet.

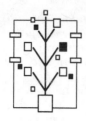

October 16, 2016

TWENTY-NINTH SUNDAY IN ORDINARY TIME

Today's Focus: How are You Holding Up?

Even Moses needed assistance in prayer, having his arms held up so they would not tire. Sometimes we need that same kind of help to pray—and sometimes we are called upon to hold up someone else in prayer.

FIRST READING
Exodus 17: 8–13

In those days, Amalek came and waged war against Israel. Moses, therefore, said to Joshua, "Pick out certain men, and tomorrow go out and engage Amalek in battle. I will be standing on top of the hill with the staff of God in my hand." So Joshua did as Moses told him: he engaged Amalek in battle after Moses had climbed to the top of the hill with Aaron and Hur. As long as Moses kept his hands raised up, Israel had the better of the fight, but when he let his hands rest, Amalek had the better of the fight. Moses' hands, however, grew tired; so they put a rock in place for him to sit on. Meanwhile Aaron and Hur supported his hands, one on one side and one on the other, so that his hands remained steady till sunset. And Joshua mowed down Amalek and his people with the edge of the sword.

PSALM RESPONSE
Psalm 121:2

Our help is from the Lord, who made heaven and earth.

SECOND READING
2 Timothy 3:14 — 4:2

Beloved: Remain faithful to what you have learned and believed, because you know from whom you learned it, and that from infancy you have known the sacred Scriptures, which are capable of giving you wisdom for salvation through faith in Christ Jesus. All Scripture is inspired by God and is useful for teaching, for refutation, for correction, and for training in righteousness, so that one who belongs to God may be competent, equipped for every good work.

I charge you in the presence of God and of Christ Jesus, who will judge the living and the dead, and by his appearing and his kingly power: proclaim the word; be persistent whether it is convenient or inconvenient; convince, reprimand, encourage through all patience and teaching.

Jesus told his disciples a parable about the necessity for them to pray always without becoming weary. He said, "There was a judge in a certain town who neither feared God nor respected any human being. And a widow in that town used to come to him and say, 'Render a just decision for me against my adversary.' For a long time the judge was unwilling, but eventually he thought, 'While it is true that I neither fear God nor respect any human being, because this widow keeps bothering me I shall deliver a just decision for her lest she finally come and strike me.' " The Lord said, "Pay attention to what the dishonest judge says. Will not God then secure the rights of his chosen ones who call out to him day and night? Will he be slow to answer them? I tell you, he will see to it that justice is done for them speedily. But when the Son of Man comes, will he find faith on earth?"

❖ Understanding the Word

It's important to remember that the stories in the Old Testament are told from the viewpoint of a people who had endured slavery, exodus, destruction, and exile. The vilification of their enemies was a motif that the writers used to demonstrate how their God overcame the most powerful of kings and armies. They may have been a wandering band of ex-slaves, but their God had chosen them, and through the presence of Moses and the law, continued to abide among them. In today's first reading, the might of Moses' staff alone is not enough to assure victory. Aaron and Hur must come to his aid. Thus the battle is ultimately won through the united efforts of the community.

In the continuing last will and testament of Paul, the author directs "Timothy" to remain faithful to what he has been taught. The Greek word *mēno* can mean "remain, dwell, abide." Unlike the charlatans who "wander" or lead people astray (2 Timothy 3:13), a true Christian remains, stays put in Christ. And the foundation for the believer is scripture, likely here understood as the Old Testament. The canon of the New Testament was not firmly established until the fourth century. The solemn charge to the Christian community, here personified as "Timothy," is to proclaim the word, be persistent, correct, rebuke, and encourage. The final three are to be complete through patience and careful teaching.

The force of a parable is that it draws the listeners into a familiar setting, populates it with relatable characters, and then totally upends the narrative. Though one would expect a judge to behave righteously, this judge "neither feared God nor respected any human being" (v. 2). Widows are to be protected because they have no male relatives to defend them, but this widow strikes fear into the heart of the judge. Whether her claim is legitimate isn't at issue. Rather, her persistence wins the day. Since parables eschew any single interpretation, the reader must use the parable's placement within the Gospel as a clue to meaning. In today's Gospel reading, Jesus uses the parable as an example to his disciples about the necessity of continual prayer. If a dishonest judge can be forced to offer justice through persistent petitions, how much more so will "God then secure the rights of his chosen ones who call out to him day and night?" (v. 7).

Our readings today call us to persistent perseverance. The judge in the Gospel parable neither "feared God nor respected any human being." However, a persistent widow elicits a just decision from him. Whether her claim was just or not, her perseverance had a profound impact on him. He feared how she might respond if he did not answer her. Her personal persistent perseverance was powerful.

The reading from Exodus paints the picture of Moses' persistent prayer as having a positive effect on the Israelites' battle. "As long as Moses kept his hands raised up, Israel had the better of the fight." Did you notice that Moses needed the help of Aaron and Hur to persevere in holding up his hands in prayer? Personal persistent perseverance is not enough. We need the support of the community to persevere when we are tempted to stop or we do not have the strength to persist on our own.

Our second reading charges us to "be persistent whether it is convenient or inconvenient." We can be tempted to doubt the words of scripture at times. We can be tempted to stop praying when prayer is not answered as quickly as we would like or in the way that we would like. However, as the example of the tortoise teaches us, "Slow and steady wins the race." Persevere in prayer. Persist in turning to God in prayer. Personal persistent perseverance with the support of the Body of Christ will make a real difference in our lives.

✥ Consider/Discuss

- Name times when persistent perseverance has been effective in your life.
- Who supports you in prayer and faith like Aaron and Hur supported Moses?

✥ Living and Praying with the Word

Faithful God, you never cease to love us even when we turn away from you or doubt your word. Give us the persistence of the widow, the perseverance of Moses, and the inspiration of scripture to patiently persevere and persist in trusting you and your merciful love.

THIRTIETH SUNDAY IN ORDINARY TIME

Today's Focus: "I" Trouble

It shouldn't be that difficult to be humble when standing before God in prayer. However, in addition to telling God what "I" want/need, we must remember the needs of the world around us.

FIRST READING
Sirach 35: 12–14, 16–18

The LORD is a God of justice,
  who knows no favorites.
Though not unduly partial toward the weak,
  yet he hears the cry of the oppressed.
The Lord is not deaf to the wail of the orphan,
  nor to the widow when she pours out her complaint.
The one who serves God willingly is heard;
  his petition reaches the heavens.
The prayer of the lowly pierces the clouds;
  it does not rest till it reaches its goal,
nor will it withdraw till the Most High responds,
  judges justly and affirms the right,
and the Lord will not delay.

PSALM RESPONSE
Psalm 34:7a

The Lord hears the cry of the poor.

SECOND READING
2 Timothy 4: 6–8, 16–18

Beloved: I am already being poured out like a libation, and the time of my departure is at hand. I have competed well; I have finished the race; I have kept the faith. From now on the crown of righteousness awaits me, which the Lord, the just judge, will award to me on that day, and not only to me, but to all who have longed for his appearance.

At my first defense no one appeared on my behalf, but everyone deserted me. May it not be held against them! But the Lord stood by me and gave me strength, so that through me the proclamation might be completed and all the Gentiles might hear it. And I was rescued from the lion's mouth. The Lord will rescue me from every evil threat and will bring me safe to his heavenly kingdom. To him be glory forever and ever. Amen.

GOSPEL
Luke 18:9–14   Jesus addressed this parable to those who were convinced of their own righteousness and despised everyone else. "Two people went up to the temple area to pray; one was a Pharisee and the other was a tax collector. The Pharisee took up his position and spoke this prayer to himself, 'O God, I thank you that I am not like the rest of humanity—greedy, dishonest, adulterous—or even like this tax collector. I fast twice a week, and I pay tithes on my whole income.' But the tax collector stood off at a distance and would not even raise his eyes to heaven but beat his breast and prayed, 'O God, be merciful to me a sinner.' I tell you, the latter went home justified, not the former; for whoever exalts himself will be humbled, and the one who humbles himself will be exalted."

✤ Understanding the Word

While the Lord is a God of justice, as Sirach notes, our God is justice wrapped in mercy. So though God has no favorites, those who are weak, oppressed, orphaned, or widowed readily gain God's attention. Likewise, the servants of God and the petitions of the lowly reach the heavens and await the Most High's response. Writing in the second century BC, Ben Sira attempts to counter the influence of Hellenism by reminding the Jews of his day that the traditions of Israel and not Greek philosophy and culture were the foundations of true wisdom.

Second Timothy draws to a close as the aged and imprisoned Paul offers his final words to his beloved Timothy. In language reminiscent of the prophets, Paul recounts his loneliness and suffering. While Demas abandoned him and Alexander opposed Paul's teaching, the Lord came to his defense. The mention of rescue from the lion's mouth (v. 17) may reflect a tradition that Paul fought beasts in the arena, though in 1 Corinthians 15:32, he means it metaphorically.

The parable of the self-righteous Pharisee and the repentant tax collector is unique to Luke and echoes the themes found in Mary's Magnificat—the arrogant of mind and heart are dispersed while the lowly are lifted up. The privileged place of tax collectors is foreshadowed in Luke 3:12, where tax collectors approach John for baptism. These same baptized tax collectors acknowledged the righteousness of God while the Pharisees and scribes rejected the plan of God (Luke 7:29–30). During the Galilean ministry, the Pharisees and scribes had complained that Jesus ate with tax collectors and sinners, to which he responded that his mission was to call sinners to repentance (Luke 5:32). Jesus had introduced the theme of appropriate humility in the parable of the invited guests (Luke 14:7–14). Now, he shows that it is the tax collector and not the Pharisee who demonstrates the appropriate response to God's mercy and thus is justified. "The one who humbles himself will be exalted" (Luke 18:14).

Fr. James V. Marchionda, OP, wrote a song—"The Prayer of the Lowly"—that sets part of our first reading to music: "The prayer of the lowly pierces the clouds and does not rest till it finds God." Although Sirach proclaims that God knows no favorites, God seems to hear the cry of the lowly—that is, the oppressed, the widow, and the orphan—with sharper ears. Pope Francis keeps reminding us about this: "God's heart has a special place for the poor." We see a picture of this in today's Gospel parable.

It is the prayer of the tax collector, who did not even raise his eyes to heaven, that Jesus offers as an example of the attitude we need. He simply and honestly prayed, "O God, be merciful to me a sinner." His poverty freed him to name his utter need for God. The Pharisee, on the other hand, was full of himself, "I thank you . . . I am not like the rest . . . I fast . . . I pay tithes." It's all about him: "I, I, I, I." The Pharisee had what my Aunt Sophia called " 'I' trouble." Even when looking heavenward, he could see only himself.

Each of us is poor in our own way because we are all sinners. We need God's rich mercy to heal us, transform us, and raise us up. Each of us has "I" trouble from time to time. It's all about me. However, if we can admit our need for God's mercy, like the tax collector, and give God the glory, like the author of Second Timothy, our prayer can pierce the clouds and will find rest in the God who judges justly, affirms the right, and will not delay in answering our prayers.

✤ Consider/Discuss

- With whose prayer do you identify more, the tax collector or the Pharisee? Why?
- When has an awareness of your lowliness helped you pray in ways that pierced the clouds to reach God's ears?

✤ Living and Praying with the Word

My God, my mercy, help me name my need for you in my wealth and in my poverty. Hear my prayer and be merciful to me, a sinner.

October 30, 2016

THIRTY-FIRST SUNDAY IN ORDINARY TIME

Today's Focus: Putting on Our God Glasses

No doubt we've all come to the conclusion that God sees the world and others in a very different way than we do. Can we attempt, however, to see the world with God's vision of love and mercy?

FIRST READING
Wisdom 11:22—12:2

Before the LORD the whole universe is as a grain
    from a balance
    or a drop of morning dew come down upon the earth.
But you have mercy on all, because you can do all things;
    and you overlook people's sins that they may repent.
For you love all things that are
    and loathe nothing that you have made;
    for what you hated, you would not have fashioned.
And how could a thing remain, unless you willed it;
    or be preserved, had it not been called forth by you?
But you spare all things, because they are yours,
    O LORD and lover of souls,
    for your imperishable spirit is in all things!
Therefore you rebuke offenders little by little,
    warn them and remind them of the sins
        they are committing,
    that they may abandon their wickedness
    and believe in you, O LORD!

PSALM RESPONSE
Psalm 145:1

I will praise your name for ever, my king and my God.

SECOND READING
2 Thessalonians 1:11—2:2

Brothers and sisters: We always pray for you, that our God may make you worthy of his calling and powerfully bring to fulfillment every good purpose and every effort of faith, that the name of our Lord Jesus may be glorified in you, and you in him, in accord with the grace of our God and Lord Jesus Christ.

We ask you, brothers and sisters, with regard to the coming of our Lord Jesus Christ and our assembling with him, not to be shaken out of your minds suddenly, or to be alarmed either by a "spirit," or by an oral statement, or by a letter allegedly from us to the effect that the day of the Lord is at hand.

At that time, Jesus came to Jericho and intended to pass through the town. Now a man there named Zacchaeus, who was a chief tax collector and also a wealthy man, was seeking to see who Jesus was; but he could not see him because of the crowd, for he was short in stature. So he ran ahead and climbed a sycamore tree in order to see Jesus, who was about to pass that way. When he reached the place, Jesus looked up and said, "Zacchaeus, come down quickly, for today I must stay at your house." And he came down quickly and received him with joy. When they all saw this, they began to grumble, saying, "He has gone to stay at the house of a sinner." But Zacchaeus stood there and said to the Lord, "Behold, half of my possessions, Lord, I shall give to the poor, and if I have extorted anything from anyone I shall repay it four times over." And Jesus said to him, "Today salvation has come to this house because this man too is a descendant of Abraham. For the Son of Man has come to seek and to save what was lost."

❖ Understanding the Word

The first reading is taken from the third part of the book of Wisdom (11:2—19:22), which utilizes the Greek rhetorical form of encomium or speech of praise. The focus of that praise is God, before whom "the whole universe is as a grain from a balance" (Wisdom 11:22). God's mercy extends to overlooking the people's sin. God loves all things and cannot loathe that which God created, since everything is imbued with God's imperishable spirit.

Scholars debate the actual authorship of Second Thessalonians, dating it either during the ministry of Paul (and therefore genuine) or in the early second century (and therefore pseudepigraphic). The letter itself claims to be written by Paul, Silvanus, and Timothy (2 Thessalonians 1:1), who write to encourage a community undergoing intense suffering on behalf of their faith (1:4–6). In today's lection, Paul is responding to a rumor that the day of Lord is already present (2 Thessalonians 2:2). "Let no one deceive you in any way; for that day will not come unless the rebellion comes first and the lawless one is revealed, the one destined for destruction" (2 Thessalonians 2:3).

As the Gospel reading for last week demonstrated, tax collectors are portrayed positively in Luke's Gospel. In today's reading, we meet yet another such tax collector, Zacchaeus, whose description seems reminiscent of that of Levi (Luke 5:27–32). Both are described as tax collectors. Both receive Jesus into their homes (Luke 5:29; 19:5). Both become the occasion for a salvific pronouncement by Jesus. For Levi we have no description, only his name. But we are given a vivid portrait of Zacchaeus. He is wealthy, curious about Jesus, short and resourceful. On first encounter, Zacchaeus seems more akin to the Pharisee than the humble tax collector of Luke 18:9–14. But unlike the Pharisees, Zacchaeus's curiosity leads him to Jesus. After his encounter, Zacchaeus responds by making amends, the exact prescription John the Baptist had given the tax collectors who had sought baptism (Luke 3:12–13). Thus as Jesus leaves Jericho and begins his ascent to Jerusalem, he has realized his mission to call sinners to repentance (Luke 5:32).

✤ Reflecting on the Word

Our readings lead me to paraphrase a Christmas song: "Do you see as God sees?" Are we finding good in all that God has made? The author of Wisdom tells us that God overlooks our sins and has mercy on all to invite repentance. Do we see as God sees, finding good in all that God has made? Jesus does. He sees Zacchaeus as someone lost who can be saved. Zacchaeus climbs a tree hoping to see Jesus and Jesus invites himself to Zacchaeus' house. Zacchaeus promises to change his ways. What does the crowd see? A sinner, unworthy of Jesus' treatment. Do we look for good as God sees or do we see only sinners, unworthy of mercy and of less value than we judge ourselves?

In all honesty, I must confess that there are some people I am ready to view with God's merciful eyes, willing to look for good within them. But there are those in whom I see only sin or evil because of the harm they've done. I find it difficult to find any possibility of goodness within them. Experiences like the Holocaust, the massacres by ISIS, and the abuse of children blind me to seeing any hope for healing that God sees in all. Divine mercy does not preclude suffering consequences for one's choices. But God's vision always sees that a change of heart is possible, even where I would rather not see that. "Do we see as God sees?" Where we do, give thanks. Where we do not, climb a tree, pray that God's vision becomes ours, and hear Jesus say, "Today I must stay at your house."

✤ Consider/Discuss

- When have you experienced the mercy that Jesus shows Zacchaeus?
- What keeps you from seeing as God sees and helps you see people's sins as doors to repentance?

✤ Living and Praying with the Word

Merciful God, you rebuke offenders little by little that we might abandon our wickedness. Thank you for such merciful love. Help me to see others and myself as you do, that I might grow more merciful little by little each day.

November 1, 2016

ALL SAINTS

Tuesday

Today's Focus: Saints Make A Difference

We celebrate those holy men and women today who, through their faith in Christ, made a difference in their own time and place. Like them we are called to make—to be—that difference for those around us.

FIRST READING
Revelation 7: 2–4, 9–14

I, John, saw another angel come up from the East, holding the seal of the living God. He cried out in a loud voice to the four angels who were given power to damage the land and the sea, "Do not damage the land or the sea or the trees until we put the seal on the foreheads of the servants of our God." I heard the number of those who had been marked with the seal, one hundred and forty-four thousand marked from every tribe of the Israelites.

After this I had a vision of a great multitude, which no one could count, from every nation, race, people, and tongue. They stood before the throne and before the Lamb, wearing white robes and holding palm branches in their hands. They cried out in a loud voice:
"Salvation comes from our God, who is seated on the throne,
and from the Lamb."
All the angels stood around the throne and around the elders and the four living creatures. They prostrated themselves before the throne, worshiped God, and exclaimed:
"Amen. Blessing and glory, wisdom and thanksgiving,
honor, power, and might
be to our God forever and ever. Amen."
Then one of the elders spoke up and said to me, "Who are these wearing white robes, and where did they come from?" I said to him, "My lord, you are the one who knows." He said to me, "These are the ones who have survived the time of great distress; they have washed their robes and made them white in the blood of the Lamb."

PSALM RESPONSE
Psalm 24:6

Lord, this is the people that longs to see your face.

SECOND READING
1 John 3:1–3

Beloved: See what love the Father has bestowed on us that we may be called the children of God. Yet so we are. The reason the world does not know us is that it did not know him. Beloved, we are God's children now; what we shall be has not yet been revealed. We do know that when it is revealed we shall be like him, for we shall see him as he is. Everyone who has this hope based on him makes himself pure, as he is pure.

When Jesus saw the crowds, he went up the mountain, and after he had sat down, his disciples came to him. He began to teach them, saying:

"Blessed are the poor in spirit,
for theirs is the kingdom of heaven.
Blessed are they who mourn,
for they will be comforted.
Blessed are the meek,
for they will inherit the land.
Blessed are they who hunger and thirst for righteousness,
for they will be satisfied.
Blessed are the merciful,
for they will be shown mercy.
Blessed are the clean of heart,
for they will see God.
Blessed are the peacemakers,
for they will be called children of God.
Blessed are they who are persecuted for the sake of righteousness,
for theirs is the kingdom of heaven.
Blessed are you when they insult you and persecute you
and utter every kind of evil against you falsely because of me.
Rejoice and be glad,
for your reward will be great in heaven."

✜ Understanding the Word

The events of the first apocalyptic vision unfold on earth; those of the second take place in heaven. Both visions depict vast assemblies of the righteous. One hundred forty-four thousand is clearly a symbolic number. Twelve is squared and then multiplied by a thousand, resulting in a number that indicates completeness. The multitude gathered around the throne comes from every nation, every race, every people, and every tongue. The universality is complete. The multitude represents those who survived the distress of the end-times because they were purified through the blood of the sacrificial Lamb. This distinction entitles them to participate in the celestial celebrations.

According to the Letter of John, love is generative, transforming. It makes believers children of God. Everything that happens in their lives is a consequence of their having been recreated as God's children. They are a new reality and consequently they are not accepted by the world, the old reality. The type of behavior they choose is frequently in opposition to society at large. The "now but not yet" of Christian eschatology (teachings about the end-time) is clearly stated. Though believers have already been reborn as children of God, their transformation has not yet been completed, nor has it been fully made known to them.

In form and content, the Beatitudes are wisdom teaching, not Christian law, as is sometimes claimed. Like most wisdom forms, they describe life situations that draw a connection between a particular manner of behavior and consequences that flow from such behavior. Most if not all of the sentiments expressed in the Beatitudes are found somewhere in ancient Jewish teaching. While the teachings of Jesus are all in some way directed toward the establishment of the reign of God, the values that he advocates are frequently the opposite of those espoused by society at large. This fact offers us a way of understanding the challenges set before us in the Beatitudes. They invite us to turn the standards of our world upside down and inside out.

❖ Reflecting on the Word

Holy Trinity Parish in Georgetown, Washington, D.C., recently inaugurated a one-day operation called "The Power of One." The goal was to engage as many parishioners as possible in various kinds of service in the community during one day. The "one" is not the one day or any one individual, but one community—a community working together for the good of the greater community. The power, of course, is rooted in the love God poured into their hearts to flow out into the world.

Today's feast celebrates the power of one that entered into the world through the dying and rising of Christ, and has been a presence in the world through all those who have been drawn into the one body of Christ through baptism. It is the power that comes when men and women are poor in spirit, mourn the world's sorrows, are meek, hunger and thirst for righteousness, are merciful, clean of heart, peacemakers, and withstand persecution for the sake of living in right relationship with God, others, and the world. They not only will receive heaven, they bring it into the world during their lives.

All Saints holds up a vision reminding us of our future when we will be fully joined with those who have gone before us, but with whom we are one even now in singing praise to our God, as we are reminded at every Eucharist. With them we cry: "Salvation comes from our God, who is seated on the throne, and from the Lamb."

❖ Consider/Discuss

- Have you known the power of belonging to a community doing good?
- Who are the saints who witnessed to you through their faith and now rest in the Lord?

❖ Responding to the Word

God and Father of all, thank you for the gift of your saints, especially those now forgotten men and women who embraced and incarnated the Beatitudes in their lives. May we join with them for all eternity to sing praise to your glory in the name of Jesus, your Son and our Savior.

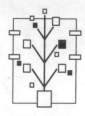

November 6, 2016

THIRTY-SECOND SUNDAY IN ORDINARY TIME

Today's Focus: Something Old, Something New

Attempting to understand the life beyond this life can be a challenge. We know that some-
how we will still live, but in a completely new way. The Risen Christ shows us the way.

FIRST READING
2 Maccabees 7: 1–2, 9–14

It happened that seven brothers with their mother were arrested and tortured with whips and scourges by the king, to force them to eat pork in violation of God's law. One of the brothers, speaking for the others, said: "What do you expect to achieve by questioning us? We are ready to die rather than transgress the laws of our ancestors."

At the point of death he said: "You accursed fiend, you are depriving us of this present life, but the King of the world will raise us up to live again forever. It is for his laws that we are dying."

After him the third suffered their cruel sport. He put out his tongue at once when told to do so, and bravely held out his hands, as he spoke these noble words: "It was from Heaven that I received these; for the sake of his laws I disdain them; from him I hope to receive them again." Even the king and his attendants marveled at the young man's courage, because he regarded his sufferings as nothing.

After he had died, they tortured and maltreated the fourth brother in the same way. When he was near death, he said, "It is my choice to die at the hands of men with the hope God gives of being raised up by him; but for you, there will be no resurrection to life."

PSALM RESPONSE
Psalm 17:15b

Lord, when your glory appears, my joy will be full.

SECOND READING
2 Thessalonians 2:16—3:5

Brothers and sisters: May our Lord Jesus Christ himself and God our Father, who has loved us and given us everlasting encouragement and good hope through his grace, encourage your hearts and strengthen them in every good deed and word.

Finally, brothers and sisters, pray for us, so that the word of the Lord may speed forward and be glorified, as it did among you, and that we may be delivered from perverse and wicked people, for not all have faith. But the Lord is faithful; he will strengthen you and guard you from the evil one. We are confident of you in the Lord that what we instruct you, you are doing and will continue to do. May the Lord direct your hearts to the love of God and to the endurance of Christ.

In the shorter form of the reading, the passage in brackets is omitted.

GOSPEL
Luke 20:27–38
or 20:27, 34–38

Some Sadducees, those who deny that there is a resurrection, came forward [and put this question to Jesus, saying, "Teacher, Moses wrote for us,

> *If someone's brother dies leaving a wife but no child,*
> *his brother must take the wife*
> *and raise up descendants for his brother.*

Now there were seven brothers; the first married a woman but died childless. Then the second and the third married her, and likewise all the seven died childless. Finally the woman also died. Now at the resurrection whose wife will that woman be? For all seven had been married to her."] Jesus said to them, "The children of this age marry and remarry; but those who are deemed worthy to attain to the coming age and to the resurrection of the dead neither marry nor are given in marriage. They can no longer die, for they are like angels; and they are the children of God because they are the ones who will rise. That the dead will rise even Moses made known in the passage about the bush, when he called out 'Lord,' the God of Abraham, the God of Isaac, and the God of Jacob; and he is not God of the dead, but of the living, for to him all are alive."

❖ Understanding the Word

The first reading is taken from the book of Second Maccabees, which recounts the struggles of the Jews under the persecution of Antiochus IV Epiphanes (175–164 BC) and the subsequent Maccabean revolt (167–140 BC). Whereas First Maccabees focuses on the military exploits of the Maccabean leaders, Second Maccabees attends to the faithful adherence to Jewish religious practices. Military success is credited to God and not to human skill (2 Maccabees 8:18, 24, 35; 9:5–6, etc.). Today's passage describes the faithful resistance of the mother with her seven sons who demonstrate fidelity and nobility in the face of martyrdom. The hope of resurrection strengthens their resolve (2 Maccabees 7:14).

Second Thessalonians is likely written by a second-generation disciple of Paul who attempts to discourage apocalyptic zeal among the community (2 Thessalonians 2:2–4). Today's reading is taken from the concluding exhortations, in which the author in the voice of Paul encourages the community to continue their good works. They are to pray for Paul and his colleagues (2 Thessalonians 3:1–2) and not neglect instruction from Paul (2 Thessalonians 3:6), trusting that the Lord is faithful and will strengthen and sustain them.

In the reading from Luke, we are introduced to the Sadducees, who did not believe in the concept of resurrection. They were a conservative, aristocratic group that controlled the temple and priesthood. They were liturgically conservative, but more liberal on Jewish practices and Hellenistic culture. In contrast to the Sadducees, the Pharisees believed in the resurrection of the dead, advocated strict adherence to the law to ensure purity, and saw the synagogue as the locus of Jewish life. Jesus explains the concept of resurrection, demonstrating that the Sadducees' question is irrelevant in light of the coming reign of God.

I was a classroom teacher. A student's question revealed either that she or he was beginning to understand a concept or that she or he had missed the point. When the Sadducees ask Jesus about whose wife the bride of seven brothers will be at the resurrection, it is clear they miss the point. Resurrected life is a new reality in which people "can no longer die, for they are like angels." The encounters between Jesus and the disciples following his resurrection reveal how long it took for his disciples to understand this. They did not have an experience that helped them wrap their minds around the concept. Neither did we until Jesus' resurrection and it is still difficult to grasp. Something of us is the same but something of us is also very different. Any change requires that an element of a reality continue while other elements are different.

However we understand the Resurrection, one thing is sure, we will live in a new way. Ours is "not the God of the dead, but of the living." The Lord is faithful to us throughout this life and into the next. God gives us strength to be faithful at all times, too. It is faith that carries us through death to new life. The seven brothers and their mother in our first reading exemplify how faith in God helps us face even death. Jesus' life, death, and resurrection is another example. So are martyrs like Archbishop Óscar Romero, Franz van der Lugt, SJ, Dorothy Stang, CND and our sisters and brothers dying for their faith today. Children of God follow the instruction in Second Thessalonians: "May the Lord direct your hearts to the love of God and to the endurance of Christ." You will find strength to be counted among those who will rise with no questions asked.

✤ Consider/Discuss

- Describe how you understand resurrected life.
- What do you fear living our faith might cost you?

✤ Living and Praying with the Word

God of life and of the living, thank you for your faithful love throughout my life. Direct my heart to love of you in order that I may have the courage witnessed by the seven Maccabee brothers and their mother, by Jesus' death and resurrection, and by those who have died for their faith throughout human history.

November 13, 2016

THIRTY-THIRD SUNDAY IN ORDINARY TIME

Today's Focus: Read All About It!

The readings at the end of the liturgical year always refocus us on the end of time. As frightening as they can sometimes be, we are always assured of the ultimate love we will know at the end.

FIRST READING
Malachi 3: 19–20a

Lo, the day is coming, blazing like an oven,
    when all the proud and all evildoers will be stubble,
and the day that is coming will set them on fire,
    leaving them neither root nor branch,
    says the LORD of hosts.
But for you who fear my name, there will arise
    the sun of justice with its healing rays.

PSALM RESPONSE
Psalm 98:9

The Lord comes to rule the earth with justice.

SECOND READING
2 Thessalonians 3:7–12

Brothers and sisters: You know how one must imitate us. For we did not act in a disorderly way among you, nor did we eat food received free from anyone. On the contrary, in toil and drudgery, night and day we worked, so as not to burden any of you. Not that we do not have the right. Rather, we wanted to present ourselves as a model for you, so that you might imitate us. In fact, when we were with you, we instructed you that if anyone was unwilling to work, neither should that one eat. We hear that some are conducting themselves among you in a disorderly way, by not keeping busy but minding the business of others. Such people we instruct and urge in the Lord Jesus Christ to work quietly and to eat their own food.

GOSPEL
Luke 21:5–19

While some people were speaking about how the temple was adorned with costly stones and votive offerings, Jesus said, "All that you see here—the days will come when there will not be left a stone upon another stone that will not be thrown down."

Then they asked him, "Teacher, when will this happen? And what sign will there be when all these things are about to happen?" He answered, "See that you not be deceived, for many will come in my name, saying, 'I am he,' and 'The time has come.' Do not follow them! When you hear of wars and insurrections, do not be terrified; for such things must happen first, but it will not immediately be the end." Then he said to them, "Nation will rise against nation, and kingdom against kingdom. There will be powerful earthquakes, famines, and plagues from place to place; and awesome sights and mighty signs will come from the sky.

"Before all this happens, however, they will seize and persecute you, they will hand you over to the synagogues and to prisons, and they will have you led before kings and governors because of my name. It will lead to your giving testimony. Remember, you are not to prepare your defense beforehand, for I myself shall give you a wisdom in speaking that all your adversaries will be powerless to resist or refute. You will even be handed over by parents, brothers, relatives, and friends, and they will put some of you to death. You will be hated by all because of my name, but not a hair on your head will be destroyed. By your perseverance you will secure your lives."

❖ Understanding the Word

The reading from the prophet Malachi depicts the coming Day of the Lord, at which the just will be separated from the wicked (3:18–21). Elijah, a prophet like Moses, would come to announce this Day of the Lord (3:22–13). As it would develop, Jewish apocalyptic eschatology resolved the disparity between the crisis of this evil age and the promise of God so that "God's elect will be vindicated." The in-breaking of this new moment would be heralded by historical and cosmic catastrophes. The turning point would be "the day of the Lord," a day of judgment and salvation.

The reading from Second Thessalonians echoes many Pauline themes found in the undisputed letters. Paul received the rights of an apostle (1 Corinthians 9:4), and here pseudeo-Paul reminds the community that neither he nor his companions took free food (2 Thessalonians 3:8a). In addition to his apostolic ministry, Paul also worked so as not to burden the Thessalonians (1 Thessalonians 2:9), a fact repeated here (2 Thessalonians 3:8b). Paul and his companions are a model to be imitated (Philemon 2:17, 2 Timothy 3:9). Restating Paul's work ethic was intended to counter current practices among some members of the community who had simply stopped working (2 Thessalonians 3:11), believing that the *parousia* had already arrived (2 Thessalonians 2:1).

The Gospel reading from Luke has its origins in Mark 13, but Luke has included some interesting additions that likely reflect the concerns of his original community. Whereas Mark interpreted the desecration of the temple as an apocalyptic symbol (Mark 13:14) that would signal the coming Son of Man (see Daniel 9:27), Luke separates the event of destruction (Luke 21:6) from the coming of the Son of Man (Luke 21:27) by introducing "the times of the Gentiles" (Luke 21:24). In today's passage, the disciples ask about the timing of the coming *eschaton* ("When will this happen?" Luke 21:7). The Lucan Jesus warns the disciples not to listen to rumors, nor to think that wars and or insurrections signal the end. Luke attempts to explain the delay of the *parousia* (which Paul had expected immediately) by introducing intermediate stages of proclamation and testimony.

❖ Reflecting on the Word

Standing in line at the grocery store I often read the headlines on the papers being sold there. I often find them outrageous, playing on news that "sells" rather than news that is true. Our inquiring minds can be drawn to the bizarre, the flamboyant, and the extreme. This is true in the readings we encounter at the end of each liturgical year. They focus on the end-times, the signs of the Lord's return, and how we can know when that will occur. Inquiring minds want to know. Jesus tells us not to be deceived. Even when some of the events that signal the end occur, "it will not immediately be the end." As he indicates in another Gospel passage, only the Father knows the day and the hour, not anyone else—not even the Son.

What are we to do? We are to persevere by staying focused on the teaching and example of Jesus Christ: "By your perseverance you will secure your lives." We are to have wonder and awe in the name of the Lord. We are to look for "the sun of justice with its healing rays." We are to keep busy doing God's work rather than minding everyone else's business. We are to live each day as if it were our last, to paraphrase St. Francis de Sales. If we keep our eyes on Jesus and live his commandments each day, we will be ready whenever the end comes. The world will know justice. We will have a wisdom that our adversaries cannot resist or refute. That's the truth, even if it doesn't sell papers.

❖ Consider/Discuss

- How would you live today differently if you knew it was to be your last?
- Where do you find the wisdom of God and the strength to live Jesus clearly?

❖ Living and Praying with the Word

God of all times and places, we know not the day nor the hour. Fill us with your Spirit so that we might live today in ways that will help us persevere in following you no matter what happens.

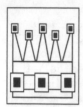

November 20, 2016

OUR LORD JESUS CHRIST, KING OF THE UNIVERSE

Today's Focus: A Crown of Contradictions

This feast celebrates majesty in humility, strength in weakness, power in gentleness. Are we able to live humble, weak, gentle lives—as Jesus did—so one day we will be crowned with his glory?

FIRST READING
2 Samuel 5:1–3

In those days, all the tribes of Israel came to David in Hebron and said: "Here we are, your bone and your flesh. In days past, when Saul was our king, it was you who led the Israelites out and brought them back. And the LORD said to you, 'You shall shepherd my people Israel and shall be commander of Israel.' " When all the elders of Israel came to David in Hebron, King David made an agreement with them there before the LORD, and they anointed him king of Israel.

PSALM RESPONSE
Psalm 122:1

Let us go rejoicing to the house of the Lord.

SECOND READING
Colossians 1: 12–20

Brothers and sisters: Let us give thanks to the Father, who has made you fit to share in the inheritance of the holy ones in light. He delivered us from the power of darkness and transferred us to the kingdom of his beloved Son, in whom we have redemption, the forgiveness of sins.

He is the image of the invisible God,
　　the firstborn of all creation.
For in him were created all things in heaven and on earth,
　　the visible and the invisible,
　　whether thrones or dominions or principalities or powers;
　　all things were created through him and for him.
He is before all things,
　　and in him all things hold together.
He is the head of the body, the church.
He is the beginning, the firstborn from the dead,
　　that in all things he himself might be preeminent.
For in him all the fullness was pleased to dwell,
　　and through him to reconcile all things for him,
　　making peace by the blood of his cross
　　through him, whether those on earth or those in heaven.

GOSPEL
Luke 23:35–43

The rulers sneered at Jesus and said, "He saved others, let him save himself if he is the chosen one, the Christ of God." Even the soldiers jeered at him. As they approached to offer him wine they called out, "If you are King of the Jews, save yourself." Above him there was an inscription that read, "This is the King of the Jews."

Now one of the criminals hanging there reviled Jesus, saying, "Are you not the Christ? Save yourself and us." The other, however, rebuking him, said in reply, "Have you no fear of God, for you are subject to the same condemnation? And indeed, we have been condemned justly, for the sentence we received corresponds to our crimes, but this man has done nothing criminal." Then he said, "Jesus, remember me when you come into your kingdom." He replied to him, "Amen, I say to you, today you will be with me in Paradise."

❖ Understanding the Word

David's ascent to the throne of Israel is a gradual one. While Saul is still alive, the prophet Samuel is directed to anoint a king from among the sons of Jesse (1 Samuel 16:1). The young David is thus anointed, and the Spirit of the Lord rushes upon him (1 Samuel 16:13). After the death of Saul, the leaders of the tribe of Judah anoint David king of Judah (2 Samuel 2:4). And in today's first reading, David is anointed for the third time and all the tribes of Israel recognize David as their king, thus confirming God's promise, "You shall shepherd my people Israel and shall be commander of Israel" (2 Samuel 5:2).

The second reading includes an ancient Christian hymn declaring Christ Jesus as cosmic Lord and peacemaker. Within the Letter to the Colossians, the setting of the hymn serves to remind the community to lead a life worthy of the Lord. Verses 15–20 describe the identity of this Lord and his effect. Engaging themes and motifs from Wisdom literature, Christ is identified as the very image of the invisible God, firstborn of creation, universal in his effect ("all things were created through him," v. 16), and unique ("for in him all the fullness was pleased to dwell," v. 19). Reconciliation and peace result from the blood of his cross.

Throughout Luke's Gospel, the evangelist employs doublets, parallel stories, or dual characters to emphasize a particular theme. The infancy narratives describe the annunciations and births of both John and Jesus. Simeon and Anna herald the infant Jesus. Jesus tells the parable of the lost sheep and follows it with the parable of the woman searching for a lost coin. In today's Gospel, we are introduced to two characters who represent two different responses to Jesus. Despite his similar predicament, the first criminal joins the rulers and soldiers in maligning Jesus on the cross. "Are you not the Christ? Save yourself and us" (v. 39). The second criminal rebukes the first, "Have you no fear of God?" (v. 40a). He then points out the irony. "You are subject to the same condemnation" (v. 40b). The second criminal confirms what Pilate and Herod had earlier announced: "This man has done nothing criminal." The final confirmation will come from the lips of the Roman centurion upon Jesus' death: "Surely, this man was innocent" (v. 47).

We celebrate a king whose throne is the cross, an instrument of capital punishment. Jesus died as a criminal, although he had done nothing wrong. He seemed powerless and yet promised, "today you will be with me in Paradise." Christ, our King, reconciled "all things . . . making peace by the blood of his cross." Christ the King models how contradictions can co-exist, if not reconcile. He was both fully human and fully divine. He was a leader who came to serve, not be served. Humbling himself, he was exalted. He found deep faith in sinners. He took on every human limitation, with the exception of sin, and was freed to the point of being raised up. He embraced death to give us life. He was of the line of David, the runt of his brothers whom God anointed king of Israel.

We often try to negate the realities that he embraced: limitation, humility, service, weakness, powerlessness, sin, and death. The irony is that when we face and embrace these realities, as Jesus did, we find new life even when others reject and ridicule us as they did Jesus. One criminal turns to Jesus. The other criminal joins the soldiers in jeering at and rebuking him. We have a choice. We can ask Jesus to help us put together life's contradictions in ways that free us, or we can jeer at and rebuke him, too. A teaching of St. Francis de Sales reminds us that nothing is so strong as gentleness and nothing so gentle as real strength. Gentle King, give us your strength and help us live with and even reconcile life's seeming contradictions.

✤ Consider/Discuss

- How do you handle life's contradictions?
- What helps you surrender to the way of the Christ whose throne was the cross?

✤ Living and Praying with the Word

Father, we thank you for becoming one with us in the life, death, and resurrection of Christ the King. You reconciled humanity and divinity in him. Help us follow Christ the King by reconciling the contradictions of our lives and deepening our union with you.

A Dominican sister of Sinsinawa, Laurie Brink, O.P., Ph.D., is an Associate Professor of New Testament Studies at Catholic Theological Union. She also serves as an associate editor for *The Bible Today*. Sr. Brink has recorded two lecture series (*Acts of the Apostles* and *Philippians*) for Now You Know Media and authored several articles on biblical topics. She is currently researching and writing a book on the biblical foundations of friendship. Having worked as a senior staff member for the Combined Caesarea Expeditions, Brink attempts to integrate archaeological research and biblical exegesis. An example of this commitment is her monograph *In This Place: Reflections on the Land of the Gospels for the Liturgical Cycle* (Wipf & Stock, 2008), co-authored with Marianne Race, C.S.J.

Author, *Understanding the Word*

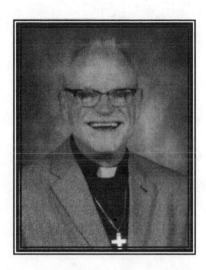

Fr. Paul H. Colloton, O.S.F.S., D.Min., is a member of the Oblates of St. Francis de Sales, Wilmington-Philadelphia Province and serves as the associate pastor for Immaculate Conception Parish, Elkton, Maryland, and St. Jude Mission, North East, Maryland. For a little over thirteen years Fr. Paul served as the Director of Continuing Education for the National Association of Pastoral Musicians (NPM). His nearly 45 years experience in pastoral ministry includes service as a liturgist, musician, spiritual director, presider, preacher, clinician, retreat director, author, and minister to and with people living with HIV/AIDS.

Author, *Reflecting on the Word, Consider/Discuss, Living and Praying with the Word*

Notes